Designing Effective Environmental Regimes

NEW HORIZONS IN ENVIRONMENTAL ECONOMICS

General Editors: Wallace E. Oates, *Professor of Economics, University of Maryland, USA* and Henk Folmer, *Professor of Economics, Wageningen Agricultural University, The Netherlands and Professor of Environmental Economics, Tilburg University, The Netherlands*

This important series is designed to make a significant contribution to the development of the principles and practices of environmental economics. It includes both theoretical and empirical work. International in scope, it addresses issues of current and future concern in both East and West and in developed and developing countries.

The main purpose of the series is to create a forum for the publication of high quality work and to show how economic analysis can make a contribution to understanding and resolving the environmental problems confronting the world in the twenty-first century.

Recent titles in the series include:

Designing Effective Environmental Regimes

The Key Conditions

Jørgen Wettestad

Senior Research Fellow, Fridtjof Nansen Institute, Norway

NEW HORIZONS IN ENVIRONMENTAL ECONOMICS

Edward Elgar
Cheltenham, UK • Northampton, MA, USA

Published by
Edward Elgar Publishing Limited
Glensanda House
Montpellier Parade
Cheltenham
Glos GL50 1UA
UK

Edward Elgar Publishing, Inc.
6 Market Street
Northampton
Massachusetts 01060
USA

A catalogue record for this book
is available from the British Library

Library of Congress Cataloguing in Publication Data

Wettestad, Jørgen, 1955–
    Designing effective environmental regimes: the key conditions /
Jørgen Wettestad.
        (New horizons in environmental economics)
    Includes bibliographical references.
    1. Environmental law, International. 2. Economic Development—
Environmental aspects. I. Title. II. Series.
    K3585.4.W483 1999
    341.7'62—dc21   98–46613
                                                                    CIP

ISBN 1 84064 000 6

Printed and bound in Great Britain by MPG Books Ltd, Bodmin, Cornwall

Contents

List of Figures and Tables

FIGURES

TABLES

Preface

The work on this book started in 1993 while I enjoyed sabbatical days of wine and roses in the lovely and inspiring surroundings of Berkeley, California. Many thanks to Director Willy Østreng at the Fridtjof Nansen Institute (FNI), Executive Director Harry Kreisler at the Institute of International Studies (IIS), and Professor Ernst Haas for making the stay possible. Moreover, Administrative Assistant Nadine Zelinski at the IIS was a great help with regard to practical matters, and the Norwegian Research Council provided crucial financial assistance. The book plans sprang out of some initial collaborative efforts on regime effectiveness and institutional design carried out with my FNI colleague and good friend Steinar Andresen; these efforts partly related to a larger collaborative research project on regime effectiveness initiated by Ed Miles at the University of Washington, with Arild Underdal at the University of Oslo in a central position. Believe it or not, my initial plan was to finish the book during my stay in Berkeley! Crazy of course, with the benefit of hindsight. The wine was too good; the CDs were too cheap; and the analytical order of regime design turned out to be far taller than I had imagined. However, it helped a lot that Ernst Haas offered kind assistance and provided useful comments on several drafts, and that my office mate, Luis Sanz, provided kind support and helpful comments.

Back in Oslo, the 'book money' was spent, and I needed to concentrate on several other fascinating projects; however, in terms of subject matter, these were clearly relevant for the regime effectiveness and design issues. Hence, I need to thank Arild Underdal, Ken Hanf and the rest of the project group within the project on national preparation and implementation processes within the Long-Range Transboundary Air Pollution (LRTAP) regime for providing me with very useful background material on national processes for my work on this regime. However, in terms of involvement, I was much more directly involved in the International Institute for Applied Systems Analysis (IIASA) project on the Implementation and Effectiveness of International Environmental Commitments, led by David Victor and Gene Skolnikoff. Many thanks to David and the rest of the project group for stimulating project meetings and discussions, and for allowing me to dive deeper into the various facets of the LRTAP regime. In addition, I have also been directly involved in a collaborative project with Steinar, Arild, and Tora Skodvin at the Center for International Climate and Environmental Research in Oslo (CICERO) on the institutional handling of the science–politics relationship in international environmental regimes. This has given me an opportunity to study the design and functioning of the scientific–political complexes within the marine pollution and acid rain contexts. Moreover, the Miles and Underdal effectiveness project mentioned earlier has proceeded further, and it has given me a lot, both in terms of very stimulating project discussions and an opportunity to do more work on the effectiveness of the acid rain and ozone regimes. And Ed's guidance on the culinary and musical gems of Seattle has been superb! In addition, I need to thank the project group related to the Nordic Council of Ministers project on the Effectiveness of Multilateral Environmental Agreements for providing an additional possibility to write about the design of the acid rain regime. Finally, thanks to the SAMRAM Energy and Environment programme financed by the Norwegian Research Council for giving me an opportunity to study the institutional design of the global climate change regime.

However, in addition to involvement in these other projects, I have found time on and off to proceed with the book work. In this process, I am deeply indebted to a number of people. Three people stand out. First and foremost, I would thank Steinar Andresen warmly for allowing me to draw upon, and develop further, ideas that we initially developed together. Moreover, throughout this process, he has offered invaluable support, comments, and ideas. Second, Arild Underdal is the Elvis Presley of political science;[1] the King of intellectual inspiration, general support, and sharp comments. Third, the work of Jon B. Skjærseth, FNI, on North Sea cooperation and the ozone regime has been extremely useful, and he has offered general support and helpful comments throughout the process.

In addition, several other people need to be thanked. Within the Norwegian Ministry of Environment, three kind and key people have in several rounds of interviews patiently addressed my questions and corrected a number of mis-interpretations: Per M. Bakken, Harald Dovland, and Per W. Schive.[2] Ed Miles has been mentioned several times already, and in addition to the contributions mentioned already, he provided helpful comments on earlier drafts. Olav Schram Stokke and Kristin Rosendal at the FNI have also provided useful comments to earlier drafts. The work of Oran R. Young has been a major inspiration for the work on this book, and Oran provided useful comments to a draft version of the analytical chapter. Michael Zürn at the University of Bremen sent me helpful comments on my 1995 conceptual note. Ann Skarstad has been a great help on the language assistance side. Øystein B. Thommesen, editor of the Yearbook of International Co-operation on Environment and Development, has provided me with various useful factual inputs and corrections regarding the regimes studied. Douglas Brubaker has advised me on book contractual matters. Ivar and Torhild Liseter have provided crucial assistance with tables, figures and final editing. Moreover, without the superb editorial and language assistance of Snorre Fjeldstad and Anne Christine Thestrup in the Spring and Autumn 1998 finishing sessions, this book would simply not have seen the light of day.

Life is definitely more than regime design. Thanks to the Rolling Stones for enduring creative inspiration and to the Bourbon Boys for providing a loud outlet for my frustrations along the way.

Finally, Lindis and Håkon: I love you.

Polhøgda, May 15, 1998
Jørgen Wettestad

NOTES

1. And this is early Elvis; in his mid and late 1950s heyday.
2. All the other helpful executive officers, both in Norway and abroad, are named and thanked in Chapters 3, 4, 5 and 7.

1. Introduction

The 1997 United Nations Special Session on the follow-up to the 1992 UN Conference on Environment and Development marks the fact that over two decades have now passed since the 1972 Stockholm United Nations Conference on the Human Environment (UNCHE). This signifies that international environmental cooperation has left its formative years and, so to speak, reached 'adulthood'. In terms of the multilateral agreements focused on in this book, many of the over 140 multilateral environmental agreements currently in operation were adopted in the wake of the 1972 Conference.[1] At the same time, cities all over the world are increasingly choked in air pollution, deforestation only accelerates, and the hot 1990s indicate that global warming is a reality.[2] Hence, although there are some positive trends, many environmental problems seem only to be getting worse. This apparent paradox indicates that the time is now ripe to begin discussing the results and organizational lessons to be learned both for analysts and practitioners from the functioning of environmental agreements, hereafter referred to as 'regimes'.[3]

Hence, a natural and central first question to ask is *to what extent have they proved to be effective instruments*, for instance in dealing with the environmental or resource depletion problems that spurred their creation? Have emissions been cut? Has the water or air quality improved enough for people to fish or go swimming safely – or indeed, breathe safely? However, in order to draw the right organizational lessons, it is of course crucially important to examine critically *why* emissions have been cut and problems solved or not solved. In other words, it is necessary to devote considerable attention to the central determinants of the degree of regime effectiveness witnessed. An undoubtedly important perspective is related to central characteristics of the environmental problems themselves. For instance, problems surrounded by high scientific uncertainty and disagreement about emissions and their effects are obviously complicated to deal with for regime negotiators. If the problems in addition stem from central societal activities, and differences between countries give rise to incompatible interests, then we can truly speak about 'malign' problems.[4] Within the more academic debate on the impact of international organizations and regimes, such a perspective is clearly given dominant weight by scholars who maintain that regimes are no more than reflections of underlying interests and power structures, and their seeming effects are mere spurious misjudgements.[5] Overall, such perspectives easily lead one to assume that the task of designing effective international regimes is a 'mission impossible'. Malign issues lead to regimes of low effectiveness; benign problems allow the development of more effective regimes – and that is that.

However, there are still several reasons to give considerable attention to the issue of organizational lessons and institutional design[6] – as done in this book. First, research carried out in other contexts indicates that the relationship between problem 'malignness' and regime effectiveness is not as simple as depicted above. Malign problems *are* sometimes dealt with effectively.[7] Not least in situations with temporarily increasing concern about environmental issues and the opening up of political 'windows of opportunity', the existence and design of international institutions may become critically important in order to transform political opportunities into new or stronger commitments.[8] Take for instance the whaling regime, where the use of majority voting played an important part in getting the whaling moratorium adopted when conservationist sentiments increased in the late 1970s and an international political 'window of opportunity' opened up for conservationists.[9] Moreover, central characteristics of the problems addressed, such as emission sources and their societal importance, are difficult to change and not easy to play around much with. In comparison, institutional factors can in principle be more easily designed and changed deliberately in order to enhance – or impede! – effectiveness. In addition, studies of national institutions clearly suggest that 'organization matters',[10] and findings from national contexts may have increasing international relevance in a world of increasing interdependence, and with the blurring of the distinctions between international and national boundaries. Taken together, such factors explain why it is natural to take an interest in organizational and institutional factors in the international regime context.

By using the term 'institutional design', I furthermore signal that the ambition in this book is clearly to move beyond the much debated 'do regimes matter' question[11] and discuss more specifically *to what extent* and *how* do regimes possibly matter? In other words, are we able to say anything more specific about the *types* of regimes – and their *specific regime features* – which of these are likely to make more impact and contribute to higher effectiveness than others? Six more specific institutional factors are focused upon in this context: access and participation procedures; decision-making rules; the role of the secretariat; the structuring of the agenda; the organization of the science–politics interface; and verification and compliance mechanisms.[12] These factors certainly touch upon controversial issues in international environmental politics and actual dilemmas for negotiators. For instance:[13]

- *should access to decision processes be inclusive or exclusive?* It has been argued that inclusive processes, for instance in terms of the inclusion of Non-Governmental Organizations (NGOs), mean effective decision-making with varied inputs and broad-based legitimacy, while others have emphasized that more exclusive processes offer optimal conditions for more delicate compromise-building.
- *Should national participants be bureaucrats or ministers?* Bureaucrats often master the complex technological and political details best; while ministers are definitely freer to cut bargains, and they usually draw much more media and public attention to the issues.
- *Should decision-making be consensual or rely on majority voting?* Consensual processes and compromise-building generally mean legitimate decisions and good prospects for implementation, but for instance the 1989 Hague Declaration on the Environment sounded strong calls more ambitious decision-making and the possible use of majority-voting.
- *Should the secretariat be a low-lying stage-hand for the parties or a driving entrepreneurial actor?* Stage-hand secretariats may give the parties optimal support and allow them to concentrate on the big issues, while more active, entrepreneurial secretariats may provide more tangible solutions to the big issues.
- *Should the agenda be comprehensive or narrow?* It has been argued that comprehensive agendas allow the integrative building of 'package-solutions', while it has also been noted that narrow agendas mean more oversight and less potential blocking points.
- *Should the scientific–political complex emphasize scientific integrity or political involvement?* Emphasis on scientific independence and integrity generally means knowledge with high legitimacy, but calls have been heard for the more active political involvement of scientists, and hence knowledge more relevant and usable for decision-making purposes.
- *Should verification procedures be 'intrusive' or 'non-intrusive'?* Calls have definitely been heard for the establishment of systems of 'intrusive', independent checking of progress information provided by parties, implying less possibility for cunning free-riders to avoid implementation costs. Softer and less intrusive procedures may mean the bolstering of a general atmosphere of trust and mutual respect.
- *Should compliance mechanisms rely on 'sticks' or 'carrots'?* Finally, several calls have also been heard for the more extensive use of economic sanctions to bolster willingness to comply with environmental treaties, while others instead emphasize the use of positive financial incentives to cope with lacking compliance abilities. In other words: one is easily faced with a number of tricky dilemmas when it comes to agreeing upon the most effective design for international environmental regimes.

In this book, these issues are initially investigated on the basis of case studies of four international environmental regimes: the two clearly regional and closely related Oslo Convention (OSCON) on Marine Dumping, and Paris Convention (PARCON) on Marine Pollution from Land-Based Sources; the 'regional plus' (including both Western and Eastern Europe) LRTAP Convention on 'Long-Range Transboundary Air Pollution'; and the global Vienna Convention and Montreal Protocol on Substances that Deplete the Ozone-Layer. Moreover, as a very natural analytical 'bonus', institutional design issues within perhaps the currently most debated international environmental regime – the Framework Convention for Climate Change (FCCC) – are discussed in a separate chapter at the end of the book, in the light of lessons from the more 'mature' and long-functioning four regimes above. Given the analytical and empirical complexity inherent in studies of the effects of the institutional design of international regimes, an important reason for focusing on these regimes has simply been data availability and the general knowledge base established at the Fridtjof Nansen Institute.[14] Luckily, these cases also exhibit other characteristics which enhance the general value and relevance of the main findings and lessons learnt. For instance, both 'malign' and more 'benign' issues are included. Moreover, given that previous research leads us to expect differences in effectiveness between these regimes,[15] there are several formal institutional differences between the regimes which are interesting in a comparative perspective. In addition, in relation to the important climate regime discussion, two important 'atmospheric' regimes are included in the sample.

Compared to an increasing number of studies on international environmental cooperation,[16] this book is different in several respects. First and foremost, there is the analytical and empirical focus on a specified, explicit group of international institutional and organizational features,[17] which of course build upon a broad range of contributions to this field.[18] Moreover, in relation to comprehensive, multi-case projects,[19] and deep-probing case studies,[20] this book fulfils crucially important 'synthesizing' functions in this debate. First, the four structured, focused case studies ensure that empirical evidence is more than anecdotal. All the cases are structured in the same way, facilitating comparative overview, not least with regard to the focused institutional issues. Moreover, the case study format provides the reader with an overview within a limited space of many important and relevant issues in each of the regimes. The insights of other contributions, either more theoretically inclined or going into greater detail in relation to specific empirical issues, are summed up, and references provided for readers interested in digging deeper into the issues discussed.

Briefly then, going through the structure of the book, the next chapter is entitled 'Analysing the effectiveness and institutional design of international environmental regimes: the conceptual lenses' and provides the main theoretical and methodological foundation for the empirical material and related analysis to be presented. Three empirical case studies then follow: Chapter 3 dealing with the Oslo and Paris Conventions on Marine Pollution in the North-East Atlantic; Chapter 4 dealing with the Convention on Long-Range Transbondary Air Pollution; and Chapter 5 dealing with the Vienna Convention and Montreal Protocol on Ozone Layer Depletion. Chapter 6 is the main comparative and assessment chapter ('Combining comparative and case study evidence: institutional findings'). Chapter 7 discusses practical implications for the climate regime ('Designing an effective climate regime: a task "too hot to handle"?'). Finally, Chapter 8 ('Designing effective environmental regimes: launching the three conditional Ps') winds up the book. Let us then proceed to the construction of a theoretical and methodological foundation for the empirical and analytical chapters to follow.

NOTES

1. This number is given in Haas, Keohane and Levy (1993:6). For an overview of international environmental agreements, see the *Green Globe Yearbook/Yearbook of International Coope-ration on Environment and Development*, now published in collaboration between Earthscan Press and the Fridtjof Nansen Institute.
2. See for instance the 'State of the World' and 'Vital Signs' reports produced by Worldwatch; for example, Brown et al. (1997).
3. As further elaborated in Chapter 2, I will take as my point of departure the regime definition suggested by Levy, Young and Zürn (1994:6): international social institutions consisting of agreed principles, norms, rules, procedures and programmes that govern the interactions of actors in specific issue-areas.
4. See Underdal (1990) and Miles et al. (forthcoming 1999) for thorough analytical discussions and also empirical applications of the problem characteristics perspective and the concept of 'malignness'. For some constructive critical comments, see Young (1998:17–18). These issues are also discussed in Chapter 2 of this book.
5. See for instance Strange (1983) and Mearsheimer (1995).
6. Basically, I adhere to Oran Young's distinction between institutions as the wider concept, pertaining to 'sets of rules of the game or codes of conduct defining social practices', and organizations as a narrower concept, referring to 'material entities possessing offices, personnel, budgets, equipment, and more often than not, legal personality' (Young 1994:3–4). This distinction and the implications for the concepts used in this book are further discussed in Chapter 2.4. For the sake of simplicity, I will stick to the wider term of 'institutional design'.
7. See Miles et al. (forthcoming 1999).
8. Regarding the 'window of opportunity' concept, see for instance Kingdon (1984).
9. However, the moratorium is disputed in a broader effectiveness perspective. See for instance Andresen (1993; forthcoming 1999).
10. See for instance March and Olsen (1989).
11. According to Young (1998:15), 'we know enough to lay to rest the sterile debate about whether international regimes matter at all or are properly understood as epiphenomena that merely reflect deeper driving forces in international society'. See also Levy, Young and Zürn (1994).

12. These factors and why they are chosen are discussed in more detail in Chapter 2. For a very good general overview of various relevant institutional dimensions in this context, see Young and Underdal (1998).
13. All these elements are further elaborated in Chapter 2, complete with extensive references.
14. See for instance Wettestad and Andresen (1991); Skjærseth (1991; 1992; 1996; forthcoming 1998); Wettestad (1994; 1995A; forthcoming 1998A, B and C); Andresen and Wettestad (1995); and Andresen (1996).
15. See for instance Wettestad and Andresen (1991) and Andresen et al. (1992).
16. See for instance Zürn (1995) for a valuable overview of main contributions so far.
17. The most similar contribution so far is probably Susskind (1994). Although clearly interesting and valuable, it is empirically and theoretically quite general; has more of a negotiation perspective; and does not cover all the institutional factors discussed in this book.
18. To start at the Fridtjof Nansen Institute, Steinar Andresen and myself launched and utilized a somewhat similar approach in a couple of articles in the early 1990s (Andresen and Wettestad 1992; 1993). Arild Underdal's work has been a major inspiration, not least Underdal (1990). The work of Oran Young must also be mentioned; for instance Young (1994). See also footnote 14.
19. Several relevant, but more general and extensive, projects have recently been concluded or are underway: for example, the Tübingen regime project (Rittberger, 1990; 1993); Haas, Keohane and Levy (1993) the Oslo/Seattle effectiveness project (Miles et al., forthcoming 1999); the Dartmouth/Harvard effectiveness project (Young et al., forthcoming 1999); the Clark, Jäger and van Eindjhoven project on social learning (Clark et al., forthcoming); the Brown-Weiss project on compliance (Brown-Weiss and Jacobson, 1998); and the 'Implementation and Effectiveness of International Environmental Commitments' (IEC) project, carried out at the International Institute for Applied Systems Analysis (Victor, Raustiala and Skolnikoff 1998).
20. For instance Jon B. Skjærseth's thorough and innovative dissertation study on the North Sea cooperation and implementation efforts in the UK, Netherlands and Norway, conducted at the Fridtjof Nansen Institute (Skjærseth, forthcoming 1998).

2. Analysing the Effectiveness and Institutional Design of International Environmental Regimes: The Conceptual Lenses

2.1 INTRODUCTION

This chapter contains three main sections. The first one, 'What is this thing called effectiveness?', introduces the approach chosen for the analysis and measurement of regime effectiveness. The second part sets the stage for the focused institutional and organizational discussion to follow, discussing its 'problematic' background in the methodological and analytical sense. The final section presents and discusses the focused institutional and organizational dimensions. Why have they been chosen? Which assumptions can naturally be formulated on the basis of previous contributions and general reasoning, as guiding devices for the empirical and analytical chapters to follow?

2.2 WHAT IS THIS THING CALLED REGIME EFFECTIVENESS?

The natural starting point for such a discussion is of course the regime concept itself. Cutting a long discussion short,[1] the regime concept in this book will be defined as 'international institutions consisting of agreed-upon principles, norms, rules, procedures and programmes that govern the interactions of actors in specific issue-areas'.[2] However, all definitions in this issue-area are debatable, and this is no exception. One might for instance discuss the precise difference between 'principles' and 'norms' – and also between 'rules' and 'procedures'. In my view, the main components of regimes are rules/procedures and regulations/programmes – which can be termed the 'structural' and 'regulative' components of regimes. Hence, the *design* of regimes is related to these two components. As it seems reasonable to perceive structural aspects, for instance decision-making rules, as the main constituent features, they are the ones primarily focused on in this book. This means that the design and content of regime regulations – for instance the 1985 30% sulphur dioxide emissions reduction commitment in the acid rain context – will primarily be regarded as one of several indicators of effectiveness.[3] However, in principle, both the structural and regulative features of a regime can be discussed in an institutional design perspective. Take for instance the global climate change regime: the rough stabilization target agreed upon in connection with the adoption of the Convention in Rio 1992 can clearly be seen as an expression of the limited effectiveness of the climate regime so far; but also as an 'undifferentiated regulative regime' in itself.[4] Although both perspectives are definitely legitimate, the former will be highlighted in this connection.

Moving on to the crucial effectiveness concept, my reasoning here is generally based on the evolving debate in the 1990s.[5] I have in particular benefited greatly from taking part in the Oslo and Seattle effectiveness project,[6] in which Professor Arild Underdal at the University of Oslo has made seminal contributions to the effectiveness debate (Underdal, 1990; 1992). As a central contribution, he has proposed a distinction between two main dimensions to the question of regime effectiveness: 'distance to collective optimum', which is 'the appropriate perspective if we want to determine to what extent a collective problem is in fact "solved" under present arrangements' (1992:231); and 'relative improvement', which is 'clearly the notion we have in mind when considering whether and to what extent "regimes matter"' (ibid.). Moreover, he has elaborated the relationship between these two dimensions in Figure 2.1:

Figure 2.1   Dimensions of regime effectiveness

Distance to collective optimum

	GREAT	SMALL
HIGH	Important, but still imperfect	Important and (almost) perfect
LOW	Insignificant and suboptimal	Unimportant, yet (almost) optimal

Relative improvement

Both dimensions are clearly important to keep in mind analytically. However, based on previous efforts to apply these analytically valuable contributions to empirical analyses,[7] there are good reasons to give primary emphasis to the *latter* perspective. Essentially, this is because 'relative improvement' (as indicated in the quote from Underdal above) is the perspective that directs primary attention to the regime part and to 'political' matters so to speak.

Assessing 'the distance to the collective optimum' brings in tricky elements in terms of locating this optimum in practice. First, should it be interpreted as the environmental collective optimum, or as the collective optimum in economic terms? Given that Underdal speaks about the solving of problems, in the environmental context it makes most sense to interpret the collective optimum in terms of solving environmental problems. However, as will be further elaborated below, finding a clear, undisputed, and for social scientists easily accessible expression of environmentally optimum conditions is often not easy. Moreover, as indicated in Figure 2.1 above, there is a complicated relationship between scores on the 'collective optimum' and 'relative improvement' dimensions. Hence, downplaying the 'collective optimum' and problem-solving parts also reduces this tricky aggregation challenge. However, downplaying does not mean 'ignoring'. Before we go further into that, let us elaborate on the focused 'relative improvement' and 'political' effectiveness perspective.

In terms of political effectiveness, it makes sense to combine *three* main types of data: first, the strength of regime regulations; second, formal compliance data and reported changes in governmental policies; and finally, implementation data, specifying the actual changes in the behaviour of sub-national target groups and the background for such changes. Although these last data are in a sense the most relevant for tracing the 'actual' political effects of regimes, due to the current gaps in implementation knowledge, we have to supplement and in some cases rely *almost* entirely on the two former data sources. However, let us briefly comment upon all these three dimensions.

Turning first to *the strength of regime regulations*, there are at least four interesting dimensions to be aware of: 'ambitiousness'; 'legal status'; 'specificity'; and 'differentiation'.[8] Ambitiousness basically indicates how much behavioural change is required. In a comparative perspective, and all other things equal, it makes sense to see a regime regulation requiring an actual change in behaviour – for instance a 30% reduction in the emissions of a given substance – as a stronger, more ambitious and more potentially 'effective' regulation than one simply calling for emissions stabilization. In terms of legal status, the main difference lies between regulations that are legally binding on the states that have agreed to them, and hence requiring national ratification and parliamentary processes, and regulations having no such binding status, being cast in the form of recommendations or political statements of intent.[9] Generally, it can be assumed that states find it politically more difficult to disregard binding decisions, and hence that binding international decisions can be considered stronger and potentially more 'effective' than (political) recommendations. Specificity has to do with the degree to which behavioural implications of regime regulations are specified through quantified targets and timetables. It is on the whole reasonable to regard more specific regulations as stronger and potentially more 'effective' than more general ones. Finally, the question of differentiation has to do with the extent to which international regimes have different targets and timetables for various types of actors, taking into account variations in the parties' particular conditions and history in an environmental and political sense. If environmental and political backgrounds vary greatly among the parties, it is reasonable to regard the development of more differentiated decisions as moves towards stronger regulations. However, given that the issue of differentiation is closely related to more general institutional issues like access, participation and decision-making procedures, it may in the end make more sense to see the differentiation issue as part of the independent, institutional variables. Let us keep this question open.

Turning then to *formal compliance data* and reported changes in governmental policies,[10] the advantage of this indicator is that it is quite easy to measure. Most international environmental regimes have a system for reporting and publishing data on the relevant parties' follow-up of regime decisions. True, these data sets are national products for external use and not always directly comparable, and are often also incomplete (as will be further elaborated in the case studies). Moreover, it is a problematic indicator of 'true' relative improvement brought about by the regime in question. The reasons for the reported emissions stabilizations or reductions achieved can be purely coincidental, for instance related to a general economic recession leading to reduced industrial activity. However, the compliance data at least offer a simple, quantitative yardstick in a conceptual world filled with ambiguities and complexity. Hence, such data should definitely be utilized, though with caution.

Given the problems related to the two indicators discussed so far, we should ideally rely primarily on detailed *implementation* knowledge in order to trace the potential causal paths between regime activities and outputs and what takes place in practice at the national level – and hence determine 'true' political effectiveness.[11] As pointed out by Marc Levy and Oran Young, a necessary (though not sufficient) condition for solving international environmental problems is the capacity to influence the behaviour of those whose actions are relevant to the problem at hand.[12] Such behavioural knowledge can then help us to interpret the compliance data and hence avoid the related spurious fallacies indicated above. Generally, implementation measures can be of the more 'formal' type, since a natural first step is the adoption of national laws and reduction programmes. Nevertheless, the 'real' implementation test is whether the behaviour of problem-creating target groups can be influenced and altered in accordance with regime targets. In this specific context, this is crucial. We are not interested in the many fascinating complexities of the implementation processes as such, but essentially in the effects which can be traced back to the regime. As such effects in some cases will not mean changes in current polluting practices, but rather a stabilization or less growth than would otherwise be likely, I find it more meaningful to use the term 'behavioural impact' rather than change. Knowledge on such causal chains, often long and complex, specifying behavioural impact is of course extremely valuable in this context. However, valuable assets are often hard to obtain and costly too, and this is also the case for environmental regime implementation knowledge to date. Hence, this book builds upon such knowledge where it is available, including some limited efforts of my own.[13] However, a chief factor in further progress in the field of measuring regime effectiveness lies no doubt in the improvement of implementation knowledge.[14] *Ideally*, then, in order to measure political effectiveness and relative regime impact, we should obtain information on the development of regime regulations and decisions; compliance with these decisions as reported by the states; and detailed domestic implementation knowledge specifying the possible causal links between the international regime level, down to the level of factory practices and to whether you and I drive more or less. As noted, knowledge about the two former kinds alone is not worthless, but should be utilized with great caution. In some cases, 'strong' regime decisions and 'full' national compliance say virtually nothing about the political effectiveness of regimes.

Let us return, then, to the complex, yet surely important field of *distance to collective optimum* and related aspects of *problem-solving* and *environmental impact*. As indicated above, in an institutional and organizational context, the political component is in many ways the most interesting, as regimes never influence problems directly. They must necessarily have an effect on a range of political factors in order to solve underlying resource and environmental problems. However, despite this logic, it is clearly untenable to ignore completely the fundamental environmental problem-solving issues. After all, these are among the main topics that the general public really would like to see an answer to; for instance questions like 'can international LRTAP meetings and the fine rhetoric and papers produced make it possible for me to fish in lakes again'? Being in the lucky situation of being able to draw heavily upon my participation in a project more specifically oriented towards the science–politics interface,[15] I will provide some important 'diachronic' and 'synchronic' bits and pieces to what may be called 'the ecological puzzle'. With regard to the *diachronic* perspective, it helps us to avoid ahistorical interpretations. In other words, regime processes and decisions have to be evaluated in the light of existing knowledge and advice about environmental conditions at the time. With the benefit of hindsight, we may see clearly that regime decisions were inadequate, but that is an unfair yardstick. In this connection, scientific advice about environmental conditions and (more or less explicitly) critical limits related to emissions of pollutants is here used as an indicator of the 'collective optimum'. However, evolving scientific advice can clearly be a quite problematic indicator of 'ecological optimality'.[16] For instance, advice may refer to different and lower levels of ambition than the achievement of optimal conditions; for instance to prevent further deterioration of ecological conditions. Moreover, scientific and technical bodies very often have administrative participants, potentially acting more as the 'agents' of national bureaucracies than as independent scientific experts concerned about the collective good. Thus, the advice produced by such bodies may sometimes tell us just as much about 'politically feasible' solutions as about 'ecologically optimal' ones. In addition, in some cases, scientific committees produce first and foremost scientific *information* rather than explicit advice, complicating comparisons with policy regulations. Still, this piece of information is better than no information at all. The *synchronic* dimension is then added in order to confront more directly the crucial, though complex question 'are the environmental problems actually being solved?' The evolving match between scientific advice and regime regulations may be almost perfect, but this does not necessarily mean that the problem as experienced by fishermen, foresters or swimmers has apparently been reduced. However, this may of course have absolutely nothing to do with the functioning of the regime, and may for instance be due to natural variations and lagged effects. In other cases, it may be a signal that there are processes in operation currently not understood or addressed by regime activities. Be this as it may, it is still a piece of information which probably interests both decision-makers and the public at large. However, the general rule of 'collect and use with great caution' is also very relevant here.

Let us, then, round off with a brief discussion of the ranking of the effectiveness of the regimes studied. As indicated, this ranking will primarily be related to the political effectiveness perspective. I will utilize a simple 'high', 'medium' and 'low' ordinal scale, basing my ranking primarily on common sense and as transparent and explicit measurement operations as possible. In a comparative perspective, one particular aspect to appreciate in this connection is the time dimension and the maturity issue. It has been noted that scoring and comparing the effectiveness of two or more regimes is a straightforward exercise, only if these regimes are measured at similar stages in their 'life cycles'.[17]

Summary

This section has defined regimes as social institutions consisting of agreed-upon principles, norms, rules, procedures and programmes that govern the interactions of actors in specific issue-areas. On the basis of this definition, 'structural' and 'regulative' components of regimes were discerned. Because structural aspects, like for instance decision-making rules, must be seen as the main constituent aspects, they are the ones primarily focused on in this book.

With regard to the crucial effectiveness concept, based on analytical experiences and the general progress of the broader debate, the chosen approach took as its point of departure Arild Underdal's two main proposed dimensions of regime effectiveness – that is, 'distance to collective optimum', the extent to which a collective problem is 'solved' under present arrangements, and 'relative improvement', focusing on whether and to what extent 'regimes matter'. Given several methodological and measurement problems related to the application of the 'distance to collective optimum' dimension, most attention was given to the 'relative improvement' dimension. In order to work better in an empirical context, 'relative improvement' was operationalized into a political effectiveness indicator, combining knowledge on regime outputs, national compliance, and implementation. Bits and pieces of knowledge on the 'distance to the collective optimum' will then be discussed in the case studies under the heading 'the environmental and problem solving dimensions'. Here, a diachronic perspective was first introduced, in order to avoid ahistorical interpretations. Regime processes and decisions have to be evaluated in the light of existing knowledge and advice about environmental conditions and trends at the time. A synchronic dimension was added in order to confront more directly the crucial but complex question of 'is the problem actually being solved?' Based mainly on their political effectiveness scores, the regimes will be ranked according to a simple 'high', 'medium' and 'low' ordinal scale.

2.3 SETTING THE METHODOLOGICAL STAGE FOR THE INSTITUTIONAL AND ORGANIZATIONAL DISCUSSION

2.3.1 Methodology and Cases: The General Background[18]

Having a sample of four environmental regimes, two major related methodological issues need to be addressed which may be termed 'internal validity' and 'external relevance'. 'Internal validity' involves efforts to move beyond the level of correlation in the focused case studies and to approach the promised land of causality, so to speak. To use a medical analogy, it is good to see that many patients get better with a medicine they have been given, but it would be more comforting to know with more certainty that it is the medicine that *causes* the improvement and not for instance a temporary improvement in the weather. The same goes for 'regime physicists'. 'External relevance' involves the extent to which the knowledge produced within the sample of focused cases is also relevant for other environmental regimes and possibly even for other types of regimes. In dealing with these two issues, two basic methodological approaches are in principle relevant: statistical analyses of a large number of cases, and more small-scale, qualitative approaches, utilizing some sort of comparative techniques. Both the limited number of cases and the non-random selection of cases rule out the use of statistical techniques in this connection.[19] Hence, we are left with the more qualitative approach.

In terms of maximizing internal validity, the case studies in this connection will function partly as sources of in-depth tracing of institutional pathways and partly as units in a limited comparative venture. A helpful device in the more in-depth case study analyses is the method of counterfactual reasoning, trying to imagine what would have happened in a situation with other regime designs.[20] Moreover, reasoning related to institutional mechanisms is another helpful device in case study analyses in this field.[21] In the regime context, examples of such suggested mechanisms have been regime provision of information and knowledge; of financial and other incentives; and of authority and capability to certain national and sub-national actors.[22] At the national and sub-national level, the two fundamental mechanisms of rationalism and norms have been suggested as important conditioning factors for how regime 'signals' are ultimately interpreted and acted upon.[23] In addition, 'internal validity' is of course also dependent upon the empirical evidence at hand and its interpretation. As will be further elaborated in the case study section, I rely on a series of interviews to balance the inability to read first-hand all the papers and reports produced over several decades within the regimes. Ideally of course, far more interviews should have been carried out. There is now a clear bias towards interviews in Norway in particular and also in the UK and the Netherlands. Moreover, some earlier interviews were carried out within a more general effectiveness perspective, with the institutional part less elaborated. However, during the autumn of 1995, I carried out a series of in-depth institutional interviews with key Norwegian scientists and government representatives in the four initially focused regimes. This exercise was repeated within the climate context in autumn 1997 and early spring 1998. As the institutional issues are often so complex, a more limited number of in-depth interviews can be just as valuable as a large number of more superficial conversations – although the latter may *look* better on paper. Moreover, I have received inputs to the institutional assessments from present or former executive officers in all the regime secretariats relevant for this book.

Let us turn, then, to the comparative venture. One could in principle have reduced the control problem here by looking only at regimes regulating the same basic types of activities, or being at exactly the same stage in their development. As this option is not viable here, I will instead carry out a careful scrutiny of basic comparability in terms of central control factors. Then, I will carry out a systematic comparison of regimes with similar effectiveness scores to obtain a better understanding of possible institutional similarities which may be of specific causal interest.[24] Given the limited degree of control possible in practice, this is of course a venture with less than optimal value. However, as few such comparative ventures have so far seen the light of day, both weaknesses and strengths related to the exercise carried out in this context may be of value and interest.

So, what about external relevance? As indicated, statistical generalization is out of the question and, frankly, this may not be at all a misfortune. We are, after all, discussing complex and often long chains of institutional effects and mechanisms which may in fact be quite ill-suited to statistical analysis. A technique that will be utilized to some extent is the logic of critical cases. For instance, institutional mechanisms functioning well in the cases dealing with malign issues should be of special interest and general value, and institutional mechanisms not functioning well even in the benign cases call for less general interest.[25] Overall, given that the comparative and in-depth case analyses of the complex and long causal chains are properly carried out, with careful consideration of conditioning factors, I will argue that even small-scale analyses as carried out in this book have some general relevance.

On this basis, let us elaborate the two main control perspectives to be utilized in the case studies: central problem characteristics and the issue of leadership.

2.3.2 The Main Control Perspectives: Problem Characteristics and Leadership

On the one hand, there is general agreement that some international problems are more difficult to solve than others.[26] It is certainly easier to deal with visible oil slicks caused by a small number of 'targetable' ships than a sneaking and so far more or less invisible threat of global warming, caused by a multitude of societal actors all around the globe. However, to move from this general observation to a consensual classification of problem types is not unproblematic. The approach chosen in this book is quite naturally heavily influenced by my long-term participation in the Oslo/Seattle effectiveness project. However, as shown below, it can also easily be linked to major explanatory perspectives within the broader field of regime studies. Hence, in such studies, and especially studies of regime formation processes, three main explanatory perspectives have received much attention, relating to knowledge, power, and interests.[27]

First, the *knowledge* aspects are primarily taken care of in the 'intellectual' part of the problem characteristics perspective utilized in this book. Important dimensions here are the degree of uncertainty and the level of consensus. In international negotiation processes substantial uncertainty about cause–effect relationships may be considered the political equivalent of live ammunition in the hands of actors opposed to regulatory progress.[28] However, this does not imply that the production of more advanced knowledge as such guarantees political progress. Policy choices in international negotiations are often quite crude, for instance the question of whether or not to ban a chemical, in which case a marginal refinement of knowledge may be insignificant. What matters more in the policy context is probably whether there is a fair degree of consensus on the knowledge available.[29] However, due to the sheer complexity of problems (for instance the many facets of the global climate change problem) some problems may be harder to deal with than others – although there are probably no intellectually 'simple' international environmental problems to be found.

Second, the *interests* aspect is of course a central ingredient in the political part of the problem characteristics perspective. As noted, a major distinction exists between 'malign' issues involving externalities and competition, and more 'benign' issues of cost-efficiency and coordination relationships.[30] An example of the latter within the international environmental context is the coordination of research and knowledge production, where no incentive to 'defect' exists once a standard format has been agreed on. In order to specify the issue of 'malignness' further, two central concepts are 'patterns of ecological vulnerability' and 'abatement costs'.[31] Regarding the ecological vulnerability pattern, this involves both a 'saliency' and a 'relative' dimension. The saliency dimension has to do with the extent to which the environmental damage and relevant problem are generally considered serious compared to other current environmental problems at the time. The relative dimension refers to the differences in vulnerability between states. Is there, for instance, a sharp distinction between 'upstream' and 'downstream' states, so that some states mainly contribute to the problem, while others mainly experience the effects of others' emissions? Or are all states more or less 'in the same boat', both contributing to the problem and experiencing the effects? Situations with sharp asymmetries also have important implications in terms of ill-balanced power and capabilities. 'Upstream' states automatically have control over polluting emissions that have a strong impact on the welfare of other states. Overall, it is reasonable to regard issues characterized by overall low saliency combined with sharp asymmetries in vulnerability as particularly malign issues potentially leading to low effectiveness regimes. Turning to the issue of abatement costs, this issue also involves both a 'saliency' and a 'relative' dimension. The saliency aspect in this connection has to do with the extent to which solutions of the relevant environmental problem affect core economic activities, like power supply, industry, and transportation – or if such sectors are not very involved. The relative dimension of course involves the degree of differences in regulatory costs between states, creating complex competitive effects related to international regulatory efforts. It is reasonable to regard issues that both affect core economic activities and create intricate competitive problems as particularly malign issues, potentially leading to low effectiveness regimes.

Some brief notes, then, on the issue of *process-oriented leadership*.[32] At least analytically, situations are conceivable in which a seemingly high effectiveness regime dealing with a definitely malign issue would easily lead one to expect a highly powerful institutional design as the explanation. However, an alternative, and in some instances co-varying, factor is the issue of leadership. It is possible that malign conflicts of interest have not been resolved by the use of, for instance, 'strong' majority voting procedures, but instead the sharp edges of the issue have been smoothed through skilful conflict resolution by entrepreneurial parties or systemic actors such as conference chairmen. The power base of such entrepreneurial leaders may rest on at least two main foundations: material strength and specific capabilities.[33] First, material strength due to a strong economy, for instance, may enable leaders to influence other negotiators through the use or threat of positive and/or negative incentives and possible sanctions. A classic example is the considerable US financial aid to Israel and the related coercive leadership potential of American actors in the bilateral and multilateral Middle East negotiation processes. However, specific capabilities like special negotiating skills, for instance in setting up package deals and finding creative bridging solutions, distinctive issue-relevant knowledge, or a special reputation/status as an impartial, independent actor, for example, may provide a power base for leadership efforts. The power base of the Evensen group within the Law of the Sea negotiations combined all these aspects.[34] Hence, one may generally assume that leaders able to combine several of these power bases will be especially effective.

Others have pointed to the other end – the receiving end – of the leadership relationship and hence the strategy dimension to the issue of process-oriented leadership.[35] Here, there is a 'directional' leadership strategy focusing on ways to shape actor perceptions and ambitions, for instance through the production and provision of new knowledge. For instance in the acid rain context, the German distribution of alarming forest destruction findings to neighbouring countries bolstered German ambitions to expand the group of European countries willing to address acid rain politically, and hence to avoid negative competitive effects related to costly domestic abatement programmes.[36] Another leadership strategy may be termed 'problem-solving leadership', in particular by altering the institutional context of negotiations. Benedick's detailed account of the ozone negotiations (1991) offers a vivid example of the positive effects of moving a small group of crucial actors into the countryside of the US South and exposing them to square dancing and barbecues (pp.48–49). As the institutional issues are especially focused in this book, this dimension of process-oriented leadership is particularly interesting in this context. Generally, while skilful leadership is most urgently needed to cope with malign issues, benign problems characterized by a strong positive correlation of interests seem to offer a higher probability of success. Hence, it may be assumed that leadership is a more important control perspective in the latter than in the former cases.

Finally, then, combining insights from both the problem characteristics and the leadership perspectives, one may say that *a particularly malign issue would be characterized by high uncertainty and little consensus, low saliency and sharp asymmetries in vulnerability, affecting core economic activities and including intricate competitiveness issues, and with little entrepreneurial capacity to smooth and reduce all these complications.* Hence, such situations would really represent very difficult cases in terms of institutional impact. With this background, let us turn then to the focused institutional issues.

2.4 REGIME DESIGN: THE SIX FOCUSED INSTITUTIONAL ISSUES

2.4.1 Introduction

In line with Young (1994), with regard to the relationship between the concepts of 'institutions' and 'organizations', I see institutions as the wider concept, pertaining for instance to codes of conduct defining social practices. Organizations is the narrower concept, referring to material entities possessing offices, personnel, budgets and so on. Although many of the issues discussed here are clearly of an organizational nature, I will as a general rule stick to the wider *institutional* concept, since more informal codes of conduct are also clearly interesting. There seems to be an interesting relationship between the formal decision-making rules of regimes, and the rules used in actual practice.

Turning, then, to the choice of specific institutional factors, as noted by Levy, Young, and Zürn (1994): 'there are innumerable regime properties that may be used for classificatory purposes, and we do not have good a priori criteria about what sorts of classifications may prove useful in future research' (p.8). Hence, such an identification must to some extent be arbitrary. However, without such an explicit identification of regime features, how are we to give policy advice about regime design? Consequently, my approach is to build upon and refine earlier analytical attempts at a 'specific' institutional analysis,[37] based on Underdal's three proposed institutional functions (1990): provision of incentives for adopting and pursuing a constructive problem-solving approach; provision of procedural opportunities for transcending initial constraints; and provision of capacity for integrating and aggregating actor interests and preferences.[38] It is possible to 'translate' these three general functions into at least six specific, structural institutional factors.[39]

Beginning with the integration/aggregation capacity, this involves more specifically *the number and type of participants*. It seems reasonable to assume that decision-making in a group of 40 states is vastly different from a situation involving only four states. Moreover, it also seems reasonable to assume that states behave somewhat differently within a cooperative setting when they are joined by non-state actors, who often have close media contacts and hence a capability to influence domestic public sentiments. A second, obvious feature determining aggregation capacity is *the decision-making rules*. There is of course a fundamental difference here between consensual rules and rules allowing some kind of majority (for example, simple or two-thirds) to decide the outcome. A third aspect has to do with *secretariat capacity*. Secretariats can provide crucial and on-time background information for the parties, help set 'realistic' agendas, and hence enhance aggregation capacity.

Regarding procedural opportunities for transcending initial constraints, this involves, first and foremost, *the structure of the agenda*. For instance, a 'broad' agenda makes it possible for indifferent states or even for losers on some issues to decide to consent, while expecting to be rewarded when other issues come up for discussion.

The provision of incentives for constructive problem-solving obviously involves the provision of 'objective' information about the environmental or resource problem at hand, independent of national political considerations. The most objective and independent information available is most often scientific information, though it may not be directly applicable in a decision-making context. This makes the organization of the science–politics interface a relevant topic for study in this connection. For instance, how are scientific advisory committees composed in order to balance the conflicting claims for, on the one hand, 'independent' science, and, on the other hand, politically 'useful' science? Finally, information about the follow-up of states concerning already adopted regulations is also interesting in this context. This type of reliable information can assure states that cooperative costs are not in vain. Coupled with mechanisms for helping weak states and punishing 'free-riders', verification and compliance mechanisms can bolster problem-solving ability considerably.

Let us turn, then, to a further elaboration of the institutional and organizational issues focused on, and formulate some more specific assumptions to guide the case studies and comparative analyses as heuristic devices. All assumptions are of course formulated in terms of 'all other things being equal', and they may be equally relevant both for studies of developments *within* regimes as for studies of relationships *between* regimes.

2.4.2 The Different Faces of Regime Access and Participation: Scope, the Role of Outsiders, and Ministerial Participation

As a starting point, it is important to note that access refers to rules regulating the possibility of participation; while participation refers to the actual participation of various groups. At least three different dimensions of this issue complex are discernible here.[40] First, there is the issue of the 'scope' of participating states. With the term 'scope', an important question is whether the regime is global, regional or bilateral with regard to state participation. Second, access and participation of 'outsiders' has to do with two factors. These are the *rules* regulating the participation of actors other than the formal state parties, for instance observers from other international governmental organizations (IGOs) such as regimes and international organizations, and representatives of various non-governmental organizations (NGOs) such as private sector organizations and environmental groups and organizations; and the actual participation of these groups. Third, the issue of high-level and ministerial participation refers to the extent to which important regime meetings are conducted only at the administrative and bureaucratic level, or if ministers and politicians also regularly participate, potentially contributing additional political energy to processes. There are of course various reasons for singling out these particular issues. Let us first turn to the question of state participation and scope.

The scope of state participation: problem requirements versus small group dynamics
It is possible here to distinguish between a more 'general' and a more 'specific' institutional design perspective. The more general perspective can be summed up as follows: in order to solve fully the environmental problems addressed, participatory scope should match problem scope quite closely. As a general rule, states taking on regulatory burdens within a regime context will not be satisfied with other states contributing to the problems while not participating in the cooperative context or taking on regulatory burdens related to solving the problems at issue. Although this is the general logic, it will probably be more feasible and easier to support in the case of some problems than others. First, for instance with regard to regimes dealing with land-based marine pollution, we know that important polluting inputs originate in far-off landlocked countries, passing through long rivers and eventually ending up in seas like the North Sea or the Mediterranean. Moreover, in the course of time we have learnt that significant marine inputs come from atmospheric pollution, perhaps originating from another group of inland countries. If all major problem contributors participated in such regimes, this would mean a potentially rather large group of countries with no direct interest in the specific sea at issue. Other

types of international problems, with less indirect pathways, may be easier to handle in this regard.

Hence, although seeking a perfect match between problem scope and participatory scope makes sense in a problem-solving perspective, there are other aspects which also need to be taken into consideration. As noted, it seems reasonable to assume that the broader the scope of the regime, the more multifarious the participating states and their interests will be, and the lower the highest common denominator achievable in regime decisions will tend to be. Likewise, with regard to national behavioural processes, the broader the scope of regimes, the more pronounced will be the probable differences in perceived vulnerability, as well as the priority and administrative capacity. Hence, preparedness as well as involvement will be marginal for a large number of actors, leading to an overall low level of national behavioural change and implementation. Moreover, as pointed out by Axelrod and Keohane (1985), developing 'effective reciprocity' requires that actors can identify defectors, that they are able to focus retaliation on defectors, and that they have sufficient long-term incentives to punish them. 'When there are many actors, these conditions are often more difficult to satisfy.'[41] Such factors probably explain why authors like Peter Sand (1990A) propose setting standards at a regional rather than a global level.

Let us, then, briefly introduce the more specific organizational design perspective in this connection. The keyword here is 'flexibility', and given its roots in the negotiation literature,[42] it is first and foremost relevant in connection with regime meetings of the parties and related outputs. Especially in comprehensive or global settings, it seems obviously reasonable, in certain phases and related to certain limited problems within a larger totality, to temporarily limit participation, and work in smaller groups, shielded from public attention.

Outsiders' access and participation: inclusive legitimacy versus exclusive effectiveness?

The classic dilemma here is of course related to the conflicting general concerns for openness and legitimacy versus decision-making effectiveness. On the one hand, to include all interested actors in decision-making, be they states or non-governmental organizations, provides high legitimacy to the final decisions. On the other hand, such broad inclusion may potentially mean a very large number of actors. Moreover, involving actors without a national mandate and a related broad range of interests and considerations in mind may complicate discussions and compromises with regard to sensitive national interests. However, this issue has more than one dimension. Much can be said for considering open access, practised with some flexibility, as a quite effective approach. It has for instance been noted by Levy, Young, and Zürn (1994:11) that: 'it is more or less uncontested that the participation of non-state actors (e.g. Greenpeace or Amnesty International) and epistemic communities, at least in the rule-implementation stage, does improve the effectiveness of international environmental regimes'. With regard to the impact on regime decisions, a high degree of inclusiveness will give actors that are interested in environmentally 'strong' regulations ample scope to provide the formal parties with up-to-date briefing notes, to function as communication links to the media, and in some cases to address their concerns directly to the negotiators in plenary sessions. Hence, environmental NGOs may take on 'entrepreneurial' functions.[43] However, general open access will seldom mean the actual participation of environmental NGOs only. It is for instance likely that private industry groups will frequently use their lobbying skills to obtain contrary goals to the green NGOs. Hence, although inclusive decision-making will generally score high in terms of legitimacy, it will by no means automatically mean 'greener' decision-making.

Also with regard to the impact on national ratification and implementation processes, a good case can be made for regarding openness and inclusiveness as generally positive features. It has for instance in this connection been maintained that the participation of NGOs can bring to bear a wide range of information and viewpoints at an early stage in the process, and thereby improve the ultimate prospects for ratification.[44] Less attention has been given to the link between broad participation and the prospects for successful implementation. For instance Haas, Keohane and Levy (1993) point out that although intergovernmental organizations are 'extremely reticent' in criticizing governments, NGOs do not face such constraints: 'They play an active role, using information gained at formal international meetings, as well as public statements made by government officials, to embarrass governments and criticize national policy' (p.399). Hence, at the general level, it is possible to expect that the participation of environmental NGOs at regime meetings would increase the chances of effective implementation. However, as indicated, there are also some clear weaknesses associated with an inclusive and open approach. General openness in negotiations can easily lead to 'playing to the gallery' as well as rhetorical and tactical moves meant to satisfy domestic clients. Such a development may easily reduce the ability to tap integrative potentials, and hence the possibility for producing strong decisions. These weaknesses also point to the obvious probable advantage of a flexible approach, with smaller groups and more closed sessions in certain crucial decision-making phases.

Ministerial and political participation: the challenge of keeping processes 'reasonably' dynamic

The final dimension shifts the attention back to the state level and focuses on the question of the *type* of state representatives. A central distinction here is between administrative-level bureaucratic participants and higher-level political participants like ministers. As indicated in Chapter 1, bureaucrats often master the complex technological and political details best, while ministers are definitely freer to cut bargains, and they usually draw much more media and public attention to the issues. Hence, with regard to impact on regime decisions, it generally seems reasonable to assume that regular high-level and political gatherings can provide sorely-needed political energy to regime negotiation processes, given the existence of continuous bureaucratic 'footwork' and follow-up. Hence, a crucial *interplay* between politically dominated and administratively dominated processes can be noted. Administratively dominated processes are generally apprehensive and finely tuned to political realities. It has also been maintained that the most flexible and creative pre-negotiation problem-solving often occurs between relatively low-level officials in informal consultations before the start of public negotiations.[45] But 'administrative' processes may also over time become routine-oriented as well as short on visions and political direction. On the other hand, processes dominated by ministers and a generally high level of politicization may easily turn into rhetorical and symbolic show-off sessions, with plenty of vision but somewhat removed from ecological and political realities. With regard to the potential impact on national policy processes, much of the same logic as indicated above seems to apply: it generally seems reasonable to assume that regular high-level, 'political' gatherings can provide crucial political energy to the programme implementation processes of regimes. For instance with regard to the production and assessments of follow-up reports to such high-level meetings, it may be assumed that such high-profile processes tend to act as implementation stimulants to a greater extent than the more low-key reporting processes of the regular party conferences. Hence, in this respect, issues and mechanisms related to participation, verification and compliance may be related.

Compared to most of the other institutional issues covered in this context, the issues of access and participation are definitely complex and multi-faceted. Hence, the topics selected for analysis in this connection cover only a part of the access and participation issue universe. The first dimension involved the fundamental scope of the cooperation, with the most relevant distinction being between a regional versus a global scope. This 'choice' in the initial regime formation process is of course closely related to important problem characteristics, but there are also regional, more limited options related to basically global problems. Anyway, the basic assumption here is that *in a short-term perspective, regimes with few and homogeneous participants tend to be more effective than regimes with many and heterogeneous participants – regardless of the actual problem scope.* However, in a more long-term perspective, it is more doubtful whether regimes not covering all major contributors to the environmental and resource problems addressed can remain effective. Given that at the regional level it is easier to achieve both a good match between problem scope and participation, and benefit from smaller group dynamics, it seems reasonable to assume that regional regimes tend to be more effective than global ones, regardless of time perspective.

The next dimension shifted attention away from states and formal parties to the question of affected non-state actors' access to, and participation in, regime activities like party conferences. This cluster of issues raises important questions on the balance between the need for legitimate, broad-based international activities and the need for effective decision-making – although there are also tricky issues concerning representativeness and legitimacy related to the NGOs themselves. Since this involves the balancing of different concerns and needs in various phases, if regarded as an inclusiveness continuum, it seems reasonable to assume that regimes with a generally inclusive access and participation profile tend to be more effective than regimes with a more exclusive profile.

The final dimension shifted the attention again back to the state level and focused on the question of the type of state representatives. A central distinction here is between administrative-level, bureaucratic participants and higher-level political participants such as ministers. Given the need for regular political vitalization of regime activities, the basic assumption in this connection can be formulated as follows: *regimes with regular higher-level political and ministerial participation in regime activities tend to be more effective than regimes which lack, or rarely have, political participation.*

2.4.3   Decision-Making Rules: Is Consensus Underrated?

International cooperation between sovereign states is naturally oriented towards compromise and consensus. The Vienna Convention on the Law of Treaties states that the adoption of treaty texts generally takes place by the consent of all parties, and the possible use of two-thirds majority voting must especially be agreed upon by consensus.[46] In order to produce decisions with high legitimacy, this is understandable. However, in situations where decision-making rules really demand *unanimity* (that is, the positive approval of all parties), a single reluctant 'laggard' state may be sufficient to hinder the vast majority of states from agreeing to a regulation.[47] Add to this the perspective that 'vetoing' is generally far easier in international cooperation than 'engineering'. In other words, in connection with regulatory proposals discussed within regimes, it may be far easier to specify economic costs falling on specific groups in the near future than it is to portray convincingly the often equivocal and long-term environmental benefits related to such regulations.[48] Thus, a strict application of the decision-making rule of unanimity does in a sense 'structurally' favour the laggards. Such situations form the background for the formulation of the *law of the least ambitious programme* with regard to regime decisions.[49] This 'law' states that 'where international management can be established only through agreement among all significant parties involved, and where such a regulation is considered only on its own merits, collective action will be limited to those measures acceptable to the least enthusiastic party'. The calls for stronger international decision-making procedures, as voiced for instance in the 1989 Hague Declaration on the Environment, should clearly be seen in the context of such 'laggards' logic'.[50] Any institutional capability to go beyond this logic in the form of allowing decisions based on the preferences of a simple, two-thirds or three-quarters majority of the parties in question must surely be assumed to enhance decision-making capacity. Moreover, such capability may be especially important in situations with severe, value-laden conflicts. Such conflicts may be less prone to consensus-building and compromise. However, as noted by Szell (1996), there may also be institutional and decision-making possibilities in a kind of grey zone between consensus and majority voting. Such possibilities include weighted voting, 'double majorities' (that is, further qualification of the majority requirement) and 'tacit amendment procedures'.[51]

Moreover, an interesting distinction can be made between *formal* and *informal* decision-making rules. As we all know, formal stringent rules may be practised with different degrees of severity. Formal strict requirements of consensus practised with flexibility may for instance open up opportunities for a decoupling of less ambitious actors, so that regime decisions can be made beyond 'the law of the least ambitious programme'. In this connection it can be noted that a slightly revised 'law' has been formulated, perhaps more fitting for international environmental regimes, taking into account a situation often containing a few major emitters and several smaller emitters. This revised 'law of the *significantly* least ambitious' indicates that collective action will be limited to those measures acceptable to the least enthusiastic party which cannot be accepted as a free-rider, hence opening up opportunities for a more flexible situation.[52] Hence, it is important to look out for possible differences between formal rules and practised rules.

However, is the thinking above equally relevant in terms of the actual *implementation* and *effectiveness* of regulations? This is a more open question. At least in situations with a significant minority being outvoted (though not large enough to form a 'blocking minority'), it is easy to imagine these minority states being quite lukewarm implementers.[53] In addition, the more ambitious rules likely to be produced by majority voting may naturally be harder to implement as well. Hence, although the initial decision may be stronger in behavioural terms than if it had been produced under a consensus regime, the final behavioural and environmental effects may be less different than the more ambitious implementation starting point might imply. However, a majority voting procedure may produce incentives for the leader states to go further in their implementation efforts than they would otherwise have done, as they may easily become 'captured by the pressure game'; while the laggards' reaction may at least be uncertain; they may feel some kind of pressure to strive for a more ambitious goal.[54] Moreover, as pointed out by Hagerhall (1993:75), a majority decision-making system permits a clearer identification of countries 'not willing to live up to the wish of the majority', and gives NGOs better possibilities of exerting pressure at different levels. Hence, there are clearly counteracting forces at work here.

In conclusion, the most natural basic assumption here would still be that *the decision-making rules of unanimity and consensus tend to lead to weaker regime decisions than with (qualified) majority voting rules.* However, a moderating distinction should be made with regard to effects in different phases. Although majority voting rules have at least the capacity to lead to more environmentally ambitious decisions (though it cannot be taken for granted that the majority is always on the 'progressive' side), the implications for implementation performance are more uncertain. First, more ambitious rules are generally harder to implement, and second, it is doubtless conceivable that outvoted states may 'sabotage' the follow-up process by giving little attention to compliance and implementation. Moreover, a distinction should also be made with regard to formal rules and rules in practice. Consensus practised with flexibility may further reduce the practical difference between consensual and majority voting approaches. Hence, the relationship between decision-making rules and the ultimate effectiveness of regimes may be far more open than is apparent at first glance.

2.4.4 The Role of the Secretariat: Assistant or Player?

As noted by Sandford (1992, 1994), much literature on international secretariats has focused mainly on the UN Secretary-General in international negotiations and crises of various kinds. Other secretariats, such as those related to international environmental regimes, have received far less attention.[55] In some major contributions, the potential role and contributions of such regime secretariats have been assessed quite optimistically. Sandford (1994:29), for instance, maintains that 'international environmental Secretariats are important *actors* in the negotiation and implementation of international environmental treaties' (my italics). Moreover, von Moltke and Young (1995:2) suggest that 'the effectiveness of the Secretariat is a necessary condition for the effectiveness of the regime'. However, as indicated in the title of Sandford's contribution, such secretariats may also be envisaged to play more low-key 'stage-hand' assisting roles. In other words, given the limited research carried out on the actual role of such secretariats, it may be a rather open question whether they should be regarded primarily as national–state assistants or more independent process players.

Ideal differences between these roles in various phases can be identified.[56] As regards agenda-setting, the player secretariat initiates and actively participates in agenda setting and protocol development. The assistant secretariat acts more as a behind-the-scenes adviser on agenda. In the negotiation stage, the player secretariat consults with the parties about negotiation requirements, and facilitates, and in some cases initiates, the development of parallel or single negotiating texts. Moreover, it not only helps to organize the meetings of the scientific and technical advisory bodies, but also contributes to the process by framing central questions and selecting participants. It is also at hand to act as moderator or mediator in the event of negotiation stalemates. An assistant secretariat does not participate directly in the negotiations; instead it provides administrative assistance to the parties in document preparation as requested. In relation to the implementation stage, the assistant secretariat collects and compiles follow-up reports from the parties. The player secretariat takes a more active role in the analyses and dissemination of such data, as well as the development of more independent data sources in addition to the parties' own reports.

The ability to play these different roles is of course partly dependent on the budgetary resources and manpower available to the secretariat. It is by no means a logical necessity for an active secretariat to be large, or vice versa. The optimal combination may very well be a rather small secretariat (not drawing more than necessary on the parties' resources) which is active and efficient. Moreover, 'player' secretariats may very well prefer to be perceived as 'assistant' secretariats, since some of the more active functions may no doubt be controversial. If this is the case, the true activism and hence influence of such secretariats will easily be underestimated in empirical analyses. Given the general, underlying premise that organizational factors may play different roles in different cooperative phases, is it then reasonable to assume that a more resourceful and active secretariat will necessarily lead to stronger regime decisions? To some extent, though not unconditionally. Most regime participants are likely to prefer a 'basic' degree of administrative strength and effectiveness.[57] However, the need for and thus interest in a considerably more resourceful and active secretariat will probably depend on the parties' own administrative resources. For instance, in the case of the Mediterranean cooperation it seems as if the active role of the United Nations Environment Programme (UNEP) was more or less a necessary condition for making the cooperation work in the initial phases. UNEP financed much of the work up to 1979 and was also an active player in the political process, sponsoring workshops, among other things.[58] In other cases, when the parties generally have more advanced administrative capacities, it is reasonable to assume that a similar secretariat effort would be unnecessary and doubtless also unwanted.

Is the above reasoning also applicable to the implementation phase? To a large extent, I would hold that view. As indicated by Haas, Keohane and Levy (1993), it is conceivable that institutions can foster the transfer of the information, skills, and expertise necessary for implementation of effective domestic programmes. The role of UNEP within the Mediterranean cooperation again springs to mind as a possible example. However, it is also reasonable to assume that in other, more 'resource-rich' settings, the role of the secretariat in this connection will be much more limited. Finally, the discussion on the role of the secretariat is an apt illustration of a basic, underlying policy paradox in this connection. The strength of the secretariat obviously involves the fundamental willingness of states to give up basic control over international decision-making processes. This can also be witnessed in the discussions regarding decision-making rules (for example, the willingness to accept majority rules) and verification and compliance (such as the readiness to accept assessments independent of the states). Hence, a sort of paradox can be formulated: if the parties within a regime were initially really so inclined to cooperate as to accept a strong, independent secretariat, majority voting and 'independent' compliance reports, then none of these features would in practice be necessary in order to achieve considerable cooperative progress.

Finally, an interesting assumption then to investigate further here is that *regimes with secretariats with a financially strong and relatively autonomous and active position (up to a certain optimal point) tend to be more effective than regimes with less financially strong and active secretariats*. A strong financial position (either achieved directly with contributions from the parties or indirectly through a link to a supportive organization like UNEP) and a relatively autonomous position can be conceived as allowing the secretariat to enhance the parties' and regime's capacity to establish and implement agreements. As indicated, some have even suggested that the effectiveness of the secretariat is a necessary condition for the effectiveness of a regime. However, the importance of the role of the secretariat should probably be regarded as being contingent on the administrative capacities of the parties. It seems reasonable to assume that the role of the secretariat can be crucial in a situation where several or all the cooperative parties have poor domestic administrative capacities. Conversely, the functioning of the secretariat may be less critical when the parties' administrative capacities are quite high.

2.4.5 Organizing the Agenda: The Virtues of Flexible Comprehensiveness

At the outset, it should be noted that the reasoning behind the structure of the agenda is naturally oriented towards the effects on decisions made at party conferences and other regime meetings. Hence, in the broader effectiveness context, which includes national policy and implementation processes, the causal chain becomes more complex. This being noted, let us examine two main, partly related, ideas in this connection, summarized with the keywords 'comprehensiveness' and 'flexibility'.

With regard to *comprehensiveness*, several authors note the advantages and drawbacks of both 'narrow' single issue approaches and broader, comprehensive packages.[59] It may for instance be argued that a large number of issues under consideration implies many potential controversies and blocking points. Thus, a narrow approach incurs less risk of 'holdouts' that impede agreement. However, Sebenius (1990) reminds us that in the Law of the Sea (LOS) negotiations context, it was precisely the failure to negotiate separate 'mini-conventions' in around 1960 that led to the comprehensive approach chosen in 1973. A comprehensive approach can then offer participants at least *something* they like, and hence increase the possibility of putting together acceptable package deals. Moreover, as Oran Young reminds us, broadening the scope of the negotiations may thicken the participants' 'veil of uncertainty', that is, reduce their ability to calculate precisely the consequences for themselves of the rules under consideration.[60] Generally, Sebenius argues for finding 'a constructive path between the Scylla of a comprehensive agenda that risks LOS-like complexity, and the Charybdis of independent, single-issue protocols (that may lack sufficient joint gain and risk very selective adherence)'.[61] His main proposition is that organizers should seek to permit issues to be creatively linked into packages that promise a sufficient joint gain to be attractive to a large number of parties, yet that are not so comprehensive as to risk excessive complexity and delay. Moreover, both Sebenius (1990) and Underdal (1990) emphasize *flexibility* as a keyword in this connection. Underdal states that the institutional setting should provide procedural opportunities for transcending initial constraints. This requires 'first and foremost a flexible agenda ... permitting ... the adding and subtraction of parties' (p.15). For his part, Sebenius recommends organizers to proceed sequentially with specific agreements or protocols, and pick 'easy' subjects first. However, it should be noted that the idea of the adding and subtraction of issues seems to necessitate a fairly comprehensive agenda in order to be workable (that is, it is important to have a 'critical' mass of issues in order to subtract and add).

Can we then identify a 'comprehensive' agenda when we see one? It is probably useful here to envisage a continuum. Valid, albeit very different, examples of quite comprehensive approaches are the European Community (EC) and the Law of the Sea negotiations and regime. The EC is often referred to in the debate on international environmental regimes as an interesting institutional model, though in no respect primarily an environmental organization. The EC covers a wide range of sectors, from agricultural policy to research and education policy. Moreover, the EC has a comprehensive environmental policy agenda encompassing air, water, wastes, chemicals, noise, and flora and fauna.[62] Such a comprehensive agenda creates *in principle* opportunities for the establishment of package deals including trade-offs both within the broader environmental field and across several sectors – although such trade-offs are probably not easy to achieve in practice. With regard to more specific resource regimes, the Law of the Sea negotiations and regime are in many ways an extreme example of comprehensiveness, encompassing rules on rights to fish, on hydrocarbons and deep seabed minerals, and on the protection of the marine environment, along with the conduct of marine scientific research. Examples of somewhat less, though still fairly comprehensive regimes, are the regional Baltic and Mediterranean marine pollution regimes. Both these regimes cover various types of marine pollution. Closer to the narrow end of the continuum, we find regimes which focus on a specific type of activity, substance or resource, such as, for instance, regimes focusing on marine dumping.

In summary, on a very general level, it may be argued that an 'optimal' agenda belongs more to the comprehensive end of the continuum than the narrow end, in order to provide possibilities for the flexible adding and subtracting of issues in different phases of the development of the regime. Hence, the following main overall assumption can be formulated: *regimes with comprehensive agendas, achieving a flexible adding and subtracting of issues, tend to adopt stronger regulations than regimes with narrower agendas and fewer possibilities for such flexibility.* However, the practical importance of the structure of the agenda in the effectiveness context is clearly more complex. Among other things, utilizing the flexibility benefits requires effective political leadership. Workable package deals must be constructed by skilful entrepreneurs.

2.4.6 The Organization of the Scientific–Political Complex: Balancing Scientific Integrity and Decision-Making Involvement

Given the complex nature of environmental problems and the technological dimension generally involved in potential solutions, knowledge production and technology diffusion aspects are bound to be important issues for the founding and functioning of international resource and environmental regimes. One of the first books on international environmental management, Kay and Jacobson (1983), concluded: 'We are struck ... by the differential effectiveness of inter-national organizations in cases where problem identification is given a clear priority, as contrasted to cases where activity takes place in the absence of any such consensus or of a major effort on the part of the Secretariat concerned to build and maintain a consensus on the nature of the problem' (p.324). This perspective was given support in our own 1991 effectiveness report.[63] Furthermore, in Haas, Keohane and Levy's important 1993 *Institutions for the Earth* contribution, out of nine possible institutional pathways, at least five touched upon knowledge aspects.[64] However, what has been lacking in this discussion is a more precise identification and assessment of the specific international organizational and institutional components in this connection. Hence, the distinction provided in Underdal et al. (forthcoming 1998) between the need to balance the autonomy and *integrity* of science against *involvement* and responsiveness to the concerns and needs of decision-makers, is analytically helpful.[65] Moreover, the 'buffer' idea launched by Ed Miles (1987) can be seen as one possible organizational solution to this balancing dilemma. Let us now take a closer look at these perspectives.

The formulation of rational and effective environmental policies requires that findings from relevant scientific research be communicated to decision-makers, and 'translated' into premises for policy decisions. However, this communication process is not uncomplicated. Generally speaking, decision-makers value 'accessibility' and 'feasibility' just as much as scientists value 'autonomy' and 'integrity'. This clash of values and priorities can result in scientists producing answers which decision-makers fail to comprehend or have less need for. In other instances, scientists can conduct research that has direct implications for sensitive questions concerning allocations within regimes, for instance research directly pointing out winners and losers in political controversies over fishing quotas. This will make it very tempting for the probable losers to try to influence the scientific work along the way. If such efforts at influence are successful, the result may be what Susskind (1994:69) has termed 'adversary science'. Hence, it has been maintained that the 'constructive use of inputs from scientific research in the making of environmental policy decisions seems to require that we find some way to combine or balance the integrity and autonomy of the scientific undertaking with "involvement" in the practical problems faced by decision-makers and responsiveness to the "needs" of decision-makers for "diagnostic" and "therapeutic" knowledge'.[66]

As mentioned earlier, a specific organizational solution which has been suggested to handle such interface problems is the 'buffer' idea, launched first and foremost by Ed Miles (1987; 1989). Miles found that one of the main factors in scientific consensus-building was the presence or absence of direct distributive and regulatory links, and that 'indirect rather than direct links to management decisions will facilitate the emergence of consensual knowledge'.[67] Particularly in situations where the level of political conflict is high, direct links to the regulatory body may 'contaminate' scientific research. Hence, on the one hand, and mainly emphasized by Miles, an organizational buffer body may facilitate the *separation* of the scientific and political activities and avoid politicization of regime activities. However, the buffer idea can also make sense in a different way.[68] Hence, an organizational buffer body may also facilitate the *integration* of scientific and political regime activities, by contributing a politically less tense meeting ground for better communication between scientists and decision-makers. I suspect that the latter dimension may in fact be the most important one in the environmental context, where the distribution and political implications of scientific findings are often more diffuse than in the fishing quotas context. However, what, more precisely, qualifies as an organizational buffer, and what does not? In order to fulfil the requirements of non-politicized communication and 'translation' of scientific and technological knowledge into potential policy premises, it makes sense, as a starting point, to look for specific, formal bodies within the regimes, staffed with administrators with a natural science background, and with the mandate of discussing (but not deciding on) questions in the science–politics interface.

In summary, knowledge production processes related to international environmental regimes may be assumed to be important. However, to what extent and in what way this importance is dependent on specific forms of organization is more uncertain. A central theme is the need to balance the autonomy and integrity of science on the one hand and involvement and responsiveness to the concerns and needs of decision-makers on the other. Given the fact that important regime decisions and substantial progress can probably be made in the initial regime phase based on fairly approximate knowledge and imperfect communication, it is reasonable to assume that the balancing and communication challenges identified above become increasingly important, when regime regulations need to be revised and adjusted in relation to environmental and societal conditions in order to remain legitimate and effective. Hence, an assumption to be investigated further in this connection may be formulated as follows: *regimes which have come to succeed in balancing the need for both independent and applicable scientific inputs tend to be more effective than regimes with less success in this regard.* A specific organizational idea in this connection is the establishment of a 'mediating buffer' between scientific processes and policy processes. This idea has two dimensions: on the one hand, 'integration' in order to increase and facilitate communication between scientists and decision-makers, on the other hand 'separation' of scientific and political activities, precluding a politicization of regime meetings. Hence, although a precise understanding of the nature of such buffer bodies is lacking, a related sub-assumption can be formulated in the following manner: *regimes with a buffer body in the interface between science and politics tend to become more effective than regimes without such buffer bodies.*

2.4.7 Institutional Questions Related to Verification and Compliance: 'Non-Intrusive' versus 'Intrusive' Elements; and 'Carrots' versus 'Sticks'

Compared to many of the factors discussed so far, the issues related to verification and compliance are clearly oriented more towards the implementation phase. However, as there is a continual interplay between regulatory development and implementation processes in most environmental regimes, these issues are of course also relevant for the processes of (re)negotiating regime regulations. Inadequate or lacking implementation reports will probably not exactly increase the parties' willingness to strengthen and further develop regime regulations. On the basis of the previous and current scholarly attention given to these issues,[69] it also seems reasonable to assume that these factors are, in terms of causality, among the chief institutional and organizational factors. To pick just two examples from the effectiveness literature: Young (1992:176) suggests that the effectiveness of international institutions varies directly with the ease of monitoring or verifying compliance with their principal behavioural prescriptions. In the same vein, according to Haas, Keohane and Levy (1993:22), 'the monitoring activities of international institutions can be vital to the ability of states to make and keep agreements'. Furthermore, issues of verification and confidence-building should clearly be related to issues of participation, and hence also to fundamental problem characteristics in several ways. First, it is of course generally easier to monitor activities within relatively small groups than within larger ones. Hence, it can be envisaged that smaller groups may in fact develop some sort of 'diffuse reciprocity', which makes careful verification and 'specific reciprocity' less important.[70] However, as indicated earlier, the fundamental scope of environmental problems and issues of legitimacy will of course often limit the extent of participation experiments. Second, it has been pointed out that some problems and some activities are by their nature easier to monitor compliance with than others, with the difference between visible oil pollution and dumping operations versus a myriad of 'diffuse' land-based marine pollution sources as an obvious example.[71] Likewise, as hinted at by Young (1992) above, some types of regulations are also easier to monitor than others. For instance, Ron Mitchell's (1994A and B) study of intentional oil pollution at sea and the differing 'monitorability' of equipment standards versus discharge standards is interesting in this connection.

I would further suggest distinguishing between two main, related issue complexes within this broader field: first, the verification part, related to state reporting and possibilities for related checking of compliance, and, second, what may be referred to as compliance strengthening mechanisms, either 'negative' (for instance some form of sanctions) or 'positive' (for instance economic incentives like compensation funds). Let us take a closer look at these issue complexes in turn.

The verification and review dimensions

A 'non-intrusive' verification cornerstone within international environmental regimes is the parties' own reports on emission policies and reductions. As indicated by Levy and Young (1993), reports on state follow-up are an important aspect of the functions of regimes as 'enhancers of cooperation'. At least two major causal pathways may be envisioned. First, as already indicated, follow-up reports can be confidence-building by generally increasing transparency and mitigating fears of cheating. Second, such reports may influence effectiveness by contributing to various forms of technological and regulatory learning. In other words, states may discover smarter ways of cutting emissions or handling resources by discussing relevant information provided by the other parties. In terms of institutional design, at least two partly related dimensions can be discerned, related to the role of the secretariat and the establishment of specific review mechanisms. Starting with the role of the secretariat,[72] the organizing of the state reporting process can no doubt be carried out in a more or less structured and effective manner. The initial regime convention provisions will often be formulated rather generally and provide limited organizational guidance. Hence, the development of well-structured and effective reporting procedures may in some instances depend upon the presence of persons within the secretariats taking a special interest in developing such procedures. In other cases, a need for a strengthened secretariat effort may follow directly from more complex and detailed regulations being developed within the regime, necessitating revised, more structured reporting procedures. In cases with a substantial proportion of regime parties with weak administrative capacities, the need may easily arise for the secretariat to take on important functions in assisting with reporting.

But should the parties' own reports constitute the only inputs to regime discussions on compliance, or should such reports be supplemented by independent inputs of some sort? This brings up the issue of specific and potentially more 'intrusive' review mechanisms. Ideally, more or less independent inputs would strengthen the general confidence-building effects related to the state reporting process. Such an independent assessment is the very basis of the 'performance review' mechanism in operation in other international organization settings.[73] For instance Sand (1990A) summarizes the International Labour Organization's (ILO) experience as an interesting model: 'annual or biannual reporting by governments, combined with regular auditing by an independent technical Committee of Experts to ascertain compliance in each member state, followed by public debate of these audited reports by the Conference Committee on the Application of Conventions and

Recommendations'.[74] According to Chayes and Chayes (1991; 1993; 1995), similar features are found in international organizations like GATT (General Agreement on Tariffs and Trade) and the International Monetary Fund (IMF). Hence, these experiences seem to point to the probable benefits of also having specific implementation committees, staffed with relevant expertise, within international environmental regimes. The staffing and degree of independence of such bodies may be assumed to give rise to complicated balancing discussions between, on the one hand, the need for legitimacy in relation to the states and, on the other hand, the professional integrity of such bodies. Moreover, the possible inputs to such bodies by NGOs is also likely to give rise to parallel, complicated balancing discussions. However, given that the design and content of regime regulations change in the course of time, does that not mean that reporting requirements and review mechanisms also vary in different phases of the development of regimes? It seems reasonable to think that they do. In the early phases of regime development, decisions and regulations are often crude and rather general, and hence do not necessarily require very advanced verification and review procedures. When regulations are developed in a more precise and complex way, the need for improved verification procedures and review mechanisms becomes more pertinent.

Compliance-strengthening mechanisms

As indicated, it is possible to distinguish here between the creation of 'sticks', for instance in the form of economic sanctions, and 'carrots', for example in the form of economic assistance provided by specifically established compensation funds. Let us start with the question of possible 'sticks'. On the one hand, international environmental politics has so far been different from 'high politics' issue areas like arms control and disarmament. In environmental politics, the stakes are generally lower, and the agreements have until now often been quite generally worded. In addition, the environmental issue area has probably been characterized by more scientific, technological and political uncertainty than the arms control field. Counting missiles may be hard enough, but assessing the emissions, not to mention environmental impacts, of often innumerable emission sources, is really a formidable intellectual challenge. Add to this the regulatory crudeness often witnessed in 'first generation' environmental agreements. All these factors weaken the relevance of formal (economic) sanctions in international environmental politics. Hence, it has been argued that 'the common feature that replaces coercion in international compliance systems is the exploitation of the accountability of states by rendering their performance transparent to scrutiny by the international community'.[75] In other words, we have to make do with systems of reporting and 'performance review'. On the other hand, it is inherent in this logic that if the stakes are generally raised in international environmental politics, the question of coercion and 'sticks' may also take on a new meaning. If issues go to the economic 'cores' of societies, seriously affecting for instance the energy sector, and agreements get tougher and more specific, and hence more precisely verifiable, then the potential significance of instruments such as sanctions could increase.

Hence, the issue of 'carrots' and positive incentives is of more general interest and practical relevance. Important aspects are access to funding, resources, markets or technology. A central factor determining the need and causal importance of such selective incentives is the economic and administrative heterogeneity of regime parties. In other words, it is reasonable to expect that such mechanisms are far more important in regimes with marked North–South and/or East–West participation than in more 'Western' regimes. In an institutional perspective, the balancing of efficiency and legitimacy is bound to be a fundamental dilemma. Donors will understandably channel their funds as far as possible through institutions that have a reputation for efficient handling of funds and projects, and where donors have substantial influence on operations and policies. Recipients will equally understandably wish to see funds primarily channelled through institutions where they have a substantial influence on operations and policies, and which hence enjoy high legitimacy.[76]

In summary, the issue of verification and compliance-strengthening mechanisms is clearly a multi-faceted and complex institutional issue, in which design and effective operation is probably conditioned by central problem characteristics. Two main clusters of questions have been identified. The first cluster is related to issues of reporting and the existence of specific, more or less independent review bodies to assess and follow up compliance and implementation questions that may be produced by such reports. Without well-functioning reporting systems and implementation bodies, it seems reasonable to assume that a general lack of confidence and possibly more specific suspicions of cheating will undermine the stability of the regime over time – although initial requirements for effective procedures may be more moderate. Hence, it seems reasonable to assume that, other things such as regulatory development being equal, *regimes with well-functioning reporting systems and related implementation review bodies tend to be more effective than regimes with lax reporting systems and no specific review bodies.*

The second cluster of questions is related to the 'carrot' part, and highlights the positive incentive part of the issue of compliance-strengthening mechanisms. This is of course primarily relevant in international contexts where a significant number of the parties have weak economic and administrative capacities and hence a poor capability to take on and follow up regime requirements. The founding of a particular fund for the assistance of economically and administratively weaker parties is the most obvious organizational idea. Hence, the following assumption seems very reasonable: *in international settings with a significant number of economically and administratively weak parties, regimes which succeed in establishing a well-functioning, compliance-supporting financial mechanism tend to be more effective than regimes which fail in this regard.*

2.5 THE CONCEPTUAL APPROACH SUMMARIZED

For the crucial effectiveness concept, two suggested principal dimensions of regime effectiveness were taken as point of departure – 'distance to collective optimum' and 'the extent to which a collective problem is "solved" under present arrangements'; and 'relative improvement' focusing on whether and to what extent 'regimes matter'. Given several methodological and measurement problems related to the application of the 'distance to collective optimum' dimension, most attention was given to the 'relative improvement' dimension. In order to work better in an empirical context, the 'relative improvement' perspective was operationalized into a political effectiveness indicator, combining knowledge on regime outputs, national compliance and implementation. Segments of knowledge on the 'distance to the collective optimum' will be discussed in the case studies under the heading of the environmental and problem-solving dimensions. Here, a diachronic perspective is introduced, in order to avoid ahistorical interpretations. A synchronic dimension is added to confront more directly the crucial but complex 'is the problem actually being solved' question. Based mainly on their political effectiveness scores, the regimes will be ranked according to a simple 'high', 'medium' and 'low' ordinal scale.

Methodologically, in order to maximize 'internal validity' and 'external relevance', in-depth case study analysis will be a central ingredient, drawing upon techniques like the tracing of institutional pathways, counterfactual reasoning and the logic of 'critical cases'. In addition, a comparative institutional venture will be carried out. Two central control perspectives in relation to the focused institutional and organizational perspective will be utilized: first and foremost, the character of the problems addressed, with related preferences or interests and capabilities; and, less focused due to empirical complexity, process-oriented leadership. With regard to the problem type perspective, a basic distinction between knowledge about the problems ('intellectual aspects') and characteristics related to the affected actors and the relationship between them ('political aspects') is introduced. Primary intellectual dimensions are level of uncertainty and degree of consensus. The political problem part centres on the degree of 'malignness', with patterns of ecological vulnerability and abatement costs as central dimensions shaping interests, preferences, and capabilities. In sum, it is suggested that a particularly malign issue will be characterized by high uncertainty and little consensus, low saliency and sharp asymmetries in vulnerability, affecting core economic activities and including intricate competitiveness issues – and with little entrepreneurial capacity to smooth over and reduce all these complications.

Building upon a distinction within the central regime concept between 'structural' and 'regulative' components, the attention in this connection is given to the structural components. Six such structural factors are singled out for further scrutiny: access procedures and participation patterns; decision-making rules; the role of the secretariat; the structure of the agenda; the organization of the science–politics relationship; and verification procedures and compliance mechanisms. The main ceteris paribus assumptions related to these factors can be summed up as follows:

2.5.1. Access and Participation

- In a short-term perspective, regimes with few and homogeneous participants tend to be more effective than regimes with many and heterogeneous participants – regardless of the true problem scope. However, in the longer-term perspective, it is more doubtful whether regimes not covering all major contributors to the environmental and resource problems addressed can remain effective. Given that at the regional level it is easier to achieve both a good match between problem scope and participation, and benefit from smaller group dynamics, it seems reasonable to assume that regional regimes tend to be more effective than global ones, irrespective of time perspective.
- Regarding the access and participation of NGOs and other 'outsiders', this is partly a question of *balancing* different considerations and needs in various phases. However, if seen as an inclusiveness continuum, it seems reasonable to assume that regimes with a generally inclusive access and participation profile tend to be more effective than regimes with a more exclusive profile.
- Regarding the *type* of state representatives, given the need for regular political vitalization of regime activities, the basic assumption in this connection is that regimes with regular higher-level political and ministerial participation in regime activities tend to be more effective than regimes lacking, or with rare, political participation.

2.5.2 Decision-Making Rules

- The decision-making rules of unanimity and consensus tend to lead to weaker regime decisions than (qualified) majority voting rules. However, moderating distinctions related to effects in different phases, as well as formalities and realities, indicated a more open relationship with regard to effects on regime effectiveness.

2.5.3 The Role of the Secretariat

- Overall: regimes with secretariats which have a financially strong and relatively autonomous and active position (up to a certain optimal point) tend to be more effective than regimes with less financially strong and active secretariats.
- However, the importance of the role of the secretariat may be seen as contingent on the administrative capacities of the parties themselves. It seems reasonable to assume that the role of the secretariat can be critically important in a situation where several or all the cooperative parties have weak domestic administrative capacities. Conversely, the functioning of the secretariat may be less critical when the parties' administrative capacities are quite high.

2.5.4 The Structure of the Agenda

- Regimes with comprehensive agendas and the achievement of a flexible adding and subtracting of issues tend to adopt stronger regulations than regimes with narrower agendas and less possibility for such flexibility. However, the practical importance of the structure of the agenda in the effectiveness context is clearly more complex.

2.5.5 The Organization of the Scientific–Political Complex

- Regimes which over time succeed in balancing the need for both independent and usable scientific inputs tend to be more effective than regimes with less success in this regard.
- Regimes with a buffer body in the interface between science and politics tend over time to be more effective than regimes with no such buffer body.

2.5.6 Verification and Compliance

- Regimes with well-functioning reporting systems and related implementation review bodies tend to be more effective than regimes with lax reporting systems and no specific implementation bodies.
- In international settings with a significant number of economically and administratively weak parties, regimes which succeed in establishing a well-functioning compliance-supporting financial mechanism tend to be more effective than regimes which fail in this regard.

As a final reflection before we turn to the case studies, let me briefly introduce an institutional dimension which is related to several of the issues discussed above and which may tentatively be termed 'institutional density'. Regimes as arenas function as meeting-places for a range of different actors – states, NGOs, international organizations, and scientists – within scientific, technological and political bodies.[77] In terms of fostering general confidence and learning, it may be reasonable to assume that regimes which contain many such meetingpoints tend to be more effective than regimes which contain relatively few meetingpoints.

NOTES

1. For some seminal contributions to this discussion, see for instance Ruggie (1975); Krasner (1983); Keohane (1985; 1993); Young (1986; 1989; 1994); Haggard and Simmons (1987); Levy, Young, and Zürn (1994).
2. This is roughly in line with Levy, Young and Zürn (1994:6).
3. However, in studies focusing primarily on domestic implementation it would be natural to regard regime regulations as a central independent variable.
4. Hence, when authors like Mitchell (1994) talk about 'regime design', it is this regulative dimension of the discussion which is focused upon.
5. For summaries of this debate, see for instance Young (1994); Andresen and Wettestad (1995); Wettestad (1995A); and Young (1998). Other important contributions include Underdal (1990; 1992); Wettestad and Andresen (1991); Levy, Young and Zürn (1994); Bernauer (1995); and Skjærseth (forthcoming 1998).
6. Around 1987/88, the Oslo and Seattle effectiveness project was started, with Ed Miles and Kai Lee in Seattle, and, on the Oslo side, Arild Underdal, Steinar Andresen, Jon B. Skjærseth and the author of this book as main participants. Preliminary outputs from the Oslo team include Wettestad and Andresen (1991); Skjærseth (1991, 1992A, B and C) Andresen et al. (1992); Andresen (1993); and Andresen and Wettestad (1995). There is a project book forthcoming in 1999 (Miles et al., 1999).
7. These problems are summed up in Andresen and Wettestad (1995) and Wettestad (1995A).
8. This draws heavily on Andresen, Skjærseth and Wettestad (1995). Note that all assumptions here are of course formulated on the condition that 'all other things are equal'.
9. For an elaboration of this issue in the international environmental context, see for instance Nollkaemper (1993).
10. For some important contributions to the regime compliance debate, see for instance Mitchell (1994A and B); Chayes and Chayes (1995); Nollkaemper (1993); Cameron, Werksman and Roderick (1996); Brown-Weiss and Jacobson (1994; 1998); Victor, Raustiala and Skolnikoff (1998).
11. For a broader discussion of implementation studies in the international environmental regime context, see for instance Andresen, Skjærseth and Wettestad (1995); Skjærseth (1996; forthcoming 1998).
12. See Levy and Young (1993).
13. Primarily Wettestad (1996) and (1998).
14. Among the major projects so far have been the Hanf and Underdal LRTAP project; the IIASA IEC project (Victor, Raustiala and Skolnikoff, 1998); and to some extent the Social Learning Project (Clark et al., forthcoming).
15. See Andresen et al. (1994) and Underdal et al. (forthcoming 1999).
16. Andresen and Wettestad (1995).
17. See Underdal's Chapter 1 in Miles et al. (forthcoming 1999).

18. For more in-depth discussions of the issues in this section, see for instance Lijphart (1971); George (1979); Yin (1989); King, Keohane and Verba (1994); Bernauer and Mitchell (1997).
19. For interesting moves in that direction, see Miles et al. (forthcoming 1999), and the regimes database project (Breitmeier et al., 1996).
20. The true value of this method is disputed however. See for instance Fearon (1991) and Biersteker (1993).
21. Understanding the concept of 'mechanism' as something that simply connects a cause with an event. See for instance Elster (1989) and King, Keohane and Verba (1994).
22. For an elaboration, see for instance Keohane (1990); Haas, Keohane, and Levy (1993); and Levy, Young, and Zürn (1994).
23. See Skjærseth (forthcoming 1998) for an analytical and empirical discussion.
24. This venture will be further elaborated in Chapter 6.
25. However, a less pragmatic choice of cases could no doubt have increased the value of this exercise. This is further discussed in Chapter 8.
26. The problem characteristics perspective has been a cornerstone in the Oslo/Seattle effectiveness project. See Miles et al. (forthcoming 1999). See also Young (1998:16).
27. For an elaboration of these perspectives, see for instance Young and Osherenko (1993); Underdal (1995); and Hasenclever, Mayer and Rittberger (1996).
28. Underdal (1989).
29. Underdal (1989). More generally, on the role of consensual knowledge, see for instance Haas (1980).
30. See Underdal (1997:13–18) for an elaboration of the distinction between these two main types of problems.
31. Thanks to Kjell Dørum for reminding me about these concepts, discussed for instance in Levy (1993) and Sprinz and Vaahtoranta (1994).
32. Time and resources do not allow a really detailed investigation of the many fascinating facets of this issue in this connection. Generally, research on entrepreneurial leadership requires detailed studies of negotiation processes and the role of individuals within such processes.
33. As pointed out by Underdal (1991) and Young (1991).
34. Skodvin (1992).
35. See Malnes (1992).
36. See for instance Hajer (1995).
37. Especially Andresen and Wettestad (1992; 1993); and Wettestad (1995A).
38. Underdal (1990).
39. One institutional issue that is not given specific mention in this connection is the role of Conference Chairs and Bureaux, except to some extent in discussions of the related issue of leadership.
40. An obvious fourth and additional dimension has to do with the composition of state delegations. Due to time and resource constraints, this dimension will not be further investigated in this context.
41. Axelrod and Keohane (1985:235). See also Olson (1965); Snidal (1995); and Oye (1986).
42. See for instance Sebenius (1990).
43. For some interesting contributions on the role of NGOs in this connection, see for instance Stairs and Taylor (1992); Hagerhall (1993); Princen and Finger (1994); Susskind (1994); Raustiala (1997) and Ringius (1997).
44. See Morisette et al. (1990).
45. See Parson (1997:170).
46. Vienna Convention on the Law of Treaties, paragraphs 9.1. and 9.2. See for instance Blix and Emerson (1973:330–355).
47. However, as further discussed by Szell (1996), requirements for unanimity are exceptions rather than the rule in international environmental politics. More weight is given to the notion of consensus, which may be defined as 'the absence of formal objection'.
48. Underdal (1989; 1990).
49. Underdal (1980:36).
50. The Hague Declaration on the Environment (1989).

51. See Szell (1996:212–213).
52. See Sætevik (1988:135).
53. Underdal (1990:7) notes that 'in the absence of supranational implementation or enforcement, "imposed" collective decisions yielding non-integrative outcomes seem more likely to suffer defection(s), particularly if coercive leadership is slackened for some reason'.
54. Compare in this context Levy's (1993) concept of 'toteboard diplomacy'.
55. In addition to the Sandford contributions, see primarily von Moltke and Young (1995).
56. This draws upon both Sandford (1992; 1994) and Von Moltke and Young (1995). The latter discusses the main secretariat functions under headings like 'regime adaptation and development'; 'capacity building and resource flows'; 'liaison and networking'; 'reporting, verification and data gathering'; and 'implementation review and assessment'.
57. It should also be noted of course that some actors participate in regimes for 'destructive' purposes, in order to slow down the cooperative process. Such actors will probably prefer a weak secretariat.
58. See Haas (1990B) and Skjærseth (1992).
59. For instance, Haggard and Simmons (1987:497) note: 'The jurisdictional scope of a regime is not incidental to its success. Overly broad jurisdiction raises administrative costs and complexity, but overly narrow agreements may allow little room for bargaining and issue-linkage'. See also Sebenius (1990); and Underdal (1990).
60. Young (1989).
61. Sebenius (1990:16).
62. See for instance Skjærseth (1993).
63. Wettestad and Andresen (1991).
64. These five pathways were formulated as: 'institutions can generate new information'; 'institutions can shape domestic politics by providing information that is useful to particular domestic factions'; 'institutions can reduce the costs of negotiating agreements by generating information'; 'the monitoring activities of international institutions can be vital to the ability of states to make and keep agreements'; and 'institutions can foster the transfer of information, skills, and expertise necessary for effective domestic programs'.
65. An earlier version was published as a report in 1994 (Andresen et.al, 1994).
66. Andresen et al. (1994:1).
67. Miles (1989:49).
68. This reasoning is derived from Arild Underdal.
69. See for instance Young (1979); Chayes and Chayes (1991; 1993; 1995); Victor and Ausubel (1992); Mitchell (1994A and B); Victor et al. (1994); Victor et al. (1998).
70. Regarding the concepts of 'diffuse' versus 'specific reciprocity', see Axelrod and Keohane (1985).
71. On the concepts of 'monitorability' and 'verifiability', see for instance Greene (1994).
72. As noted by Von Moltke and Young (1995:7), 'the collection, analysis and dissemination of such data (on the activities and operations of the regime) is one of the central functions of international Secretariats'.
73. See for instance Schram Stokke (1992). In the environmental context, the OECD Performance Reviews should be mentioned as a specific example.
74. Sand (1990A:33).
75. Chayes and Chayes (1991).
76. For a more comprehensive design discussion in this connection, see for instance Keohane and Levy (eds) (1996).
77. For a discussion of the distinction between regimes as arenas and regimes as actors, see Underdal's Chapter One in Miles et al. (forthcoming 1999).

3. Increasing Concern and Improving Design: The Oslo and Paris Conventions on Marine Pollution in the North-East Atlantic[1]

3.1 INTRODUCTION: INSTITUTIONAL BACKGROUND

It was the ocean dumping issue that gave the main impetus to the establishment of international conventions to regulate marine pollution in the North Sea and the north-east Atlantic in the early 1970s. Due to increasing economic activity in the post-war years and rapid growth in the production of industrial and public waste, an initially attractive disposal option was to dump the waste into the sea. A catalysing event was the 1971 'Stella Maris' incident, drawing attention to potential marine pollution activities under little or no international or national surveillance and control.[2] This contributed to the start of an international negotiation and regulatory process, and The Oslo Dumping Convention (OSCON) consisting of 27 Articles and three Annexes was signed in 1972 by all 13 West European maritime states.[3] The Convention covered the wider north-east Atlantic area,[4] but with the North Sea as the main dumping area. The Oslo and Paris Commisions (OSPARCOM) 10th Anniversary book (1984) notes that: 'After the signing of the Oslo Convention, international opinion in environmental matters was favourably disposed towards the conclusion of agreements to establish rules for the prevention of pollution' (p.6). Given that land-based, more numerous and diffuse sources were undoubtedly a potentially much more important source of marine pollution than the dumping activity, a first diplomatic conference was held in 1972 at the initiative of the French government to establish a convention on land-based marine pollution. Reflecting the more complex and complicated nature of the land-based issues, the drafting of the land-based convention took a longer time. The initial Convention for the Prevention of Marine Pollution from Landbased Sources (hereafter: PARCON) was signed in Paris in 1974 and came into force in 1978.[5] It originally covered marine pollution from land-based sources such

43

as emissions via watercourses, both directly from the coast and from offshore installations under the jurisdiction of the coastal states. It was amended in 1986 to include pollution of the sea from atmospheric sources. Both OSCON and PARCON were initially structured around a blacklist/grey list system, and these lists indicated priority substances to be regulated. The blacklisted substances were either banned (as in the case of OSCON) or targeted for elimination (as in the case of PARCON).[6] The grey-listed substances required a specific permit (OSCON) or were targeted for reduction or elimination (PARCON).[7]

The main goals of OSCON were, first, to take all possible steps to prevent the pollution of the sea by the dumping of substances liable either to be hazardous to human health, to harm living resources and marine life, to damage amenities, or to interfere with other legitimate uses of the sea. A second element, relating to prevention of marine pollution, was the ban on dumping harmful substances from ships and aircraft, and the provision of a system of permits or approvals for dumping other substances. In a similar way, the main goals of PARCON were to take all possible steps to prevent pollution of the sea by adopting measures individually and jointly to combat marine pollution and by harmonizing the parties' policies in this regard.[8]

The main political bodies within the regimes have been the commissions (OSCOM and PARCOM). The commissions have consisted of all the parties, meeting annually, and making decisions either in the form of binding decisions or non-binding recommendations.[9] In addition, the Commissions have been assisted by technical working groups: the Standing Advisory Committee for Scientific Advice (SACSA) in the case of OSCON, and the Technical Working Group (TWG) in the case of PARCON. These bodies have themselves been assisted by ad hoc working groups. Finally, there was a Joint Monitoring Group (JMG) and a permanent, shared secretariat in London.

In addition to the Convention context, it is especially important that both dumping and land-based pollution matters have been on the agenda of four regular ministerial North Sea Conferences (NSCs): Bremen 1984; London 1987; The Hague 1990; and Esbjerg 1995 (with intermediate meetings held in Copenhagen in 1993 and in Bergen in 1997). The North Sea Conferences have produced non-binding, political Declarations.[10] In terms of knowledge improvement, the establishment of the North Sea Task Force (NSTF) at the 1987 London Conference should be emphasized. Although formally separate institutions, it makes much sense to see the North Sea Conferences as in practice parts of the OSCON and PARCON regimes. There are numerous and complex links both at the international and national levels between these processes. At the international level, OSPAR (see below) has for instance in practice run the nutrient reduction process and reported to the NSC meetings. With regard to hazardous substances, the NSC and PARCON processes have been more separate, with PARCON working more within a 'Best Available

Technology' (BAT) approach, more indirectly related to percentage reductions targets.[11]

In September 1992, the Oslo and Paris Conventions were merged into one revised convention: The Convention for the Protection of the Marine Environment of the North-East Atlantic (OSPAR). In terms of land-based issues, the main new elements were the incorporation of the precautionary principle into the Convention, and also the obligation to use the best available technology (BAT) and best environmental practices (BEP).[12] Moreover, the 1992 Convention does not distinguish between black- and grey-listed substances – a uniform regime for all substances has been established. Institutionally, as indicated above, the two former Commissions have merged, and the technical working groups (SACSA and TWG) have formed a 'Programmes and Measures Committee' (PRAM). The Joint Monitoring Group has been reorganized into an 'Environmental Assessment and Monitoring Committee' (ASMO), incorporating the work of the North Sea Task Force.[13] It should also be mentioned that a specific Action Plan for the Oslo and Paris Commissions has been agreed upon. The OSPAR Convention entered into force on 25 March 1998. (See Figure 3.1 for an overview of the current organizational setup.)

The focus on OSCON and PARCON as separate 'regimes' in this connection deserves some brief comments. This separate treatment is partly based on the fact that dumping and land-based marine pollution can in one sense be seen clearly as separate and 'specific issue areas' with quite different characteristics. Moreover, given the complicated character of the regime design discussion, it is important to have as simple and clear-cut units of analysis as possible. However, alternative, broader interpretations of the 'specific issue area' component of the regime concept can clearly be envisaged in this context.[14] In a sense, dumping and land-based pollution could have been seen as parts of the broader issue area of north-east Atlantic marine pollution. Moreover, in addition to OSCON and PARCON and the North Sea Conferences, other institutions with regulations influencing this marine area, like the European Community and the International Rhine Commission, could have been included in such a broader regime definition and discussion.[15] But again, such broader points of departure would have complicated the already complicated regime design discussion considerably.

Turning finally to the more specific organization of this chapter, it is not only the establishment of the North Sea Task Force that points to the 1987 North Sea Conference as an important turning-point within the regime. For instance, in connection with an earlier study of this regime, a panel of referees almost unanimously singled out this conference as a turning-point in the cooperation.[16] Hence, it makes sense to organize discussions on effectiveness, problem and process development, and institutional design into two major parts: before and after the 1987 North Sea Conference. Moreover, it should generally be noted that most attention is given to the PARCON story, partly because it is the most complex one, but partly also as a reflection of the author's past research priorities and related competence. On this basis, let us first turn to the important question of effectiveness.

Figure 3.1   OSPAR: current organizational setup

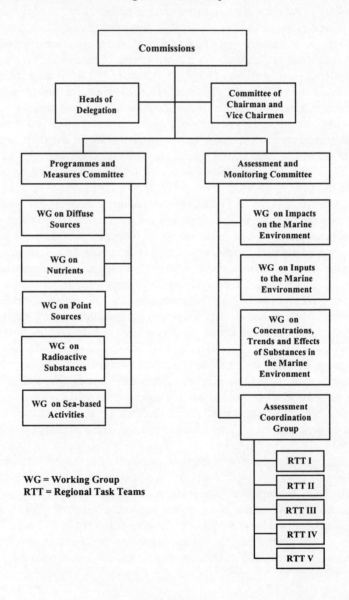

3.2 THE QUESTION OF EFFECTIVENESS: SUBSTANTIAL IMPROVEMENT OVER TIME

3.2.1 'The Early Years': 1974–87

Political effectiveness: a period of inertia
Turning first to the strength of Paris Commission regulations, during the period 1978–85 PARCOM managed to agree upon a total of 12 binding decisions on regulation measures and 14 non-binding recommendations.[17] Most of these outputs focused on the blacklisted substances of mercury and cadmium. Although on paper this represented in principle quite a respectable performance, serious questions can be raised with regard to the specificity and actual ambitiousness inherent in this regulatory development. As indicated by several observers, the regulations generally contained vague and imprecise formulations, with few precise and verifiable targets and timetables.[18] Take for instance the 1985 decision on the use of aldrin, dieldrin and endrin, stating that 'all Contracting Parties will phase out the use of aldrin, dieldrin and endrin *as soon as practicable*' (my italics). As noted by Pallemaerts (1992), this is ambiguously worded, and it seems reasonable to interpret the statement to the effect that the parties to the Paris Convention intended to maintain their full discretion in determining how soon this phasing out would be considered 'practicable'.[19] Moreover, the fact that the parties would choose to commit themselves to marine pollution quality standards which were shrouded in high scientific uncertainty and were in practice unverifiable, only strengthened the behavioural leeway inherent in these regulations.[20]

Although national behavioural impact data from this period is limited, Skjærseth's dissertation in particular (forthcoming 1998) provides us with important national information on water and ocean pollution politics in the UK, the Netherlands and Norway. The overall impression supports the 'suspicions' created by the loosely formulated international regulations: *these regulations had very little national behavioural impact*. In Norway domestic goals were more ambitious than PARCOM policies. For instance in the 77 page Parliamentary Report summing up the achievements and experiences of a major domestic clean-up programme targeting both municipal and industrial emissions, less than a page was devoted to 'international cooperation'. The main perspective here was Norway's opportunity to learn from measures undertaken by other countries and the potential to influence the process in other countries in order to avoid negative competitive effects for Norway.[21] Also in the Netherlands, most domestic action taken was based on domestic concerns and causes. In the UK, domestic legislation lagged behind international developments, but there are few indications that PARCOM decisions made the

British undertake more or different measures from those they would have done anyway during this period.

Turning briefly to the case of dumping and OSCOM, the essential picture is parallel to the 'lenient' PARCOM picture. OSCOM dealt with a wide range of waste and pollution problems, from dumping of wartime ammunition to industrial waste. The main problems were dumping of industrial waste, contaminated sewage sludge, incineration at sea, and dredge spoil. Before 1987, the key word was control of dumping operations, not significant reduction of them. Hence, more specifically, during the decade 1977–87, two decisions and ten recommendations and 'agreements' were produced, mainly establishing cooperative procedures to control dumping. It is not surprising, then, that the total amount of industrial waste dumped by the parties was actually higher in 1983 than in 1976 (although dropping slightly from 1983 to 1987) and more toxic waste was incinerated in 1987 than in 1980.[22] The most notable commitment was the 1980 recommendation to take all possible steps to reduce at source the contamination of sewage sludge with heavy metals, probably having a certain impact on British operations.[23] The first North Sea Conference in Bremen in 1984 also deserves some brief remarks in this connection. The Conference may generally be characterized as a 'necessary first step', producing few specific new measures. For instance, with regard to the dumping issue, the ministers drew general attention to the need for reduction of pollution at sea by dumping, but no specific measures were decided upon.[24]

Summing up, based mainly on the moderate international regulatory progress and available national evidence, it seems reasonable to conclude that the political effectiveness of the OSCON and PARCON regimes was quite low during this period.[25]

The environmental and problem solving dimensions: moderate concern, high uncertainty

The key phrase which describes the pollution situation in the north-east Atlantic during this period, with the North Sea receiving the bulk of the inputs and hence of most interest, was definitely high uncertainty.[26] The reason for the establishment of the OSCON and PARCON regimes seems to have been a rather general concern for the North Sea and north-east Atlantic environment and not specific, alarming reports about the quality of the marine environment. Moreover, the main international marine scientific organization – the International Council for the Exploration of the Seas (ICES) – had long been chiefly preoccupied with fishery science, and its 'Advisory Committee on Marine Pollution' (ACMP) was established in 1972 – the same year as OSCON. However, the more general concern about environmental issues was of course quite high in the 1970s.[27]

In the early 1980s, there was also growing issue-specific concern, especially in Germany, about increasing pollution in areas like the Wadden Sea. This increasing concern was an important factor behind the decision to arrange a specific North Sea Conference in 1984. As part of the preparatory work for this conference, a scientific 'Quality Status of the North Sea' report (QSR) was produced. Concerning evidence of ecological and other effects, the report concluded that 'observations and investigations known up to now ... do not in general allow clear cause–effect relationships between contaminant inputs and effects on marine organisms to be identified' (Quality Status of the North Sea Report, 1984:27). Uncertainty was high both with regard to inputs and effects. Regarding the more general development of the pollution situation, the report did not give any indications of a developing 'ecodisaster' in the North Sea. Local problems were acknowledged, but the overall situation was not seen as alarming. The main picture was very much the same in the better prepared and more detailed QSR produced prior to the 1987 North Sea Conference.[28] A central conclusion in the 'Summary Report' read: 'In general, deleterious effects, at present, can only be seen in certain regions, in the coastal margins, or near identifiable pollution sources. There is as yet no evidence of pollution away from these areas'. Moreover, a general 'variable quality of scientific evidence' was noted. The report noted that good trend data on the development of the pollution situation were scarce. However, 'the few sufficiently long time series available indicate that with a few exceptions, contamination has been reduced or at least has not increased over the last decade'. For instance, with regard to the black-listed PCBs, reports from the UK, Denmark and Sweden indicated reduced concentrations in PCBs, PCTs and DDT in fish. A specific relationship to PARCOM activity was rather unlikely though – in this period, PARCOM was only able to come up with a recommendation on PCBs, and that was not until 1983.

In summary, there was high uncertainty about the development of the pollution situation in this period. There were growing indications of local problems, but the Quality Status Reports produced in connection with the North Sea Conferences gave an impression of a situation that was overall quite stable, but again highly uncertain. How this development was related to OSCON and PARCON activity is uncertain, but given the few and rather vague decisions produced, there is little reason to assume that these regimes meant much for the development of the north-east Atlantic pollution problems in this phase.

3.2.2 The Recent Years: Increasing Effectiveness after 1987

Political effectiveness: international breakthrough and domestic action
As already indicated with the identification of the reduction measures agreed to at the 1987 North Sea Conference as a symbolic turning-point, the general

willingness of states to commit themselves internationally increased towards the end of the 1980s. This can be seen both in the number of measures, and their contents with regard to specific emission targets and timetables. The most visible and clear-cut measures in this connection are the North Sea Conference measures. At the 1987 conference, the most important measures with regard to land-based emissions were agreed emission reductions of nutrients and toxic substances 'of the order of 50%', to be achieved by 1995, with 1985 as the baseline. Concerning the dumping issues, it was decided to phase out the dumping of industrial wastes in the North Sea by the end of 1989, and to reduce marine incineration by at least 65% by the end of 1990 and to phase it out completely by the end of 1994. Moreover, the so-called 'precautionary approach' was formally adopted, and as mentioned, the parties agreed to establish a specific North Sea Task Force (NSTF) for the general enhancement of scientific knowledge.[29]

Progress continued at the 1990 Hague North Sea Conference and the 1987 measures were elaborated and specified. First, 36 pollutants were specified for 50% cuts, and in addition it was decided to reduce emissions of substances 'that cause a major threat to the marine environment' by 70% or more (that is, dioxins, mercury, cadmium and lead). Moreover, the parties also agreed that the 50% targets should apply to atmospheric emissions of 17 of the 36 substances by 1995, or by 1999 at the latest. With regard to the dumping measures, the termination of incineration was brought forward to the end of 1991. Moreover, dumping of sewage sludge should stop as soon as possible, and programmes should be drawn up by the end of 1990 to phase out the practice completely, by the end of 1998 at the latest.[30] At the 1995 Esbjerg Conference, a new fundamentally important step ahead was taken with the adoption of a 25-year elimination target for the input of hazardous substances. In addition, the parties agreed to reduce hazardous substances (especially organohalogen substances) to non-harmful levels by the year 2000, and expressed general support for the implementation of several European Community Directives and Regulations.[31]

Focusing more specifically on the OSCOM and PARCOM activities, they have increased substantially, partly as a response to the North Sea Conference measures summed up above. In more quantitative terms, as many recommendations were adopted during 1986-89 as during the first eight years of the cooperation (1978–1985). Moreover, it has been indicated that PARCOM accomplished an average of 3.8 decisions per year up to 1985, increasing to an average of 5.7 from 1986; after 1990, the number of decisions annually increased to 7.5.[32] Regarding the more qualitative contents of this increased activity, PARCOM adopted an approach focused on industrial sectors and the specification of Best Environmental Practices and Best Available Technology related to these sectors.[33] Within OSCOM, spurred on by the North Sea Conference measures, important decisions were taken during the years

1987–90 on the reduction and cessation of industrial waste, dumping of sewage sludge and incineration at sea within specified time limits.[34]

Concerning national compliance, have these sharpened international measures been followed up nationally? In the case of dumping, the answer is quite simply a positive one. Available national evidence clearly indicates that various forms of marine dumping in this area will soon become a thing of the past.[35] On the *land-based* side, more complex and technology-related international decisions, coupled with reporting problems, hamper the more specific PARCOM assessment.[36] Hence, let us primarily focus on the compliance picture with regard to the North Sea Conference (NSC) measures, summed up in the 1995 'Progress Report' produced for the Esbjerg Conference. The overall picture can be summed up as follows: compliance is substantial, though not uniform and in some cases somewhat uncertain. Regarding the hazardous substances targets, the picture is mixed, but a 'fairly high compliance' assessment seems reasonable. Concerning the 70% targets agreed to in The Hague in 1990, although 'significant progress appears to have been made' (p.9), only a minority of the countries are expected to reach the mercury targets, while a majority are expected to achieve the dioxins, cadmium and (especially) lead targets. In the case of the 50% reduction target for other heavy metals, good progress has apparently been made in terms of point sources, but less success has been reported in terms of diffuse sources (like fertilizers, atmospheric depositions, run-off from roads). A prevalent complication in all these assessments is the methodological reporting differences between the countries. Turning to the nutrients picture, the overall impression is one of 'high phosphorus and medium nitrogen' performance. All countries except France (25%) expect to achieve the phosphorus target. However, all countries have problems with the nitrogen target, and an overall achievement around 25% in relation to the defined problem areas is expected.[37]

Does there then exist more detailed implementation knowledge that indicates more precisely if the reported national behavioural changes have been related to regime activity? The aforementioned 1995 NSC Progress Report generally states that 'the reductions have been achieved as a result of a combination of measures taken nationally, some in consequence of international obligations from the EC and the Oslo and Paris Commissions' (p.10). In order to dig at least a little deeper, let us again focus first on the case of Norway.[38] Domestic concerns have long been important in terms of hazardous substances, but international commitments have affected the extent of substances focused on. For instance, a 1995 governmental report on the use of regulatory instruments in Norwegian environmental policy stated that several PARCOM measures in recent years have influenced Norwegian regulatory activities, for instance concerning the chloralkali industry and chlororganic substances from paper mills.[39] Second, regarding the nutrients issue, the recent controversy over

Norwegian municipal reductions clearly indicates that the Norwegian reduction efforts have been more extensive than they would have been without the NSC measures and related PARCON activity. The need to fulfil international obligations has been explicitly referred to by environmental authorities in their defence of the reduction programmes.

In the Netherlands, rather like in Norway, there has been a turn from mainly domestically driven processes to more internationally influenced processes after 1987/1990. For instance, as a response to the 1990 NSC Declaration, a specific North Sea Action Plan was developed. Moreover, the follow-up programme on industrial sectors was directly related to international developments. The UK marine pollution policies changed radically after 1987, and this change seems to have been influenced to a varying extent by the Conference and Convention activities during the last decade. In the case of dumping of industrial wastes and sewage sludge, this influence is strong and clear-cut. Land-based emission policies have also been influenced, though methodological differences complicate precise assessments.

The environmental and problem-solving dimensions: overall status quo so far?

As may be recalled, although good trend data were scarce, the 1987 Quality Status Report (QSR) concluded that 'the few sufficiently long time series available indicate that with a few exceptions, contamination has been reduced or at least has not increased over the last decade'. Overall, the conclusion read: 'In general, deleterious effects, at present, can only be seen in certain regions, in the coastal margins, or near identifiable pollution sources. There is as yet no evidence of pollution away from these areas'. How does this relate to the main picture indicated by the most recent 1993 QSR? Overall, with regard to trends, it is difficult because of different methodologies to make sensible comparisons with historical data or, perhaps more surprisingly, even with the data reported in the 1987 QSR (Quality Status Report of the North Sea 1993:107). Moreover, uncertainty is generally emphasized, due to natural variability: 'because of this variability, effects of abatement measures may not be observed and, at the same time, anthropogenic inputs may remain unnoticed' (ibid.:113). Still, regarding hazardous substances, it is concluded that measures taken have at least resulted in a distinct reduction in inputs of 'certain' substances, as reflected in the lower concentrations found in water, sediments and/or biota. For example, in the central Dutch coastal zone, a significant decrease was observed in concentrations of cadmium, lead, copper, zinc, and chromium in sediments between 1981 and 1991. Moreover, the downward trends in metal concentrations related to biota noted in the 1987 QSR continue, with a few exceptions (ibid.:115). With regard to organic contaminants (PCBs, TBT, HCHs), there is evidence of serious problems, for example, the effect of high concentrations of PCBs on the reproductive success of seals. For TBT and HCH it is concluded that more stringent goals and measures are urgently needed; here, effects of TBT on the shell shape of oysters have been noted (ibid.:109, 116). Although PCBs are in the process of being phased out, there are still problems. With regard to nutrients, despite reductions, there have been no detectable effects of these reductions in most parts of the North Sea since 1985. This may of course have something to do with natural variability and lagged effects (ibid.:121).

What about the overall health of the North Sea: has it improved or deteriorated since 1987? Not being a natural scientist, and reading somewhat between the lines, my impression is one of overall status quo so far. There are scattered, marginal improvements here and there, but pollution 'hot spots' still remain. As in the 1987 QSR, the 1993 QSR indicates that there are few serious problems in the northern or central parts of the North Sea, but effects become increasingly identifiable from the western to the eastern part of the Channel, from the northern to the southern part of the North Sea, and as one approaches the coastal margins and estuaries (ibid.:109). Hence, measures taken seem at least to have prevented a deterioration of the situation. Delayed effects of measures taken and natural variability may mean that clear improvements are just around the corner, but then again increased economic activity in the 1990s may counteract such trends. Still, apart from the dumping issues, the regional pollution problems in this area are far from being solved.[40]

Concluding comments: increasing effectiveness, but several uncertainties
As a conclusion, we can state with considerable certainty that the political effectiveness of OSCON and PARCON have increased considerably during the most recent years; exactly to what extent is, especially in the case of PARCON, a task for further implementation research, with systematic compilation and checking for external international and national factors like economic fluctuations, general technological development and European Community policy processes.[41] Uncertainty remains high concerning environmental trends and solutions to the problems, despite the more concentrated North Sea Task Force knowledge improvement efforts. A picture of roughly status quo emerges from the 1993 Quality Status Report. Hence, given the considerable economic activity in the region, the positive political development is to some extent confirmed – although this relationship is very complex to interpret, due to delayed effects and natural variability, among other things.

Be this as it may: how, then, can we explain the increasing political effectiveness? Let us first set the stage for the institutional discussion by reviewing some important features of the dumping and land-based pollution problems and how they developed, related main preferences and some brief comments on the issue of entrepreneurial leadership.

3.3 ACCOUNTING FOR OVERALL INCREASING, BUT STILL DIFFERING EFFECTIVENESS WITHIN THE DUMPING AND LAND-BASED CONTEXTS: PRONOUNCED DIFFERENCES IN PROBLEM CHARACTERISTICS

3.3.1 The Background for Slow Progress during the 1970s and early 1980s: Uncertainty and Moderate Concern

As indicated, with regard to knowledge and 'intellectual' problem characteristics, uncertainty was clearly high – both in terms of inputs, concentrations and biological effects. This was for instance revealed in the 1987 Quality Status Report's effort to assess the development over time. Here, it was noted that 'good trend data, whether for inputs, concentrations or effects in the general North Sea are scarce' (p.53). On the other hand, there was apparently not much scientific discord at this early stage. As to intellectual complexity, the land-based pollution problems must be regarded as quite complex compared to the dumping problems where pollution originates from deliberate, specific operations. Land-based pollution 'has ... widespread geographical origin emanating from all sorts of human activity and is not ... the result of any single deliberate disposal operation'.[42] In the case of dumping, various types of uncertainty were gradually reduced during the first part of the 1980s. Knowledge improved considerably as to who dumped what, where and how much; but was less pronounced with regard to ecological effects. Technological uncertainty was reduced in the sense that the parties became increasingly aware of alternatives to dumping.[43]

With regard to political characteristics, because of the high scientific uncertainty, transboundary pollution was probable, but little was known with regard to 'who polluted whom'. The general anti clockwise circulation pattern in the North Sea indicated that 'export' and 'import' of pollution was taking place, but probably not much more was known. Societal and governmental concern over marine pollution in the area must be characterized as moderate, but with some NGO activity and pressure connected with the visible and more easily targetable dumping operations. Still, there were also some variations in the extent to which countries felt affected by such problems, with for instance the Netherlands showing comparatively strong concern about marine pollution. Hence, the possibility that abatement measures would affect the international competitive situation of the relevant plants and branches, and ultimately the national economies, was perhaps in reality a more widely shared and uniform concern than the concern about marine pollution in itself. In a general comparison between dumping and land-based pollution activities, the industries and activities contributing to the land-based pollution problems were considered more important for most of the states, although dumping was obviously important for countries like the UK.[44] Thus, given the high scientific uncertainty and relatively low public pressure on governments to do anything about the transboundary marine pollution problems in the area, the main reason for at least the majority of the North Sea/Atlantic states to 'go international' was probably not so much to reduce international marine pollution drastically, but rather to avoid competitive disadvantages resulting from domestic abatement efforts. In summary, a picture emerges of problems which definitely had some complicating and malign features, but also some more benign aspects. There were features such as high scientific uncertainty and complexity, and especially in the land-based context, potential abatement measures would touch upon important industrial activities and give rise to competitive difficulties among the states. In both contexts, there were some variations in the extent to which countries were affected both by marine pollution problems and measures to reduce such problems. On the more benign side, dumping was not that important as a waste disposal option for many countries, and various improvements in knowledge about the dumping issues occurred during the first part of the 1980s.

In terms of actor preferences and capabilities, some fundamental and practical asymmetries can be noted. At the very first meeting of the Interim Paris Commission in 1974, a fundamental controversy arose over which basic abatement strategy was to guide the cooperation: 'Environmental Quality Standards' (EQS) or 'Uniform Emission Standards' (UES).[45] The countries favouring EQSs argued that the ultimate objective of the convention was to protect the marine environment, and to assess the health implications for human beings (for example, through their consumption of fish). Besides, they also referred to Article 6 in the Paris Convention, that the contracting parties should take into account the nature and quantities of the pollutants and the level of existing pollution, as well as the quality and absorptive capacity of the receiving waters. The United Kingdom was the leading spokesman for this approach. The countries favouring UES emphasized the preventive effect of this approach, the fact that it could be based on 'the best existing technical methods'; and that it authorized the establishment of standards on an international scale, having a stabilizing effect on the competitive situation between the countries. The foremost advocates for this approach were France, the Federal Republic of Germany (FRG) and the Netherlands. A compromise solution was reached in 1978, deciding that both approaches should be valid on a parallel basis until 1983.

With regard to more specific regulatory preferences, the overall picture is quite similar to the one outlined above: the UK – little affected by pollution and a probable 'exporter' of polluting substances – generally seemed to prefer the more lenient and less binding regulatory measures, while more affected and 'pollution importer' countries like the Netherlands, Sweden and to some extent the FRG preferred the stricter and more binding regulatory measures.[46] Hence, the reasons for the differing preferences were probably a combination of differences both in regulatory philosophies and material interests. However, as indicated earlier, apart from the UK and the Netherlands, the general impression is that the PARCON parties did not give much priority or attention to the land-based pollution issue during this period.[47] Thus, it can be argued that in one sense, the only country during this period to actively promote the reduction of land-based pollution in the area was the Netherlands.

Also in the case of dumping, two opposite poles may be identified in this period. On the one hand, the Nordic countries were not engaged in dumping during the 1980s (except Norway, which until 1989 delivered waste for incineration at sea). At the same time, these countries were quite probably affected to some extent by dumping conducted by other actors. On this basis, they had nothing to lose and everything to gain from active opposition to marine dumping. On the other hand, the UK had been engaged in all kinds of dumping during the 1970s and 1980s. Moreover, the UK was not much affected by its own and other actors' dumping and considered the abatement costs of alternative options to be substantial. Hence, it is not surprising that the UK acted as the least ambitious actor within the regime. Overall, then, the situation was to a significant degree characterized by asymmetrical interests and incompatible preferences – despite the overall limited importance of the dumping problems.[48]

Consequently, the general picture with regard to *entrepreneurial leadership* offers few surprises. Given that 'control over major emissions important to others' is an important source of power in this context, the UK may be characterized as a kind of 'negative' entrepreneur and main stumbling block within the cooperation during this period, opposing and blocking decisions.[49] Several other countries probably often shared the British preferences, but were able to keep a low profile due to the vocal and quite consistent British position. In addition to the UK's position as a major emitter, without whose consent the impact of regulatory measures would be sharply reduced, an important general scientific capacity may also be mentioned. On the other hand, there were of course counter-forces. In the land-based context, Sætevik (1988:92) points first and foremost to a certain entrepreneurial activity on the part of the Dutch, stating for instance that 'the other delegates consider the Dutch delegation to be the most enthusiastic in pursuing compromise solutions in matters where the negotiations have come to a deadlock'. Moreover, the German and Swedish delegations also took on a leadership role on some occasions. However, since potentially like-minded countries like the other Nordic countries were apparently 'medium interested', no potent and stable driving coalition emerged.

Within the dumping context, the Nordic countries were more active, but given their own limited dumping activities, they could not morally bolster their entrepreneurial efforts with potential own domestic sacrifices related to tougher international dumping measures.

3.3.2 The Background for Increasing Effectiveness in the Late 1980s and 1990s: Towards Less Malign Problems and More Compatible Preferences

Looking through the 1987 Quality Status Report, it becomes clear that scientific uncertainty had not been substantially reduced during the first decade with the conventions in operation. For instance, when the report comes to the final 'assessment of the status of the North Sea' section, it notes that: 'problems arise because of the variable quality of scientific evidence. In some cases, although considerable evidence is available about the distribution of a contaminant, there is no evidence of it causing undesirable effects. In others, there is insufficient information on which to base a judgement' (p.65). However, although uncertainty was not much reduced, it was gradually communicated better to the decision-makers. In this respect, the 1987 QSR marked a clear improvement compared to the 1984 report. In addition, a genuine improvement in scientific knowledge over time took place from 1987 on, largely due to the work of the North Sea Task Force, as will be further elaborated in the section on institutions. Hence, it was explicitly acknowledged in the 1995 North Sea Conference 'Progress Report': 'When one compares knowledge about the North Sea environment today with the situation which existed a decade ago it is clear that, despite the gaps which remain and which were identified in the 1993 QSR, considerable progress has been made in many areas ... today we have a dependable and comprehensive statement of circulation patterns in the North Sea, a much greater knowledge of inputs and the dispersion of contaminants, greater knowledge of ecological conditions and a better understanding of the impact of human activities on the North Sea environment' (p.203). Technologically, the regular meetings in the technical working groups of the Commissions (SACSA and TWG) also contributed to a diffusion of knowledge and techniques on how to deal effectively with marine pollution problems. Economically, more was known about how different types of regulations had affected – and could affect – economic growth. On the whole, this improvement of technological and economic knowledge reduced the intellectual complexity related to this issue.

On the political side, there were still the competitive aspects related to abatement measures, but the situation was not completely unchanged: the countries' industries had been given some 'moderately quiet' years to restructure and adapt their activity. Administratively, the countries' environmental ministries and departments had been functioning for some years, and regulators and regulated industries had become better acquainted. On the other hand, increasing attention given to nutrients and algal bloom problems meant additional complexity in the regulatory process, with a sharpening regulatory focus on the agricultural and municipal sectors. As indicated by the compliance problems related to the nitrogen targets, the agricultural sector has proved to be equally as hard to influence as industry – certainly functioning in a different way from industry and hence creating the need for a different regulatory approach.

Did the situation change with regard to how states perceived environmental problems through the 1980s, both generally and more specifically related to marine pollution problems? Apparently so. More issue-specifically, alarming reports about the ecological situation in the Wadden Sea off the Netherlands, and in the German and Danish coastal areas, changed the situation somewhat towards the mid-1980s. However, the impression is that the more general shift in electorates' attitudes towards environmental questions from the mid-1980s on was at least as important. This process started before the 1987 North Sea Conference. For instance, in a public opinion poll commissioned by the UK Department of the Environment in September 1986, it was maintained that environmental problems scored markedly higher than in the 1970s. According to the ENDS-report (1987A:16–17): 'Clear majorities were "very worried" about nuclear waste disposal and chemical pollution of waters, while between one-third and one-half were very worried about agrochemicals, wildlife destruction, bathing water quality and acid rain ... Stricter legislation was particularly favoured to deal with chemical pollution of rivers and seas (85% of respondents)'. However, it should clearly be noted that the process of changing attitudes of electorates and governments shifted gears and became notable first and foremost after the 'watershed' 1987 North Sea Conference.[50] Hence, it is debatable how much this changing trend actually influenced governmental attitudes prior to 1987. Moreover, events like the 'algae invasion' and the mysterious seal deaths, which attracted major public attention at least in countries like Norway, also occurred after the 1987 North Sea Conference; more specifically, in 1988–89. Hence, these more issue-specific dramatic events very likely contributed to the gradual rise in effectiveness up through the 1990s.

In the dumping context, the industrial waste problem in particular became less 'malign' towards the end of the 1980s because France, Belgium, West Germany and the Netherlands unilaterally decided to end such dumping. This was related both to the general 'greening' of governments referred to above and to more issue-specific changes. Compared for instance to the UK, it was evident that this group of countries probably suffered more from their own dumping activities.

Finally, was the OSCON and PARCON handling of the problems influenced by developments in other issue areas and organizational settings around the mid-1980s? As indicated earlier, developments within the European Community seem to be among the most obvious potentially influencing factors. Towards the mid-1980s, the environmental dimension had become more naturally integrated in the EC cooperation – especially in connection with the agreement on the 'Single Act' in 1985. The basis was established for a more active policy in this area – and the more reluctant countries within the EC cooperation knew this, not least the UK. There was obviously an increased incentive for starting mutual adjustments. Moreover, some of the main EC countries placed heavy pressure on the UK with regard to the air pollution and acid rain issue.[51] Thus, the UK in the middle of the 1980s was stuck with environmental controversies on several issues, and in the same fundamental position: 'the dirty man of Europe'. With regard to the EC and the development of relevant directives, it should generally be noted that this development has increased substantially in pace during the 1990s. This was clearly witnessed in connection with the 1995 North Sea Conference, where previously adopted EC directives and regulations were identified as principal measures to achieve some of the NSC process goals.[52]

Turning then to changes in preferences and positions, let us begin with the land-based context and two of the most important countries within the regimes, namely the major emitter countries, the FRG (West Germany) and the UK. They are also especially important in the sense that the other countries – although many of them were quite moderately interested and active – were not very pronounced 'stumbling blocks' during the first period of the cooperation. As indicated earlier, the FRG's main position was ambiguous during the first years of the cooperation – on several occasions, for instance, it supported the strictest and most binding alternative in the PARCOM discussions, while on other occasions opposing decisions and blocking proposals. Towards the middle of the 1980s, the FRG position moved towards the 'stricter' side. In 1983, for instance, the FRG (together with the EC and France) blocked the adoption of a ban on the use of the black-listed PCBs. In 1985 the FRG had changed preferences as to PCBs because of domestic developments and was now able to support a ban.[53] In 1987, an explicit indication of this greater German urge for action was the active diplomacy shown by the German Minister for the Environment, Klaus Topfer.[54] There are probably both issue-specific and more general reasons for this change in position. Partly there was a generally increased German concern over water pollution, as is witnessed in the German initiative for the establishment of the North Sea Conference forum partly there was a general drive for greener policies in Germany, caused by the 'Waldsterben' (forest death)/acid rain issue and the related political rise of the Green Party.[55] However, through the 1990s, the impression is that the German role in the marine pollution context has again become more ambiguous, and it is not possible to characterize the country as a general leading country (interviews, autumn 1995). This is probably related to dramatic domestic political changes and increasing economic problems.

With regard to the UK, the main British position seemed to have changed little when the second North Sea Conference started in November 1987. According to informed observers commenting on the political situation just prior to the Conference, Britain was reluctant to agree to expensive new measures. It did not believe that the level of pollution in the North Sea justified new measures.[56] However, in November 1987, just before the Conference, a major UK policy shift took place on discharges of dangerous substances. This was summarized in the following manner in the well-informed ENDS journal: 'After a 12-year war of attrition with its European neighbours about the manner in which discharges of dangerous substances should be controlled, the UK is to shift its ground and apply strict technology-based controls to effluents containing the most hazardous substances'.[57] Hence, there were some indications of a British 'softening' even before the 1987 Conference. As the UK agreed to both the 50% reductions discussed at the 1987 Conference and the tightening of these measures at the 1990 Hague Conference, the crucial principal and practical shift of position on the issue of land-based substances was confirmed. However, in the 1990s, besides involvement in controversies over the dumping of sewage sludge and of radioactive wastes, the UK and France have been in conflict with the other countries over the building of secondary water treatment facilities.[58] Moreover, at the 1995 Esbjerg North Sea Conference, the UK did not join the others in the pledge to phase out substances that are persistent, toxic and liable to bioaccumulate within 25 years. Hence, despite a general decrease in the level of conflict between the UK and most of the other North Sea countries, old conflict lines are still latent.

For the other countries, the picture is of course somewhat mixed, depending on the characteristics of the various sub-issues. Generally, participants in the cooperation point to the Netherlands as the most active leader country. This has been the case particularly on the issues of nutrients, pesticides, and some heavy metals. Sweden is mentioned in connection with hazardous substances.[59] Regarding the issue of nutrients, the Danes have also been very active. Hence, in terms of the hazardous substances and nutrients issues, emerging from the late 1980s on, there has been a strong coalition including Germany, the Netherlands, Denmark, Sweden and partly Norway pushing the others to go along.[60]

In the dumping context, and with regard to dumping of industrial waste, the Nordic countries continued their proposals for a complete phase-out. Moreover, as noted, the situation changed when France, Belgium, West Germany and the Netherlands unilaterally decided to end such dumping. However, the UK, supported by Spain, Portugal and Ireland, continued to oppose their proposals up to the 1987 North Sea Conference political 'breakthrough' and the ensuing OSCOM decisions. Incineration at sea developed in a quite 'benign' direction, as it was increasingly realized that land-based treatment methods would actually be cheaper than incineration at sea.[61]

Summing up, in order to shed some light on the increase in effectiveness from the late 1980s on, it is necessary to focus on changes in problems and preferences during the preceding period – the early and mid-1980s. On the one hand, some changing trends and important events can be noted. Growing concern was witnessed in some important countries like the FRG about increasing marine pollution levels and a more general process of greater public concern about environmental problems. In the dumping context, a series of countries unilaterally stopped dumping. On the other hand, several of these important processes shifted into substantially higher gear only *after* the 1987 North Sea Conference and can only contribute to explanations for the increasing effectiveness up through the 1990s. This is for instance the case with the increase in both more issue-specific and general environmental concern, partly due to the alarming algae and seal incidents during the late 1980s. Scientific knowledge improved and was communicated better to decision-makers, but this was clearly related to regime activity and the North Sea Task Force, as will be elaborated on in the next section on institutions.

Although dumping problems are largely finding their solutions in the 1990s, several malign and complicating features of the land-based problems remain – with for instance many economically important activities to be regulated; asymmetries in the 'import' and 'export' of polluting substances; and international competitive effects. Not least, there is a growing awareness of the actual complexity of the problems on the emissions side. This has to do with an increased understanding of the importance of atmospheric inputs, emissions from the agricultural and municipal sectors, and increasing awareness of the myriad of substances not systematically understood and/or addressed at all. In sum, although improvements have been made in relation to many of the 'old' industrial problems, they have not been completely solved, and new problems and complexity have been added along the way.

With this background, we are ready to zoom in more directly on the focused institutional questions.

3.4 INTERNATIONAL INSTITUTIONAL DESIGN: SUBSTANTIAL IMPROVEMENTS OVER TIME

3.4.1 Access and Participation: From an Exclusive, Administrative Approach to More Inclusive, High-Level Processes

The first decade: 'exclusive' and bureaucratically dominated processes primarily within the Conventions

As indicated earlier, OSCON and PARCON cover a far wider geographical area than the North Sea; they also cover the north-east Atlantic area. Hence, in addition to the North Sea states (Denmark, Sweden, Norway, the Netherlands, Belgium, Federal Republic of Germany, France and the United Kingdom) Ireland, Portugal, Spain, Iceland and Finland (in OSCON only) also become participating states. Were these states, then, the main contributors to the pollution problems in this area? Did the institutional and political responses match the scope of the problems? Looking only at direct emissions to water, the answer is generally positive. The North Sea states were the major contributors and they were central participants within the conventions. However, over time it became clear that the inclusion of countries outside the most affected North Sea core of countries also led to more complicated decision-making and the 1984 first North Sea Conference gathered a somewhat smaller group of countries.[62] This conference forum was no immediate success, but with the benefit of hindsight, the 1984 Conference can be regarded as the necessary first step of an increasingly important process. Concerning the match between problems and political processes, it should also be noted that some of the polluting substances, which ultimately enter into the North Sea via rivers, have their origin in Eastern European countries. Taking atmospheric inputs into consideration, which may be the main source of heavy metals inputs, the Eastern European sources are even more important. Hence, the main direct contributors to the pollution problems were among the participating states, while a significant portion of land-based substances stemmed from Eastern European countries not included in the conventions.

A special participatory dimension relates to the role of the European Community within PARCON. As indicated earlier, the EC signed the Convention as a separate Contracting Party and the EC Commission participated along with the nation states in the PARCOM meetings. In general, the EC dimension had both positive and negative effects on the progress of PARCOM during these years.[63] The effects were positive in the sense that the Paris Commission was able to benefit from preparatory work done by the EC. On the other hand, due to policy uncertainty and thus lacking approval from the EC Council, the EC blocked decisions on the regulation of at least seven substances within the Paris Commission. Moreover, in some cases, EC regulations were used as models for PARCOM decisions, which resulted in less stringent decisions than the original Paris Commission proposals. In addition, the EC also occasionally intervened to prevent discussions on a scientific/-technical level within the Technical Working Group, due to upcoming discussions within the EC system.

Regarding the access and participation of various kinds of non-state actors, the conventions did not mention this issue at all. The only actors referred to in the texts were the 'Contracting Parties'. It was not until the subsequent adoption of procedural rules for the work of the Commissions that the circumstances governing NGO participation were clarified. These rules stated that 'the Commission may unanimously invite international organizations and non-contracting States to send observers to the meetings' (rule 4). Hence, NGOs were initially barred from the different OSCON and PARCON bodies. A moderate adjustment was made in 1983 with the decision to allow NGO access to particular meetings if there were no objections from the parties. Until 1990, NGO participation was limited to the occasional brief presentation to the Commission delegates before their annual meetings.[64] Within the North Sea Conference forum, NGOs were not allowed to attend the 1984 Conference. Moving on to the type of national participation in OSCOM and PARCOM during this period, the parties were represented by civil servants only (administrators and scientists). However, at the 1984 North Sea Conference, administrators were joined by politicians from the various countries, mostly the respective Environment Ministers. Hence, this Conference was characterized as a 'Ministerial Conference'.

Did this participation pattern influence outcomes and national policy processes in any detectable way? Would for instance a broader and more inclusive approach have been more effective? It can easily be argued that the inclusion of more state parties, for instance the Soviet Union and/or several Eastern European countries, (which would have meant a better match with the states actually contributing to the pollution problems), would not have improved effectiveness. The inclusion of these states would have considerably increased the heterogeneity of participants, and would probably have led to even weaker outcomes. In fact, it seems more apt to ask if a narrower state participation, for instance only focusing on the comparatively wealthier and similar North Sea states, would have led to more and stronger decisions. The answer here is not obviously positive and clear-cut. In this period, a central laggard like the UK would still have been present among the participants. In addition, the first Bremen North Sea Conference in 1984 had both a narrower state focus and introduced government ministers into the arena of common North Sea decision-making. Judged by the meagre outcome of this Conference, a narrower and more politically high-level forum did not automatically speed up things.

Recent years: more open and high-level processes

The further consolidation of the North Sea Conference system, with three full-fledged conferences and two more intermediate meetings organized, has meant a further regionalization and consolidation of the dual participatory approach within the regime. This development has further been reflected in the 1988 decision to allow formally for regional and differentiated decisions within the regimes. The revision process of the early 1990s and subsequent establishment of the 1992 OSPAR Convention only led to marginal participation changes in relation to the old Paris Convention, for instance with the inclusion of Switzerland and Finland among the cooperating states. The question of including Russia in the cooperation has been discussed more generally. As indicated by Andresen (1996), good reasons can be given for Russian participation, considering the country's contribution to land-based pollution, both dumping and atmospheric inputs. On the other hand, Russian participation would further increase the scope of interests represented and not least the variation in ability to deal with identified problems. Hence, such an inclusion seems unlikely, at least in the short term. Regarding the EC dimension, the hampering effects noted in the first decade have decreased in more recent years, in line with the further development of EC environmental policies. Moreover, the policy diffusion effect from the EC to OSPAR and the North Sea Conference system has increased in recent years, as witnessed for instance by the explicit reference of the 1995 North Sea Conference measures to the EC Urban Waste Water and Nitrates Directives. Still, despite these tendencies, it is questionable if an expanding and even more heterogeneous EC can develop further into a leading force within the OSPAR context.[65]

The recent decade has seen increased access for and participation of NGOs both within the convention and conference contexts. At the 1987 North Sea Conference the NGOs were permitted to attend the opening session and make brief statements. This was also the case in 1990, and access to information was improved. Actual participation has increased over time. At the 1995 Conference, 36 delegates represented environmental NGOs while 32 delegates represented industry and other target groups.[66] From 1990 on, the Conventions also allowed further access for NGOs. At the 1990 PARCOM meeting, the rules regulating observer entry were changed in a more NGO inclusive direction by adding the formal mention of non-governmental organizations to Rule 4.1. Increased participation followed. By 1992, eight out of twelve applying NGOs had been accredited as PARCON observers.[67] In connection with the 1992 PARCON revision process and the ensuing OSPAR meetings, it was discussed whether to allow NGOs to participate in the work of subsidiary bodies like the TWG. There was extensive disagreement over this issue, but in the end it was decided that NGOs were allowed to submit written comments on decisions and recommendations forwarded to the technical groups from the Commission, and also apply for the opportunity to make oral presentations at working group meetings. In practice, due to their exclusion from the working groups, NGOs instead present 'technical' papers and inputs at the Commission meetings, something that is not always popular.[68] Regarding the level of proceedings, the three regular North Sea Conferences and two intermediate meetings in the recent decade have meant a considerable strengthening of political input into the cooperation in the recent years. In addition, the first Ministerial OSPARCOM meeting was held in 1992, in connection with the final negotiations on the new OSPAR Convention.

What, then, has been the impact of this changing picture? Most importantly, the North Sea Conferences and related implementation processes have definitely been a central factor in the increasing effectiveness process. First, the North Sea context has meant a narrower and more homogeneous group of states. Moreover, the conference context has meant a generally higher degree of politicization, with more frequent involvement of politicians and ministers in the decision-making process. Ministers, and more explicit and visible political fights, have attracted the media, and hence at least temporarily placed these issues higher on the public agenda. This process has gradually permeated the wider OSCON and PARCON regimes. Still, the NSC effect must be qualified in at least three respects: first, the initial 1987 London political breakthrough came as the result of a lucky interplay of several factors, like for instance the British host factor.[69] Moreover, and most importantly, both the 1987 breakthrough and the results of later conferences have built upon scientific, administrative and political groundwork carried out within the wider convention context. Third, during the politically crucial immediate period after the Conference, the process was somewhat boosted by the headline grabbing algae 'catastrophe' and the mysterious seal deaths. With regard to the changes in access for NGOs and other non-state actors, these modifications are too recent to have significantly influenced the effectiveness question. Has effectiveness 'suffered' from the lack of outside insight and input? Not necessarily. It is important here to remember that the green NGOs' interest in this issue was moderate during most of the 1980s.[70] However, their interest has increased over time, and Greenpeace especially has been active in this field. There seems to be a clear majority view within the regime that increased access and participation is good.[71] Hence, it is somewhat paradoxical that the NGOs are barred from the working group meetings, where their alternative and supplementary scientific and technical expertise could potentially be most valuable.

3.4.2 Decision-Making Rules: An Increasingly Flexible Consensus

Article 18 in the Oslo Convention explicitly required unanimity both for procedural and substantial matters. The PARCON picture was a little more complex. After first stating that 'the Commission shall adopt, with unanimous vote, programmes and measures for the reduction or elimination of pollution from land-based sources', PARCON's Article 18 went on to state that 'should unanimity not be attainable, the Commission may nonetheless adopt a programme or measures by a three quarters majority vote of its members', being binding only for those states that voted for the measures. However, the majority voting option was not utilized in the first decade, except in administrative cases. Majority decisions were regarded by most parties as environmentally ineffective, as long as the minority had the right to reserve their position against the decision, which would then fail to apply in these states. Furthermore, the unanimity rule functioned in practice in a modified form, since reservations from comparatively insignificant polluters like Spain and Portugal were largely ignored.[72] Hence, the convention approach must be characterized as a strongly consensual one – giving substantial weight to the preferences of the least enthusiastic actor who could not be accepted as a 'free-rider'. Being more ad hoc processes, the North Sea Conferences have operated without any formal decision-making procedures. At both the 1984 and 1987 Conferences, all decisions were unanimous.[73]

In more recent years, some interesting changes can be noted. First, there is the issue of regionalization, related to the follow-up of the North Sea Conference process. This can be seen as a participation issue, but has also obvious decision-making implications. In order to accommodate more easily the interests of both North Sea and non-North Sea OSCON and PARCON states, the Commissions decided in 1988 to open up opportunities for regionalization and differentiation of the cooperation. More specifically, decisions or recommendations could apply to a specified part of the convention area and different timetables could also be applied, related to various ecological and economic conditions in the different regions and sub-regions covered by the conventions. This regionalization option was further and formally codified in Article 23 of the 1992 Convention. Within OSCON, this opened up the way for progress on the issue of industrial waste dumping, since Spain and Portugal were allowed longer time limits. Within PARCON, regulations both on nutrients and PCBs benefited from this approach.[74]

Second, the 1990s have seen an increased use of the majority-voting option in practice. In 1990, and for the first time in the history of PARCOM, a binding decision was adopted by a three-quarters majority vote.[75] This development has accelerated, and the majority of decisions in the 1990s have been three-quarters majority decisions.[76] However, as noted by Hey, Ijlstra and Nollkaemper

(1993:40), this does not signify 'real' majority type decisions, in which the majority binds the minority. Instead, it should be interpreted as part of a general tendency towards greater differentiation and flexibility within the cooperation. A certain change could also be witnessed within the North Sea Conference context, with a 'footnote practice' developed at the 1990 Conference, implying that resistance from one country would not block the whole process.[77]

Overall, despite the interesting developments summed up above, the general impression is one of basic continuity: the practical decision-rule has been and will continue to be a flexible consensus. As can be recalled, dissent did not automatically stop earlier decision-making; this depended on the issue-specific importance and to what extent objections could be disregarded. However, the degree of flexibility and differentiation has clearly increased. According to some, this is not necessarily an improvement, since reluctant parties may for instance get away with reservations and references to 'inapplicable conditions', instead of several years of politically embarrassing objections and vetoes.[78] On the other hand, since water conditions and pollution vulnerability do vary quite a bit between the participants, there is the obvious advantage of not having a few scarcely affected reluctant parties blocking a majority's steps in the right direction. It is too early to say how the balance between these somewhat contradictory factors will turn out.

3.4.3 The Role of the Secretariat: Increasing Resources and Leeway over Time

In the rules of procedure adopted at the first PARCOM meeting in 1978, it was the Secretary's functions that were most precisely defined. These functions were mostly administrative: drawing up budgets, receiving and distributing to participants various reports of the Commission and of the Working Groups and so on. However, the precise boundaries of the role were not given once and for all, namely: '(he) shall perform any other tasks that may be entrusted to him by the Commission or by the Chairman' (Rule 8). In practice during the first decade, the Secretariat produced, for instance, over 70% of the PARCOM documents.[79] Moreover, the Secretariat sometimes played a mediating role, for instance by drawing up new proposals based on the various countries' proposals. In addition, the Secretary sometimes put forward his own proposals for solutions.[80] In cases where the Secretariat and the Chairman could work closely together, outcomes could clearly be influenced.[81]

In terms of manpower and budgetary resources, OSCON and PARCON shared secretarial services. During the first decade, the Secretariat consisted of one secretary, two deputy secretaries and three clerks. The budget was provided by contracting parties according to a United Nations allocation formula based on gross national products. According to participants in the Commissions, the

Secretariat's resources were clearly limited. But it was also stated by some that a larger and more resourceful Secretariat would not necessarily be more effective, given the mediocre national priority given to the provision of information and general follow-up.[82] Viewed from the outside, the manpower situation does seem to have been sparse, given the task of administering two conventions and several subsidiary bodies covering a broad range of marine pollution issues. However, the contracting parties themselves were overall very satisfied with the work of the Secretariat. Furthermore, they emphasized the personal element, that is, that much depended on individual efforts and qualifications.[83] With regard to the North Sea Conferences, secretarial services here have been ad hoc, primarily provided by the varying host countries.

In recent years, a significant increase in budgetary resources and administrative capacity has taken place. In the 1990s, the Secretariat has numbered eleven persons – five executives and support staff,[84] the Secretary for the North Sea Task Force and an NSTF clerk. The budget for the two Commissions was roughly £750 000 in 1994.[85] Still, has the role of the Secretariat also changed in more qualitative terms? Apparently to some extent, though not drastically. In a generally greener and more progress-oriented atmosphere, it is reasonable that the Secretariat has experienced both an increased need and scope for a more active role. Participants in the cooperation point out that the less active first decade of the cooperation in terms of policy implied a limited set of tasks for the Secretariat, and that the increased activity and development of the cooperation has naturally required additional Secretarial efforts – for instance, in connection with the BAT process, and not least data collection and reporting. Hence, although resources have increased, tasks have increased substantially also. Moreover, they indicate that the Secretariat has in practice several ways to exercise a more or less subtle influence, for instance by discussing and clarifying matters ahead of formal meetings, before positions are more fixed and the need to 'play to the gallery' sets in; by consciously choosing lead countries and group chairmen who are interested and not directly opposed to regulations in the particular field; and by initiating procedural development and streamlining, as for instance witnessed in the case of reporting procedures (see section 3.4.6).[86] Combined with the trend of increasing resources and manpower, it may be assumed that the ability to utilize these instruments has increased.

Overall, has the Secretariat influenced the course of the cooperation, then? Yes, I think so, although not very dramatically. If we imagine an even smaller Secretariat with an incompetent and lazy Secretary, the cooperation would obviously have proceeded less 'technically' smoothly than seems to have been the case here. But would outcomes have been much different? I doubt it. In relation to the main driving economic and political controversies within the regime, the Secretariat has had little leverage. Hence, the increasing resources and somewhat changing role of the Secretariat are much more reflections of a generally more effective process than independent driving forces in themselves.

3.4.4 The Structuring of the Agenda: Moderate Success in Dealing with a Complex Issue

Given the complex character of the agenda issues, this section will mainly focus on PARCON. Generally speaking, the agenda of PARCON has been concerned with 'land-based marine pollution'. Potentially, this is definitely a broad agenda, both because of the variety of input pathways and the various polluting activities involved. Let us first have a look at the pathways. Compared to marine dumping, for instance, land-based pollution reaches the marine environment via several quite different pathways. One important pathway is riverine emissions, and rivers often receive emissions from many different activities along their way, and perhaps even run through several countries. There are also direct emissions to coastal and ocean areas, and emissions via the atmosphere. Much air pollution eventually ends up as marine deposition. Second, land-based pollution stems from various types of societal activities.

At least three main groups of activities can be discerned: industrial emissions; agricultural runoff and emissions; and municipal emissions like sewage.

How, then, did the PARCON parties approach these challenges in terms of structuring the agenda? First, some sequential elements may be noted. A broad priority was signalled already in the drawing up of the black and grey lists. In the first years of PARCOM, monitoring and regulatory action focused on a small group of substances (mercury, cadmium, and PCBs), related first and foremost to industrial riverine and coastal emissions. Moreover, most scientific and technical matters were delegated to TWG, JMG and other subsidiary bodies. This allowed the Commission meetings to concentrate on resolving complicated problems related to differences in regulatory philosophies and practices among the parties. Towards the end of this first phase, in addition to PARCOM decision-making, land-based marine pollution issues were also part of the agenda for the 1984 North Sea Conference. Even though OSCOM and PARCOM decision-making had been closely related from the start, for instance with coordinated Commission meetings, this Conference gave decision-makers an additional opportunity to see marine pollution issues in a broader perspective, as the agenda combined both land-based and marine dumping issues. Moreover, within the land-based part of the agenda, both industrial, agricultural, and municipal emissions were indirectly addressed.

The agenda of PARCOM was gradually expanded throughout the 1980s and more of the substances on the black and grey lists were brought into the regulatory focus. The main marine pollution problems relating to agricultural and municipal emissions, that is, nutrients 'overload' and algal blooms, gradually caught the attention of decision-makers. In 1986, a specific, supplementary PARCOM protocol on atmospheric marine pollution was established. Towards the mid-1990s, the environmental effects of fishery activities were placed on the agenda. However, as several issues and substances in this manner have been added to the agenda, with very few being 'solved' and withdrawn along the way, the agenda of the PARCOM meetings has in recent years become very packed. According to participants in the cooperation, this has reduced both the Paris Commission's effectiveness in general, but also in particular its opportunities to discuss more fundamental, long-term issues, such as the adequacy and effectiveness of the Commission's work in the light of available scientific and technical evidence. Hence, if one looks upon the establishment of the black and grey lists as a conscious effort at sequencing and structuring the agenda, it seems only moderately successful. In the 1992 Convention, the black and grey list approach was abandoned, and a uniform approach adopted.

In connection with a discussion concerning approaches and structuring of the agenda, the gradually increasing emphasis on the BAT (Best Available Technology) and BEP (Best Environmental Practices) approaches should be mentioned. This has meant a gradual shift from a substance-by-substance approach based on the distinction between black and grey lists to an approach entailing the prevention of pollution by the prescription of particular technological processes.[87] BAT as a principle was endorsed at the 1987 North Sea Conference and adopted in 1989 by PARCOM. Moreover, a specific Industrial Sectors Working Group was established to review BAT in ten industrial sectors. However, even if the PARCOM agenda has become increasingly packed, it should be noted that the even broader agendas of the 1987 and 1990 North Sea Conferences seem to have been quite productive, as this broadness made it possible to strike some bargains between dumping (OSCOM) and land-based (PARCOM) issues. This was especially important at the 1987 Conference: it is quite possible that the earlier main 'stumbling block' – the UK – would never have agreed to the 50% land-based reduction measures had the country not been given special treatment in connection with the dumping issues. Moreover, the NSCs have made significant contributions to the focusing and specification of the regulatory agenda with regard to hazardous substances. Still, it is of course difficult to distinguish the separate effect of this dimension of the NSCs in relation to aspects like ministerial participation and more media and public attention. Nevertheless, the 1992 Convention included both dumping and radioactive substances, and in an issue-linkage perspective, the potential in the 1992 OSPAR Convention in this respect was undoubtedly improved.

How can this development be interpreted? The picture is definitely complex, with contradictory tendencies and lessons both within PARCON and the NSCs. Could agenda matters have been handled differently? Thinking for instance in terms of models applied in several other environmental regimes, the establishment of protocols focusing on one or two substances at a time (in this case for instance mercury and/or cadmium) is a theoretical alternative and a more strongly sequenced route. In this connection, it can be argued that land-based marine pollution long lacked the dramatic, visible external shock of the 'Waldsterben' in the acid rain context or the 'ozone hole' in the ozone context. When the 'algae catastrophe' struck in the late 1980s, it no doubt helped to place the issue of nutrients and algal blooms high on the political agenda in some countries, but this process was already in motion within the North Sea Conference system. One may wonder what would have happened if the algaes had struck a decade earlier. Would such an event have led to a more focused regulatory process – or would it have mattered little, due to a general lack of national administrative preparedness and international quarrels over regulatory approaches? My hunch is that it would have mattered somewhat. Be that as it may, instead it was the comprehensive North Sea Conferences that gave important inputs to a further focusing and specification of the regulatory agenda.

3.4.5 The Organization of the Science–Politics Interface: Initial Weaknesses, but Improvements Over Time

Let us first briefly recapitulate the structure of the scientific–political complex in the first decade. The main decision-making bodies were the Commissions, composed of national delegations (ranging from one delegate up to five or six), meeting annually and separately for three to four days, followed by a joint session of the Oslo and Paris Commissions lasting two to three days. The 'Standing Advisory Committee for Scientific Advice' (SACSA/OSCON) and the 'Technical Working Group' (TWG/PARCON) were the scientific and technical advisory bodies, composed of technical bureaucrats from all the contracting parties, meeting three or four times annually, giving advice and reporting to PARCOM. The work of the Joint Monitoring Group (JMG) was based on national marine monitoring programmes. Hence, the JMG was mainly composed of representatives of various marine monitoring and ocean research institutes in the respective countries. The JMG reported directly to the TWG, and more indirectly to the Commissions as parts of the TWG's report. In addition, an 'external' body within this structure was the International Council for the Exploration of the Sea (ICES). Initially, the input of ICES into the work of the Commissions consisted of some limited advice on monitoring questions and a general briefing on the work of ICES at Commission meetings.

As this brief overview indicates, the organizational structure included a sort of buffer between scientific research and decision-making, in the form of the technical working groups. Although these groups were intended to be 'politically neutral' forums, their focus on possible technical solutions as well as the practical implementation of measures, inevitably introduced economic and political aspects into the discussions. With regard to the TWG, despite some scattered complaints about politicization of its work, the contracting parties seemed quite content with the functioning of the TWG in this period.[88] Moreover, the TWG's buffer function lay clearly towards the integrative and communicative side. However, the scientific–political complex as a whole did not function very well in this period. This is most clearly seen on the input side, where the work of the Joint Monitoring Group was in several ways flawed: it covered only the major estuaries and coastal zones of the participating states and no open sea sites. Moreover, it was based on the already existing monitoring programmes of the states and little mutual adaptation took place.[89] However, the malfunctioning of the JMG was probably mainly a reflection of the general low priority given to OSCON and PARCON matters by the participating states. Also with regard to the administrative capacity and functioning of the Commissions, some flaws were apparent, like superfluous discussions on matters already debated in the technical working groups and inadequately prepared participants.[90] Within the North Sea Conference context, under the leadership of Germany, a specific 'Quality Status of the North Sea' report (QSR) was produced in connection with the 1984 Bremen Conference, based on national submissions. However, as the report was completed just in time for the actual Conference, and had not been discussed by the delegations in advance, parts of the report were disputed at the Conference.[91]

Did the somewhat malfunctioning scientific–political complex influence outcomes and national policy processes in this period? In reality, only marginally, I think. Looking for instance through PARCOM's Annual Reports from these years, scientific uncertainty does occasionally turn up in the discussions. But this was related first and foremost to lacking national input data, and hence reporting deficiencies, and not to scientifically underpinned assessments and suggestions introduced by TWG/JMG. In fact, these annual reports clearly indicate that, most often, reluctant parties used other arguments than data inadequacies and scientific uncertainty. Such arguments included economic difficulties, legal obstacles for the implementation of measures (for instance the discussions on PCBs and PCTs), the lack of available substitutes (for instance the discussions on aldrin, endrin and dieldrin), and EC-related competence problems (PCBs and PCTs) – to mention a few.

During the recent decade, the main change has undoubtedly been the establishment of the North Sea Task Force (NSTF). The NSTF was part of the outcome of the 1987 North Sea Conference, with ministers and administrators identifying several knowledge deficiencies in connection with the production of the 1987 Quality Status Report. These deficiencies were related to the trends in inputs of contaminants, the linking of inputs to actual contaminant levels, and the environmental impact of contaminants. The NSTF comprised delegates from the eight North Sea states and the Commission of the European Communities, under the co-sponsorship of OSPARCOM and ICES.[92] The Task Force had two main functions: first, the preparation of a new Quality Status Report (QSR) on the North Sea, presented in 1993, and, second, the coordination of monitoring, modelling and research activities. As the 1987 report was put together mainly on the basis of (differing) national contributions, leading to compatibility problems, the approach taken in connection with the 1993 report was more differentiated. Based on the advice of ICES, the North Sea was separated into subregions, and 13 reports were prepared including the Channel, the Skagerrak and Kattegat and the Wadden Sea.[93]

Overall, the work of the NSTF has no doubt meant a general 'boost' for North Sea monitoring, modelling and research activities. Moreover, as indicated by the 1995 North Sea Conference 'Progress Report', the 1993 Quality Status Report represents the most comprehensive assessment yet made of the health of the North Sea (p.200). However, with regard to the core NSTF, delegates represented their governments, and a certain 'negotiated science' aspect crept into the venture. Having the prime responsibility for the two concluding QSR chapters on conclusions and recommendations, discussions naturally took on a more political flavour. Still, according to Ducrotoy (1997:188), the conclusions reached by the research scientists were not altered in any significant way. When the QSR was discussed at a specific scientific symposium in Denmark in 1993, the overall conclusion was that while some new data were presented, most merely complemented those already included.[94] From an outside perspective, the stronger role played by ICES has added a more substantial scientific 'core' which was necessary for the monitoring and research work in this region, and the administrative quality of this work has apparently not become dominant.[95] In fact, it is quite possible that this dual scientific–political character has functioned mostly positively, giving the work a more explicit action-oriented and feasibility dimension than what a purer scientific/academic venture could easily have turned into.

In connection with the establishment of the 1992 OSPAR Convention, and also related to the fact that the mandate of the NSTF was fulfilled with the publication of the 1993 Quality Status Report, the technical working groups (SACSA and TWG) have merged into a 'Programmes and Measures Committee' (PRAM). PRAM has five standing subordinated working groups on diffuse sources, nutrients, point sources, radioactive substances and sea-based activities. The Joint Monitoring Group has been reorganized into an 'Environmental Assessment and Monitoring Committee' (ASMO), incorporating the work of the North Sea Task Force. ASMO has four subordinated working groups on assessment and coordination, impacts on the marine environment, inputs to the marine environment, and a regional task team for the preparation of a regional quality status report. Both these restructured committees, and their working groups, have been in operation since 1994.

How fundamental are these institutional changes, then? Judging by the terms of reference for the two groups, the changes in the functioning of the system initiated by the establishment of the NSTF will be strengthened. The terms of reference for ASMO clearly indicate that basic features of the NSTF organizational model and way of working will be maintained: close cooperation with ICES; the publication at regular intervals of reports on the quality status of the marine environment; and the development of analytical tools such as modelling for assessment procedures and so on. On the reporting side, in line with the more explicit advisory North Sea Task Force, it is probable that the work of ASMO will emphasize advisory and communication issues more than the old JMG. As to PRAM, which has replaced the earlier technical working groups, a more action-initiating role is signalled in its first obligation: 'in accordance with the priorities established in the Action Plan of the Commissions, prepare proposals for decisions and recommendations for consideration by the Commissions to prevent and eliminate pollution of the maritime area' (Annex 24, point 2.a). In comparison, the terms of reference for the TWG only contained what is now formulated as a second obligation for PRAM, namely to 'advise the Commissions on technical and scientific questions remitted to it by the Commissions'. An aspect which is definitely new, is the obligation to 'review reports for assessing compliance with, and the effectiveness of, agreed Decisions and Recommendations' (Annex 24, point 2.e). On the more administrative/political side of the scientific–political complex, partly as a response to the reduced ability to discuss the adequacy and effectiveness of the Commission's work in light of available scientific and technical evidence, the tendency has been to increase the frequency and importance of Heads of Delegations and Group of Chairmen and Vice-Chairmen (CVC) meetings. Especially the Heads of Delegations meetings are important in this context.[96]

Summing up, there have certainly been changes in the organization of the scientific work and the science–politics interface more generally – both within the North Sea Conference context and the more specific convention context. However, it should be noted that the establishment of the NSTF was primarily a result of generally increasing attention and priority, and specific effects so far seem hard to trace. Moreover, the new PRAM and ASMO working groups definitely seem to indicate a more action-initiating and critical effectiveness assessment role for these bodies, and the continued important position of ICES, initiated by NSTF, means a strengthened role for more independent scientific expertise. Still, the reorganization is too recent to pinpoint any practical effects. Hence, the main practical effects of a clearly strengthened scientific–political complex lie ahead of us.

3.4.6 Verification and Compliance Mechanisms: an Evolving Interplay with Regulatory Development

In terms of verification in PARCON, the main elements of the reporting system were first laid out in Article 12 in the Convention: 'The Contracting Parties shall inform the Commission of the legislative and administrative measures they have taken to implement the provisions (of the Convention)'. Moreover, Article 17 contained additional reporting duties: 'The Contracting Parties, in accordance with a standard procedure, shall transmit to the Commission ... the results of monitoring ... and the most detailed information available on the substances listed in the Annexes to the present Convention and liable to find their way into the maritime area'. The role of the Commission was laid out in Article 16: 'It shall be the duty of the Commission ... to exercise overall supervision over the implementation of the present Convention ... (and) to review generally ... the effectiveness of the control measures being adopted and the need for any additional or different measures'. Similar obligations were laid out in Articles 11 and 17 of the Oslo Convention. In practice, this led to the establishment of standard reporting procedures, with annual forms to fill in for each country regarding types of substances emitted, quantity and so on. These forms were sent to the Secretariat, which in turn produced a draft report. This draft was then sent back to the contracting parties to ensure that the figures were correct before official reports were published by the Secretariat. No independent assessment of the reported figures was carried out, either by the Secretariat or any external body. In general, within PARCON, reporting did not function very well. Data were often lacking or inadequate.[97] This picture of an initially quite sloppy system with missing and incomparable data has been confirmed by more recent interviews with regime participants.[98] Moreover, as national reports were not designed in relation to international commitments, the basis for assessments of 'the effectiveness of the control measures being adopted and the need for any additional or different measures' by the Commissions was simply not available. However, within OSCON, the reporting system functioned much better,[99] probably because of the more 'monitorable' character of the dumping operations.

The Paris Convention also contained a dispute settlement procedure. Article 21 of the Convention stated that 'any dispute between Contracting Parties relating to the interpretation or application of the present Convention, which cannot be settled otherwise by the parties concerned, for instance by means of inquiry or conciliation within the Commission, shall, at the request of any of those parties, be submitted to arbitration under the conditions laid down in Annex B to the present Convention'. A key element in the arbitration procedure was the establishment of an arbitration tribunal, consisting of one representative of each of the parties and a third, independent chairing arbitrator. The outcome of this procedure was described as 'binding', and no further 'penalizing' steps were mentioned. In practice, this procedure was not utilized.

Did the overall lax PARCON system give rise to grave cooperative impediments during the first phase of the cooperation? To my knowledge, no. As indicated earlier, the issue of lacking data and reporting inadequacies turned up quite regularly in PARCOM discussions on possible regulatory measures. At least judged by the annual reports, this never led to heated complaints from any of the contracting parties. Rather, the Commission as a whole confined itself to mild requests for more and better data from the parties. This seemingly relaxed atmosphere may be interpreted in several ways. First, as binding outcomes were few and regulatory wording not always crystal clear, the parties may understandably have come to regard PARCOM regulations as not much more than general guidelines. In brief, there were not many clear policy yardsticks available which 'suspicious' parties might have referred to. And very few seemed to miss such yardsticks during this period. A supplementary interpretation is that, at least over some time, the parties acquired the information they needed about other states' pollution policies through more informal channels than official reports – for instance through personal contacts in the various subsidiary bodies of the regime. In other words, a sort of 'diffuse reciprocity' was developed. Be this as it may, the important thing to note is that although low effectiveness and lax compliance checking are correlated in this period, the latter probably contributed very marginally to the former.

In the 1990s, both reporting routines and actual reporting have improved quite considerably. This is due to a conscious structuring effort from the Secretariat, partly based on signals given in the 1992 OSPAR Convention and Action Plan. The 1992 Convention signalled a strengthened emphasis on implementation and compliance issues, both relating to the roles of the contracting parties and the Commission.[100] Hence, OSPAR has developed procedures whereby all parties report on the implementation of decisions and recommendations one year after their entry into force. In addition, if there is a deadline, implementation reports are to be submitted in the first year following the deadline. If there is no deadline, reports are to be submitted every four years until full implementation.[101] Moreover, reports are produced by the Secretariat, where reported achievements are contrasted to the action plan, thus making the relationship between plans or goals and actual achievements much more explicit than the earlier situation, when there were only general emission statistics reports from the parties. A related issue is the general development towards increased transparency within the cooperation. Until 1993, all documents produced were considered private unless the Commission had specifically agreed to make them publicly available. In 1993 this policy was reversed and Commission documents are now available to all – NGOs, media and the public alike. However, despite several procedural improvements, participants in the cooperation indicate that practice and critical compliance discussions are lagging somewhat behind.[102] Although actual reporting has improved, this is more so in terms of nutrients than of diffuse sources. On substances like PCBs, mercury and toxic chemicals, only a small minority of the parties have been reporting as required.[103] Moreover, in practice, the relevant working group does not have a clear responsibility for examination of the national reports. Overall, developing a well-functioning 'compliance chain' from the working groups via PRAM to the Commission meetings clearly takes time.

In addition to reporting within the conventions, progress reports have been produced in connection with the North Sea Conferences. For the 1995 Esbjerg Conference, a 200 page 'Progress Report' was published, explicitly ranking the North Sea countries in terms of compliance with percentage reduction targets. The general impression is clearly that transparency and accountability are better taken care of within the NSC system than within PARCON, primarily because central targets and timetables are both more specific and less complex than the more diffuse mass of PARCOM decisions. However, participants in the NSC processes point out that national procedural and methodological differences still hamper comparative assessment efforts within this context.[104] It should also be mentioned that, related to the NSC processes, there have been separate and 'independent' progress reports produced by Greenpeace and 'Seas at Risk', both in 1989–90 and in the process leading up to the 1995 Conference.

In summary, reporting and transparency have increased considerably in the 1990s – much as a response to regulatory sharpening over time. As with many of the other institutional changes in recent years, these changes have been more effective in contributing to a broader effectiveness improvement process than in initiating one. Moreover, much of the reporting and transparency improvement is too recent to have influenced the cooperative processes in any noticeable way yet. A specific international compliance checking system, for instance in the form of the establishment of a specific implementation committee, is not on the drawing board. This may be a reflection of the rather homogeneous character of the participants and the relatively long history of cooperation. Although international routines and practices still leave something to be desired, participants in the cooperation emphasize that there is a balance to this process: tougher and tighter procedures may improve transparency further, but may also lead to a growing unwillingness among the parties to commit themselves internationally.

3.5 CONCLUDING COMMENTS: FROM INCREASING CONCERN AND BETTER DESIGN – TO DECREASING CONCERN AND IRRELEVANT DESIGN?

Were the initial OSCON and PARCON regimes 'designed for weakness', for instance reflected in the moderate administrative and financial resources allocated to the Secretariat and the lack of priority given to the establishment of a well-functioning monitoring programme? To a certain extent, but it is important to remember that these conventions were definitely parts of the 'first generation' international environmental regimes and there was not much issue-specific experience to build on. It is understandable that states were apprehensive with regard to the creation of new international instruments in this field, even before several of them had much administrative experience at home to build on and rely upon in environmental matters. A country like Norway established its Ministry of Environment in 1972, the same year as OSCON. Hence, it may be argued that the conventions were designed apprehensibly and tentatively rather than as intentionally weak.

Still, the main causes for slow progress both in terms of regime activity and national behavioural change in the first years lie elsewhere. First, there was high scientific and technological uncertainty. Moreover, abatement measures would to a varying degree touch upon important economic interests and, due to asymmetries in activities, create competitive difficulties between the states. For instance, the UK was responsible for about half of all waste dumped. In addition, there were more general differences in regulatory philosophies and practices between the UK and most of the other countries. All these basic elements were reflected in differences in preferences, both with regard to emission control principles and more specific measures. Moreover, a striking feature of the land-based marine pollution issues in this first phase was the overall moderate concern about the problems in the area and related lack of real political urgency in most of the states involved. Concern was generally higher in the more 'visible' dumping issue area, but it was mostly a case of small or non-dumping countries attacking the dumping countries.

From the early 1980s on, this picture started gradually to change. First, there was increasing issue-specific impatience. Some alarming specific and issue-related reports appeared in the early 1980s, like the 1980 German report. Moreover, over time, a feeling of slow progress bothered an increasing number of countries. Several countries unilaterally stopped marine dumping. Even within the main 'laggard' country, the UK, a gradual reorientation of marine pollution policies began to take form. In addition, general environmental concern started to increase again somewhat from the mid 1980s on. These elements help to shed light on the political 'breakthrough' at the 1987 London North Sea Conference. In the wake of this Conference, alarming algae and seal events, and especially substantially increased general environmental political concern in the late 1980s and early 1990s, contributed to the gradual acceleration of the process, and rising effectiveness.

So what about the role of institutional factors? Well, there have been some institutional changes, but many of them have occurred too recently to have influenced positively the effectiveness of the cooperation. Examples here are the increased scope for NGO participation and the improved reporting routines and practices. Other changes probably belong more to a middle category, being the results of and linked to the general shift in cooperative mood, but also contributing to it. Examples here are the strengthened Secretariat, increased regionalization and decision-making flexibility, and not least the important work of the North Sea Task Force, leading up to the reorganization of the OSPAR scientific–political complex. Hence, the most conspicuous positive institutional change has been the three North Sea Conferences held during the past decade, creating the NSTF, among other things. First, the North Sea context has meant a narrower and more homogeneous group of states. Moreover, combining dumping and land-based issues has created an issue linkage and bargaining potential. Third, and not least important, the NSCs have meant a generally higher degree of politicization of the cooperation in the form of a more frequent involvement of politicians and ministers in the decision-making processes. This has meant the involvement of actors both sensitive to the changing demands of society and with the power to transform potential issue linkages and bargaining opportunities into political realities, and in the process, naturally attracting media attention. Fourth, the fact that the conference declarations have only been 'politically binding' may have contributed to a looser atmosphere than within the convention context. Still, the NSC effect must be qualified in at least two respects: first and foremost, both the 1987 breakthrough and the results of later conferences have built upon scientific, administrative and political groundwork carried out within the wider convention context. Hence, there has been a crucial interplay between the convention and conference contexts – with the conventions carrying out important legal and political groundwork for the 'vitalizing', more political conferences, and the conventions in turn transforming the conference commitments into binding international law.[105] Moreover, it turned out to be lucky that the important 1987 Conference took place in London; with the Conference host factor contributing to a more general policy change process in development in the UK, which was a crucially important regional marine actor.

Overall, the institutional design of the conventions seems to have developed from a mild impeding force into an asset for the cooperative process. There is now the potential to draw upon the expertise of non-governmental organizations. Moreover, the possibility of adopting flexible decisions, adapted to various environmental conditions and problems, has been established. In addition, institutional routines are in place which increasingly allow meaningful assessments and comparisons of the implementation performance of the various states. However, improved institutions may definitely be needed, in order to clarify and implement regulatory challenges successfully, like the 1995 North Sea Conference target to eliminate completely the inputs of hazardous substances by the year 2020. We should not forget that crucial malign features of the land-based problems remain – with for instance many economically important activities to be regulated; asymmetries in import and export of polluting substances; and international competitive effects – and not least the growing understanding of the real complexity of the problems. This latter aspect has to do with increased awareness of the importance of atmospheric inputs, emissions from the agricultural and municipal sectors, and a growing comprehension of the myriad of substances not systematically understood and addressed at all.

Looking ahead, at least two more general question marks can be noted. First, there is clearly a general reduced attention and priority given to environmental issues in many of the relevant countries.[106] Have the states in the region (only moderately intentionally) then succeeded in building a smooth-running machine which only a declining minority will be interested in utilizing effectively? Second, there is the uncertainty related to an expanding and developing European Community. Norway and Iceland are now the only OSPAR countries that are not members of the EC. At the same time, EC policy-making in the issue area is becoming more important, and the expanded EC is clearly a sort of a regime Goliath. Will Goliath in the future move on alone, then, ignoring the interests of the small Davids and leaving old institutions behind as empty shells?

NOTES

1. This case study draws upon several types of sources: an earlier version of the chapter (Wettestad and Andresen, 1991; Wettestad, 1992) benefited from interviews with Per W. Schive in the Norwegian Ministry of Environment and Jens H. Kofoed in the Norwegian State Pollution Control Authority. Moreover, in 1988–89, I conducted interviews with relevant civil servants and scientists in Denmark, the Netherlands, Belgium, the Federal Republic of Germany, and the UK. In addition, a questionnaire was sent out to the 12 participating countries in PARCON and to a group of six more independent observers and scientists. Seven answers from the participant group were received, and three answers from the group of observers. In the more recent round of revisions, I conducted some in-depth interviews on institutional issues in autumn 1995 with Per W. Schive and Stig Borgvang, in the Norwegian Ministry of Environment. Borgvang has also served for several years with the OSPARCOM Secretariat. I received written comments on a draft from Stan Sadowski, OSPAR Secretariat, in July 1997. Moreover, in the final round, I have benefited greatly from

Jon B. Skjærseth's doctoral dissertation (forthcoming 1998), and his comments on parts of this chapter.

2. In 1971, the coaster 'Stella Maris' left the port of Rotterdam with 650 tonnes of chlorinated hydrocarbons on board, destined to be dumped in the northern part of the North Sea. The incident caused immense public alarm and was met with protests from a number of European governments. See for example, Skjærseth (1992C).

3. That is, Denmark, Sweden, Norway, Portugal, Spain, Iceland, France, United Kingdom, the Netherlands, Federal Republic of Germany, Belgium, Finland, and Ireland.

4. This area extends to Greenland in the West, Gibraltar in the South, and to the North Pole.

5. Except for Finland, the same countries as in the case of OSCON (see note 3); in addition, the European Community (EC) also signed the Convention as a separate contracting party.

6. Blacklisted substances in the case of OSCON and PARCON were initially organohalogen compounds; mercury and mercury compounds; cadmium and cadmium compounds; persistent synthetic floating materials; and persistent oil and hydrocarbons.

7. Grey-listed OSCON and PARCON substances were organic compounds of phosphorus, silicon and tin; elemental phosphorus; non-persistent oils and hydrocarbons; and the following elements and their compounds: arsenic, chromium, copper, lead, nickel and zinc.

8. See for example, Green Globe Yearbook (1994:192, 194).

9. This is for instance discussed by Hayward (1990:93).

10. See for example, Mensbrugghe (1990).

11. A summary of NSC issues and related PARCOM activities is found in the 1995 North Sea Conference Progress Report.

12. For a discussion of this Convention, see for example, Hey, Ijlstra, and Nollkaemper (1993).

13. The Terms of Reference for the new ASMO and PRAM Committees are outlined in the Summary Record of the fifteenth joint meeting of the Oslo and Paris Commissions (1993), Annexes 23 and 24.

14. I am thankful to an anonymous reviewer for pointing this out to me.

15. See for instance Nollkaemper (1993) and Skjærseth (forthcoming 1998) for such broader discussions.

16. Wettestad and Andresen (1991); Wettestad (1992).

17. See Skjærseth (forthcoming 1998; ch.5).

18. See for example, Sætevik (1988: ch.5); Pallemaerts (1992); Skjærseth (forthcoming 1998: ch.5).

19. See Pallemaerts (1992:16). Pallemaerts's overall assessment is very similar to Sætevik's (1988:17): 'Finding itself unable to adopt more than a few binding decisions of limited significance, the Paris Commission has resorted to making non-binding recommendations on various policy-matters relating to emissions of dangerous substances. Apart from their non-binding nature, these recommendations are generally so vague and non-committal in their wording that their real significance may equally be questioned'.

20. This is further discussed in Skjærseth (forthcoming 1998). See his Chapter 5 for a brief summary of the debate on uniform emissions standards versus environmental quality objectives within PARCOM during the first decade.

21. Stortingsmelding (Norwegian Parliamentary Report) 107 (1974–75). See Skjærseth (1998: ch.6).

22. Skjærseth (1991:45).

23. Skjærseth (1998: ch.5).

24. See for instance Pallemaerts (1992:6).

25. Against this conclusion, it may be argued that all regimes need some 'warm up' time in order to become really effective. This is a valid point, but it is hard to set an 'objective' and general time limit for when regime effectiveness 'should' start to increase, like, say, after five years. Such an assessment must be based on a careful comparison of cases.

26. Wettestad (1989).

27. See for instance Skjærseth's (1998: ch.10) discussion of different data sets about the development of 'green' attitudes.

28. See Wettestad (1989) for a comparison and discussion of the 1984 and 1987 QSRs.

29. 1987 London North Sea Conference Declaration.

30. 1990 Hague North Sea Conference Declaration.
31. More specifically, the 1991 Urban Waste Water Treatment Directive; the 1991 Directive on nitrate losses from agriculture; and the 1992 Regulations on agro-environmental measures. See the 1995 Esbjerg North Sea Conference Declaration.
32. See Haas (1993) and Andresen (1996).
33. See for instance Nollkaemper (1993:128–146).
34. See Skjærseth (1998: ch.5).
35. Skjærseth (ibid.).
36. See Broadus et al. (1993) and Andresen (1996).
37. North Sea Conference Progress Report (1995:89).
38. The information here on Norway, the Netherlands, and the UK is mainly based on Skjærseth (1998: ch.6).
39. NOU 1995/4, "Virkemidler i miljøpolitikken", p.182.
40. See Wettestad (1994; forthcoming 1999A) for a more in-depth discussion of the science–politics relationship within this regime.
41. Jon B. Skjærseth's doctoral dissertation, which focuses on Norway, the Netherlands and the UK, of course provides an excellent point of departure for such further efforts (Skjærseth, 1998).
42. The Oslo and Paris Commissions (1984:39).
43. See Skjærseth (1991).
44. According to Skjærseth's 1991 thesis on the effectiveness of the Oslo Convention, the importance of dumping activities varied between the various countries. For countries like the UK, the dumping option has probably been regarded as nationally quite important, given perceptions of alternative options.
45. See for example, Sætevik (1988); Boehmer-Christiansen (1990); Nollkaemper (1993: ch.3); Skjærseth (1998: ch.5).
46. See Sætevik (1988: ch.8).
47. For instance, Sætevik (1988:82) comments upon the FRG: 'In the FRG there seems to have been a development in the past few years towards preferences for stricter regulatory measures and a higher level of activity ... On the other hand, there are other factors which might indicate rather low priority of the Paris cooperation, in particular the FRG's constant reluctance towards contributing financially to the administration of the cooperation and its enterprises, which has been reflected for instance in its opposition to establishing working groups and to maintaining the allocations for the Secretariat'.
48. See Skjærseth (1991).
49. According to Sætevik (1988:78), 'on at least twelve occasions the UK has opposed the adoption of proposals, which in three cases has resulted in blocking decisions'.
50. See Skjærseth (1998: ch.10).
51. As indicated by Brackley (1987:4): 'Britain has been severely criticized by some of its European neighbours for "dragging its feet" on some prominent environmental issues, in particular for not undertaking to reduce SO_2 emissions more quickly, and for resisting or delaying proposals for Community legislation'.
52. More about the development within the EC in relation to these issue areas can be found in Nollkaemper (1993: ch.3) and Skjærseth (1998: ch.5).
53. Sætevik (1988:82).
54. As commented in *New Scientist* in 1987: 'Five weeks before the Conference, Klaus Topfer visited all the North Sea states to put forward his government's stance ... West Germany is ... claiming that the North Sea has already received so much waste that it would be foolish to continue discharging into it materials known or suspected to be hazardous' (Milne, 1987:55).
55. According to Peter Haas (1993:153) 'The new German interior minister, whose responsibility included the environment, found this proposal to be a convenient way for a weak and low-profile ministry to appeal to growing domestic environmental concern, while also promoting his own political career. He called for a North Sea Ministerial Conference'. For some further information on the emergence of German environmental policy, see Boehmer-Christiansen and Skea (1991), especially Chapters 4, 5 and 10.

56. 'Britain is reluctant to agree to extra controls, which will involve large sums of money ... It does not believe that the level of pollution in the North Sea justifies general measures over and above existing controls' (Milne, *New Scientist*, 1987)
57. ENDS Report (1987B:17–18).
58. See for example, *International Environment Reporter* (1993).
59. Norwegian interviews, autumn 1995; see also Haas (1993:140).
60. Compare in this connection P. Haas's (1993:138) thesis on a 'leader-laggard' process-driving dynamic: 'Leader governments are pressed by both industry and public opinion to draw other governments up to their levels of environmental protection. "Leaders" are countries with stringent sectoral environmental measures, which promote their sectoral standards for universal adoption'. However, it is indicated by participants in the cooperation that it is harder to identify 'leaders' and 'laggards' in the 1990s, as there is an increasing tendency for new initiatives to come from working groups and not directly from specific countries (Norwegian interviews, autumn 1995).
61. Skjærseth (1991).
62. That is, only the eight North Sea states bordering directly on the North Sea proper: Belgium, Denmark, France, Germany, the Netherlands, Norway, Sweden, and the UK. In addition, Switzerland has been a participant, due to its geographical position as a source of inputs to the River Rhine.
63. This is mainly based on Sætevik (1988: ch.9).
64. Sadowski (1996:14).
65. See Andresen (1996).
66. Skjærseth (1998: ch.8).
67. Although the balance between environmental organizations and industrial organizations has not been a formal concern, practice seems to indicate the operation of such an informal norm. See Skjærseth (1998: ch.8).
68. Norwegian interviews, autumn 1995.
69. See Wettestad (1988).
70. For instance, according to Haas (1993:136–137): 'Non-governmental organizations exercised little regional influence until the late 1980s. Other than Greenpeace International and Friends of the Earth, few regional NGOs existed, and there was little transnational logistic support for coordinating efforts by national groups. Most national environmental groups were not involved with marine issues, focusing instead on energy and nature conservation'.
71. See Sadowski (1996).
72. See Sætevik (1988: ch.10).
73. Skjærseth (1998: ch.8).
74. Ibid.
75. PARCOM Decision 90/1 'on the reduction of discharges of chlorinated organic substances from the production of bleached kraft pulp and sulphite pulp'.
76. Norwegian interviews, autumn 1995.
77. Skjærseth (1998: ch.8).
78. Hey, Ijlstra and Nollkaemper (1993:42).
79. Skjærseth (1998: ch.8).
80. Sætevik (1988:117–118).
81. Skjærseth (1998: ch.8).
82. Sætevik (1988:117–118).
83. Ibid.
84. Communication with Stan Sadowski, OSPAR Secretariat, July 1997.
85. *Green Globe Yearbook* (1995:154).
86. Norwegian interviews, autumn 1995.
87. Hey, Ijlstra and Nollkaemper (1993).
88. Sætevik (1988:117–118).
89. Wettestad (1989).
90. Sætevik (1988:117–118).
91. Interview with Norwegian civil servant, 1989.

92. Its main objective was formulated in the Declaration from the London North Sea Conference: 'to carry out work leading, in a reasonable time scale, to a dependable and comprehensive statement of circulation patterns, inputs, and dispersion of contaminants, ecological conditions and effects of human activities in the North Sea'.

93. See Reid (1990) and Ducrotoy (1997).

94. The 1995 Progress Report, p.201.

95. See Wettestad (forthcoming 1999A). I find Haas's (1993:155) assessment a little too bombastic: 'the NSTF is high profile and politicized ... Consequently, domestic administrative forces prevail over transnational scientific ones in establishing priority concerns and identifying future problems'.

96. Norwegian interviews, autumn 1995.

97. See Sætevik (1988:116).

98. Norwegian interviews, autumn 1995.

99. Skjærseth (1998: ch.8).

100. See Articles 22 and 23 in the 1992 OSPAR Convention.

101. See Andresen (1996:78).

102. Norwegian interviews, autumn 1995.

103. Information from the Secretariat, referred to in Andresen (1996:78).

104. Norwegian interviews, autumn 1995.

105. See for example Hayward (1990); Wettestad (1991; 1992); Skjærseth (1996; 1998); Andresen (1996).

106. Various data sources for instance indicate a marked decline in the UK and Norway, with more uncertainty related to the Dutch development. See Skjærseth (1998: ch.10).

4. More 'Discursive Diplomacy' than 'Dashing Design'? The Convention on Long-Range Transboundary Air Pollution (LRTAP)

4.1 INTRODUCTION

In 1968 the Swedish scientist Svante Oden published a paper in which he argued that precipitation over Scandinavia was becoming increasingly acidic, thus inflicting damage on fish and lakes.[1] Moreover, it was maintained that the acidic precipitation was to a large extent caused by sulphur compounds from British and Central European industrial emissions. This development aroused broader Scandinavian concern and diplomatic activity related to acid pollution, and played a part in the adoption of 'Principle 21' at the 1972 Stockholm UN Conference on the Human Environment. This principle stipulated that states have an obligation to ensure that activities carried out in one country do not cause environmental damage in other countries, or to the global commons. The specific background for formal negotiations on an air pollution convention was the East–West détente process in the mid-1970s, in which the environment was identified as one potential issue for cooperation. Due to the East–West dimension, the United Nations Economic Commission for Europe (UNECE) was chosen as the institutional setting for the negotiations. ECE is one of five UN regional economic commissions concerned with information and generally facilitating collaboration, with a membership of 34 parties, including the US and Canada.[2]

The ECE Convention on Long-Range Transboundary Air Pollution (LRTAP) was signed by 33 contracting parties (32 countries and the EC Commission) in Geneva in November 1979. Four main aspects of the 1979 Convention may be discerned: first, the recognition that airborne pollutants were a major problem; second, the declaration that the parties would 'endeavour to limit and, as far as possible, gradually reduce and prevent air pollution, including long-range transboundary air pollution' (Article 2); third, the commitment of contracting parties 'by means of exchange of information, consultation, research and monitoring, to develop without undue delay policies and strategies which should serve as a means of combating the discharge of air pollutants, taking into account efforts already made at the national and international levels' (Article 3); and fourth, the intention to use 'the best available technology which is economically feasible' to meet the objectives of the Convention.[3] The Convention did not specify any pollutants, but stated that monitoring activity and information exchange should start with sulphur dioxide (SO_2).

The Convention has been in force since 1983, with a current membership of 43 parties. Moreover, the Convention was to be overseen by an 'Executive Body' (EB), which included representatives of all the parties to the Convention as well as the European Community (EC). Furthermore, the ECE secretariat was given a coordinating function. The institutional structure has also included several Working Groups, Task Forces and 'International Cooperative Programmes' (see Figure 4.1 for an overview of current organizational setup). One of these was the Cooperative Programme for Monitoring and Evaluation of Long-Range Transmissions of Air Pollutants in Europe (EMEP). Rooted in the Convention's strong initial focus on knowledge improvement and monitoring, a specific financing protocol for the EMEP monitoring programme was established in 1984.

After the signing of the Convention, and the 1984 EMEP Protocol, the first main regulatory step in the cooperation was the 1985 Geneva Protocol on the Reduction of Sulphur Emissions, calling for a reduction by at least 30% of emissions and transboundary fluxes of SO_2 as soon as possible, though by 1993 at the latest, with 1980 levels as baseline. In the 1988 Sofia Protocol on Nitrogen Oxides (NO_x), the signatories pledged to freeze NO_x emissions at the 1987 level from 1994 onwards and to negotiate subsequent reductions. The next step was the 1991 Geneva Protocol on Volatile Organic Compounds (VOCs), which called for a 30% reduction in VOC emissions by 1999, based on 1988 levels – either at national levels or within specific 'tropospheric ozone management areas'. The latest step so far is the new Sulphur Protocol, signed in Oslo in June 1994 by 28 parties, based on the 'critical loads' approach. The aim of this approach is that emissions reductions should be negotiated on the basis of the (varying) effects of air pollutants, rather than by choosing an equal percentage reduction target for all countries involved. Several new protocols are underway within the regime regarding new and combined NO_x and VOC requirements; heavy metals; and persistent organic pollutants (POPs). (See section 4.2.1 for more details on the various protocols and processes).

As in the case of OSCON and PARCON discussed in Chapter 3, other institutions with regulations influencing this area could have been included within a broader regime definition and discussion. I am especially thinking about the role of the European Community. But as noted in the previous chapter, despite the merits of such a broader approach, it would have complicated the already complicated regime design discussion considerably.

Given the central role of monitoring and knowledge improvement within the regime, as indicated by the specific 1984 financing protocol on the EMEP monitoring system, and the steady process and protocol development, the concept of 'discursive diplomacy' seems relevant as a key phrase describing this regime.[4] However, does this also automatically mean that the LRTAP is a regime with a 'dashing institutional design'? This is one of the central questions addressed in this case.

Figure 4.1   LRTAP: current organizational setup

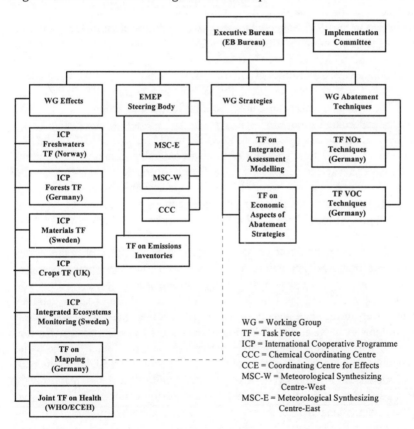

4.2 REGIME EFFECTIVENESS: STEADY INTERNATIONAL PROGRESS AND BEHAVIOURAL CHANGES – BUT FOR WHICH REASONS?

4.2.1 Political Effectiveness: Impressive Facade, but More Modest Contents?

The strength of regime regulations: steady development
Turning first to the 1979 Convention, it was definitely binding, but its ambitiousness and specificity were low, generally talking about the 'limitation and gradual reduction and prevention' of transboundary air pollution.

Moving to the 1985 Sulphur Protocol, at the third meeting of the Executive Body of the Convention in Helsinki, July 1985, 21 countries and the EC signed this Protocol, which stipulated a reduction by at least 30% of emissions and transboundary fluxes of SO_2 as soon as possible, although by 1993 at the latest, with 1980 levels as baseline. It came into force in September 1987. However, some major emitter states chose not to join the agreement, among them the UK, the US, and Poland. Hence, compared to the Convention, it was also binding, but with higher specificity and ambitiousness, including both the 30% reduction target and the 1993 time limit. Flexibility was naturally quite low, as countries with widely varying emissions, regulatory histories or baselines, and environmental conditions, were obliged to reduce with the same percentage rate. However, the opening up of opportunities for reductions only of 'transboundary fluxes' introduced a flexible element, especially pushed by the Soviet Union.[5]

In the 1988 Sofia Protocol on Nitrogen Oxides (NO_x), the signatories pledged to freeze NO_x emissions at the 1987 level from 1994 onwards and to negotiate subsequent reductions. Twenty-five countries signed the Protocol, including the UK and the United States. Moreover, 12 European signatories went a step further and signed an additional (and separate) joint declaration committing them to a 30% reduction of emissions by 1998, with a flexible baseline between 1980 and 1986.[6] In terms of strength, much of the same reflections apply to the NO_x Protocol as to the Sulphur Protocol, but in the NO_x case one should also be aware of the separate political declaration for a 30% reduction, as mentioned above. Hence, many of the countries have had two related international commitments to live up to, although of quite different characters. In this connection, it should be noted that the 30% declaration was not formally a part of the LRTAP regulatory system. The ambitiousness of the NO_x Protocol's stabilization target was quite clearly lower than the 30% sulphur requirement. However, given the role of transport and the generally more complex emission picture in the NO_x case, the 30% NO_x declaration target was probably far more ambitious than the 30% sulphur target.

The next step was the 1991 Geneva Protocol on Volatile Organic Compounds (VOCs). VOCs are a group of chemicals that are precursors of ground level ozone. The Protocol called for a 30% reduction in VOC emissions by 1999, based on 1988 levels – either at national levels or within specific 'tropospheric ozone management areas' (TOMAs). Some countries were allowed to opt for a freeze of 1988 emissions by 1999.[7] Twenty-one parties signed the Protocol in 1991; Portugal and the EC joined in 1992. Russia and Poland chose not to sign. By April 1998, the Protocol had been ratified by 17 parties and is hence now formally in force.[8] In terms of strength, the Protocol was also binding and quite specific. Moreover, this Protocol marked a further move towards greater flexibility with the TOMAs, and a certain flexibility with regard to baseline or starting point. Given the complexity of the VOC issue, ambitiousness was probably higher than in the case of the NO_x Protocol.

The latest step so far is the new Sulphur Protocol, signed in Oslo in June 1994 by 28 parties, based on the 'critical loads' approach. The aim of this approach is for emissions reductions to be negotiated on the basis of the (varying) effects of air pollutants, rather than by choosing an equal percentage reduction target for all countries involved.[9] Hence, the Protocol sets out individual and varying national reduction targets for the year 2000 alone for half of the countries, and additional 2005 and 2010 targets for the other half with 1980 as base year. By April 1998, the Protocol had been ratified by 14 parties.[10] In terms of strength, the Protocol is both binding and specific, including both detailed targets and timetables. However, the key point is how these elements are combined with flexibility on the basis of the 'critical loads' approach, resulting in somewhat differentiated targets. Ambitiousness is substantially increased compared to the 1985 Protocol.

As indicated, several new protocols are underway within the regime regarding new and combined NO_x and VOC requirements; heavy metals; and persistent organic pollutants (POPs). While the two latter processes were concluded in June 1998, the combined NO_x and VOC Protocol will not be concluded until 1999.

In summary, a steady regulatory development may be discerned, with regulations gradually becoming both more ambitious and specific, but also more fine tuned to ecological and economic variations among the countries.

National compliance: generally impressive[11]
Turning first to the *sulphur* compliance picture, as will be recalled, the Protocol called for a 30% reduction by 1993, with 1980 as baseline. The largest European polluters who abstained from signing the Protocol were the UK, Poland and Spain; these three accounted for about 25% of Europe's 1980

sulphur emissions. Let us take a look at the final compliance picture which emerged from the 1995 LRTAP progress report.[12] Two of the signatories, although non-compliers mid-term, had changed considerably. The main part of the former USSR – Russia – joined the compliers with a fair margin (around 50%). Ukraine and Belarus also managed to comply with the Protocol. Although East and West Germany had merged, the united Germany achieved compliance with a fair margin (close to 50% reductions). Several countries had achieved around 70% reductions (Austria, Denmark, Finland, France, the Netherlands, Norway and Sweden). Regarding the non-signatories, there were some interesting features. The UK had landed on 37%, making it a *de facto* complier. Portugal had actually increased its emissions, while there were no figures for Spain after 1990. Summing up: given that the 21 parties overall had reduced emissions by around 48% by 1993, and that all parties had reached the target, the Sulphur Protocol part of the LRTAP regime must be said to be characterized by very high compliance.

Regarding the NO_x compliance picture, as will be recalled, the 1988 NO_x Protocol called for the stabilization of emissions at the 1987 level from 1994 onwards, and the related political declaration (signed by 12 countries) called for a 30% reduction by 1998. The main compliance picture may be summed up in the following manner:[13] existing data indicate that 19 of the 25 parties have stabilized their emissions and overall reduced them by 9%. Three parties have increased emissions by 4–41% above 1987 levels. However, considerable data problems complicate compliance assessments. There were for instance problems with the NO_x emission reports of Italy, Liechtenstein, Luxembourg, Spain, and the European Community for the years after 1991. Moreover, several parties have been slow in reporting emission data for the base year 1987. Furthermore, as indicated by the overall 9% emission reduction so far, progress in relation to the 30% declaration target has been modest (although this target only applies to 12 of the parties). Austria, Denmark and Switzerland are the only countries that seem to be reasonably on schedule (15–20% reductions). In summary, although assessments are complicated by considerable data problems, compliance with the 1988 Protocol has been fairly high. However, progress in relation to the non-binding 30% declaration target has been modest.

Regarding VOCs, the data here are still very scattered. However, of the eleven countries (out of 23 parties) providing data for 1993, an overall reduction of around 15% may be noted.

In conclusion, the LRTAP must definitely be characterized as a high compliance regime, but to what extent can the LRTAP regime be credited? In order to answer such questions, we have to enter the territory of implementation and regime-induced national behavioural changes.

Implementation data and the tricky causal question: a sobering perspective
First of all, available evidence indicates that major causal factors for compliance levels are not found at all within the sphere of environmental politics. Upon summarizing and discussing the sulphur and NO_x implementation processes in the UK, Germany, the Netherlands and Norway in another context, I concluded that the majority of the reductions and compliance levels achieved in three of the four countries (the UK, Netherlands, and Norway) are apparently explained by processes that are not primarily related to environmental protection, at least with regard to sulphur reductions.[14] In the UK, industrial recession and reduced energy demand in the 1980s were important factors. The NO_x picture is more varied, but privatization and the switch from coal to gas were important factors. In the Netherlands, a gradual conversion to domestic natural gas for supply, and domestic political and financial reasons were clearly important. In Norway, much has been achieved by reducing consumption of heavy fuel oil on land. The exception is Germany, where environmental regulations have apparently, in fact, been the main driving force.

Focusing more closely on the LRTAP contribution to these processes, the short, tentative answer is: it has not been very significant, at least for these particular countries. The LRTAP process has obviously been important as an arena for creating and maintaining intergovernmental confidence and learning. However, in a situation without the LRTAP, significant reductions would probably have taken place anyway, due to other economic and political processes and domestic political pressure motivated by environmental damage. It is, for instance, important to remember that Germany was almost as reluctant as the UK at the convention negotiations in the late 1970s. Without the 'Waldsterben' phenomenon, both German and European acid rain politics would have looked very different today (see section 4.3.2). Moreover, with regard to German and British acid rain politics, the European Community decision-making arena has possibly been more important than the LRTAP. However, there is still a possibility that the LRTAP has been more important for the other West and not least East European countries. This is for instance indicated by Levy (1993:118–121). He suggests that countries like Austria, Finland, the Netherlands, and Switzerland were influenced by the LRTAP through increased awareness of domestic acid rain damage. Moreover, countries like Denmark, the UK, and the Soviet Union were influenced by the LRTAP through various types of linkage effects.

In summary, a preliminary causal analysis of the regime indicates that regime activity and decisions have led to somewhat 'greener' acid rain policies – to varying degrees in varying countries – than would have been the case without this regime activity. However, more in-depth studies of countries like Germany, the Netherlands, UK, and Norway also indicate that factors not directly related to the regime seem more important in certain countries for shedding light on the compliance levels achieved so far.

4.2.2 The Environmental and Problem-Solving Dimensions: Improvements, Though Still Some Way to Go ...

Let us first turn to the evolving match between scientific knowledge and advice and the international policy measures taken in response.[15] With regard to the sulphur process, although scientific uncertainty was reduced and there was growing consensus in the early 1980s (as will be further specified later), there seems currently to be general consensus on seeing various aspects of the 30% Protocol as only remotely related to specific scientific evidence. Both the baseline of 1980, the target date of 1993, and the 30% reduction target have been characterized as quite arbitrary;[16] 20% was too little, and 40% seemed too much. However, my own interviews have confirmed the impression that most scientists definitely saw the 30% reduction as a significant step in the right direction. Hence, many scientists (at least in Germany and the Nordic countries) would probably have preferred more substantial reductions, but were evidently reluctant to rally around specific, higher reduction targets.

The NO_x science–politics story is in several ways different from the sulphur story. First, the scientific understanding of the more complex NO_x problems, at least emission-wise, was much less developed than in the case of the sulphur problems, which had been studied longer. The start of the negotiation process can be characterized as a spin-off from the successful establishment of the Sulphur Protocol.[17] Hence, initial targets discussed in the negotiations were borrowed first and foremost from the sulphur context and based more on political ambitions among pusher states than on well-developed scientific evidence. A knowledge-improving process was organized together with the negotiations. There is little doubt that improved knowledge influenced several participants' perceptions and positions and the course of the negotiations, though overall in a quite sobering direction.[18] The initial widespread support for a 30% reduction target was reduced in the course of time, largely due to increasing scientific and technological knowledge. Still, in terms of distance to an optimal environmental situation, there is little doubt that the stabilization target finally agreed upon was not a substantial contribution to narrowing this gap.

Let us then briefly turn to the science–politics relationship within the VOC process. Generally, the VOC problems are more similar to the NO_x problems than the sulphur problems – with for instance a multitude of emissions sources. It is not surprising, then, that the VOC process entailed several similarities to the NO_x process. Hence, a rapid knowledge production took place in a rather short time span and primarily within the regime context. The general impression is an overall acceptance of the scientific evidence to hand, but also a general 'sobering' recognition of the considerable uncertainty and complexity involved. This recognition was reflected in the unprecedented flexibility and complexity of the Protocol's commitments as the basic 30% reduction commitment was 'sweetened' by elements like a flexible base year (between 1984 and 1990), a freeze option for small polluters, and that some countries would only have to reduce by 30% within specific 'tropospheric ozone management areas' (TOMAs). Hence, in terms of narrowing the gap to the environmental optimum, the VOC protocol must also be regarded as a moderate contribution.

Turning finally to the 1994 Sulphur Protocol and the question of 'critical loads', this concept was already introduced in the NO_x negotiations. However, it was not until the negotiations on a new and revised sulphur protocol that this approach really moved centre-stage. A critical load is defined as 'a quantitative estimate of an exposure to one or more pollutants below which significantly harmful effects on specified sensitive elements of the environment do not occur according to present knowledge'.[19] Early in the negotiations, it was recognized that it would be impracticable to reduce sulphur depositions below critical loads by the end of the century. Based on inputs from the 'Regional Acidification Information and Simulation' (RAINS) model developed at the International Institute for Applied Systems Analysis (IIASA), it was instead agreed to reduce (first by 50%, then in 1993 by 60%) the gap between current levels of sulphur deposition and critical loads in most of Europe, except for the most acid-sensitive areas. The RAINS model then introduced tentative country-specific emission reduction targets. Hence, a period of sometimes intense bargaining followed, in which old political conflicts re-emerged.[20] The final Protocol was decided upon in Oslo in June 1994, setting out individual and varying national reduction targets for the year 2000 alone for half of the countries, and additional 2005 and 2010 targets for the other half – with 1980 as base year. Overall, then, scientific evidence played a very important role. Distinguishing this process from the foregoing, decision-makers largely accepted and actually adopted many of the policy implications inherent in the model predictions.

Given the patchy, though improving, match between scientific notions of ecological requirements and the regime regulations adopted, what is the current picture concerning actual solutions to the problems? On the one hand, if problem solutions are regarded as synonymous with the achievement of critical loads in Europe, then it is clear that most countries have some way to go before these critical targets are achieved. The targets in the 1994 Sulphur Protocol involve as a minimum a 60% reduction of the gap between 1990 sulphur depositions and the critical levels in the environment. Hence, even if the UK, for instance, achieves its 80% emissions cuts targets before 2010 (with 1980 as baseline year), then the country's emissions will still be some 40% above ideal levels. On the other hand, it must be kept in mind that the LRTAP primarily addresses the transboundary problems. Even if domestic critical loads are not met, the transboundary exports in major exporting countries may be reduced so much that the transboundary problems are more or less 'solved'. This remains to be further discussed and substantiated, but it is still important to keep the perspective in mind.

Moreover, there is definitely no direct, linear relationship between emissions cuts and environmental improvements. We are talking about gradual, slow processes, in which both positive and negative effects may not be seen for several years or decades after emissions changes have been achieved. Take for instance the Norwegian situation: at the same time that emissions in Europe were cut by around 40%, acidification damage in Norway gradually increased – up to a 1995 peak damaged area of over 110 000 km^2 receiving more sulphur than nature can handle. Moreover, although rainfall gradually became less acid, acid deposition did not decrease accordingly, due to increased rainfall patterns. However, more recent scientific reports indicate small improvements and possibly a reversed trend with regard to acidification damage.[21]

In addition, as indicated above, improved knowledge has gradually made clear that we are dealing with several sub-problems, in which the initial lake and forest acidification damage is only part of the picture. In the course of time, urban air pollution problems harming human health and causing material damage have come more to the forefront – as well as the complex interplay between the various substances and processes. However, the urban air pollution problems have a stronger local character than the more 'classic' acidification problems. Hence, there are also marked variations in the development of the urban problems. However, an outsider's overall impression is that these problems have so far shown an increasing trend due to more traffic – in spite of technological advances in the form of catalytic converters, for example.

Hence, overall, the transboundary acidification problems have been reduced somewhat, though an ultimate solution to the problem, getting below critical loads in both the rural and urban environment, is partly a matter of implementing recently adopted regulations – and of revising established regulations and addressing various new substances and sub-problems. In reality, this is a venture extending well into the next century.

4.2.3 Summing Up: 'Moderate' Effectiveness So Far? But What About the Process Dimension?

So, has the LRTAP regime been very effective so far? On the international regulatory side, progress has definitely been substantial. There has been a steady development of protocols, covering more substances, with regulations gradually becoming both binding, specific and more adapted to ecological and economic variations among the countries. Moreover, national compliance with these protocols must overall be characterized as high. Hence, it may seem somewhat paradoxical that a closer scrutiny of available national and sub-national knowledge offers doubts about the importance of the LRTAP in bringing about national and sub-national policy changes in this field. In brief, much behavioural change would apparently have occurred anyway – due to changes in energy policy, unrelated economic and industrial changes, and so on. In addition, the impact of parallel European Community (EC) processes must also be taken into account.[22] However, it must be emphasized that much national knowledge is uncertain or lacking, and the picture may vary between countries.[23] Still, as a tentative assessment, behavioural impact so far seems only moderate. Nevertheless, what about critical loads and the perhaps uniquely advanced 1994 Sulphur Protocol? Actually, this process and the substantial regulatory progress mentioned above indicate that there is a process dimension to regime effectiveness that a strict focus on 'compliance and behavioural progress so far' may easily ignore. As has been pointed out by an experienced regime analyst, 'it is hard to imagine being where we are today regarding transboundary air pollution in the absence of the LRTAP process'.[24]

Contributions to environmental problem-solving must be characterized as moderate with regard to the three first protocols within the regime. Although there was a lack of clear-cut, consensual and precise scientific advice indicating more ambitious targets, there appeared to be a widespread feeling in the scientific community that the targets agreed upon were ecologically ineffective, though still steps in the right direction. Concepts of environmental 'critical loads' were launched, though not yet sufficiently developed to be utilized in international decision-making processes – although they were, for instance, generally mentioned in the NO_x protocol. The second Sulphur Protocol is an important step ahead, both in terms of sharpening the scientific input with regard to environmental 'critical loads' and optimal conditions, and also in terms of formulating policies explicitly directed to closing the gap to the optimal conditions.

Hence, the tentative, overall assessment of the LRTAP regime must be 'only moderately effective' in terms of behavioural impact and measured against crude notions of ecologically optimal policies, but more effective in a more diffuse and less measurable awareness-raising and learning perspective.

How, then, can we substantiate and explain the overall moderate regime effectiveness so far? Let us first have a closer look at the basic problem and control perspective.

4.3 ACCOUNTING FOR MODERATE EFFECTIVENESS: MALIGN PROBLEMS – BECOMING SOMEWHAT LESS MALIGN ...

4.3.1 The Background to the 1979 Framework Convention: High Malignity and Overall Low Concern

How can the transboundary air pollution problems be characterized in the mid/late 1970s in terms of knowledge and main interests? And how can these initial problem characteristics throw light on the regime creation phase and the establishment of the 1979 Framework Convention?

In terms of knowledge and 'intellectual' problem characteristics, the overall picture was one of high uncertainty and complexity. There is of course no such thing as '*one* transboundary air pollution problem', but rather several different problems with more or less distinct structures. However, in the initial regime formation phase, both scientific and political attention was primarily directed towards sulphur emissions and related acidification problems.

Two main clusters of research problems in the international air pollution debate can be discerned: first, questions related to the international transport of substances, and second, issues related to the deposition of polluting substances and the impact of these depositions. Related to this was the important 'linearity' question: was there a linear relationship between reduced emissions and transboundary transport – and reduced national depositions and ultimately impacts on the environment? In 1978/79, some knowledge existed on both these research problems. Concerning the transport question, results from an OECD project, which started in 1972 and included the eleven European member countries, were published in 1977. Countries were here classified as either net exporters or net importers, although all countries received back to their territories a proportion of what they sent up. Denmark and the UK were, for instance, identified as net exporters, while countries like Austria, Finland, Norway, Sweden, and Switzerland were identified as net importers. The report indicated that the UK was the major exporter, producing more sulphur pollution than any other nation. However, the OECD itself emphasized the degree of uncertainty involved. Moreover, as the deposition and impact questions were in their very nature more complicated than the transport question, overall uncertainty was high – despite major efforts like the Norwegian project.[25] There was some degree of scientific disagreement, which is quite natural in such a complex field of research, but this did not necessarily follow national boundaries (see, for example, the Norwegian project). However, there seems to have been less 'pure' scientific controversy than one may be led to believe from the rather heated public debate.[26]

Intellectual complexity was in principle quite high, given that many types of anthropogenic emission sources were part of the picture (power stations, factories, vehicles, ships and so on), and also several natural sources were involved; several substances contributed to the problem (SO_2, NO_x, hydrocarbons and so on) and these substances partly interacted with each other to produce an 'acid cocktail'. However, as already indicated, most attention in this early phase was given to the sulphur and power station part of the problems.

Turning to the more political baseline, keywords were 'asymmetries and complexities'. Let us first turn to the basic interdependent relationship between the relevant states. The scientific and technological uncertainty surrounding the transboundary air pollution problems at this initial stage indicated the existence of a cost efficiency potential. A more comprehensive understanding of the regional ecosystem and a cheaper and faster route to effective abatement equipment represented the actual synergy potential. However, improved scientific and technological knowledge did not alone reduce the transboundary movements of polluting substances. In order to reduce these externalities, such knowledge had to be applied and transformed into practical, national programmes for reductions of emissions. It should be kept in mind that emissions sources were numerous, including power stations, various industrial sectors, and the transport sector. The need for such reduction programmes, affecting vital economic sectors, immediately introduced a competitive dimension to the problem. This was also largely related to the technological abatement situation at the time. There existed several technological abatement alternatives related to power stations and industry, the main ones being to lower the sulphur contents of the fuel before it was burned or to remove the sulphur from emissions. However, cheap and simple technological 'fixes' were simply not available at the time.[27]

Let us turn to the vulnerability question. With regard to environmental vulnerability, the OECD study indicated both symmetrical and asymmetrical dimensions. Symmetrical, in that regionally important countries like the FRG seemed to 'import' as much pollution as it 'exported'. However, the asymmetrical aspects seemed more striking. Due to wind currents and atmospheric conditions, several countries, for instance the UK, seemed to be net exporters of polluting substances. Moreover, the UK exported its emissions to a large extent to the net importing Scandinavian countries.[28] This particular relationship was further aggravated by the fact that the soil in Norway and Sweden has a relatively poor natural buffering capacity against acid precipitation. With regard to vulnerability related to abatement costs, the use of coal was an important factor in the energy profiles of important emitters like the UK and West Germany. In the case of Britain, the country derived more than 90% of its energy needs from fossil fuels, mostly in the form of coal-fired power stations. Thus, given the technological situation, cleaning emissions would clearly be expensive for the UK, and would apparently mainly benefit *other* countries' environments – due to wind currents and the fact that there was very low concern about British acidification damage at the time.[29]

This coal factor also had some implications for the complexity of the transboundary air pollution problems. As the UK had large domestic coal supplies of high sulphur content, coal had supply-security implications as an alternative to imported oil. Moreover, more general economic and employment implications were also involved, as coal countries like the UK and the US had suffered economic depression in mining areas.[30]

Based on the preceding problem diagnosis, one would expect quite diverging actor preferences. This of course holds true. Let us briefly take a closer look at the national positions and arguments of some of the main actors during the negotiations on the LRTAP Convention.[31]

The broad picture is not surprising: basically, there were a few, small activists versus many uninterested and reluctant parties. Mainly importer countries like the Scandinavian countries insisted on binding and specified international measures. More specifically, the Scandinavians put forward a 'standstill' and 'rollback' proposal, within the framework of a convention. The proposal called on signatories to hold the line against further SO_2 increases (standstill), and begin to abate SO_2 pollution levels by fixed, across-the-board percentages (rollback). As could be expected, major emitter/exporter countries like the FRG and the UK opposed these proposals.[32] The British delegation called for more research to establish firmly the responsibility for long-range pollution. However, it should be noted that the UK position at this point seems to have been somewhat more open than that of the FRG. The UK accepted broad, general statements of policy and even of measures to achieve this policy, as long as no positive obligations were imposed or assumed.[33] Further, it has been maintained that the British finally decided to accept the convention because they believed that their plans for increased reliance on nuclear power for generating electricity would bring about a net reduction in sulphur emissions. The FRG wanted the ECE agreement to include multilateral research exclusively.[34] They did not like the idea that the proposed coordinating function of the ECE Secretariat could authorize it to intervene in the internal affairs of member states. French and Scandinavian diplomatic pressure allegedly induced the Germans to sign.

In summary, the transboundary air pollution problems in this initial phase must fundamentally be characterized as malign and complex problems, shrouded in scientific uncertainty and to some degree also controversy. One of the most important aspects to keep in mind is that important roots of the problems have been – and to a large extent still are – tightly linked to the energy supply sector. This was illustrated, for instance, by the important role of coal-fired power stations for the British sulphur emissions. Industrial competitive ability is of course important for industrial societies, but energy supply is in addition a kind of meta-industry, being both a precondition and a basis for the development of other sectors – and an industrial sector in itself. Hence, regulatory efforts raised problems ranging from regional employment considerations to security and defence considerations. Combined with marked asymmetries with regard to environmental and regulatory impacts, the prospects were not very bright for a further development of the process.

4.3.2 The Background for Sequential and Steady Regime Development: Improved Knowledge, a Crucial Turnabout of Germany – but still a Complex Issue

The empirical ground covered in the next sections is of course simply immense. We are talking about nearly 20 years of knowledge and political development, with four protocol negotiation processes, each with its particular intellectual and political characteristics.[35] For the sake of simplicity, the years and negotiations leading up to the first Sulphur Protocol in 1985 are referred to as 'the first sulphur context' and the years and negotiations leading up to the 1994 second Sulphur Protocol are referred to as 'the second sulphur context'.

With regard to intellectual progress, there has been a development from scientific controversy to 'critical loads'. Uncertainty about the character of transboundary pollution was clearly reduced during the 1980s, at least concerning transport and depositions. This was largely due to the effort of the EMEP programme.[36] Within the first sulphur context, a certain scientific consolidation was witnessed at the 1982 Stockholm Conference on Acidification of the Environment. The Conference's final statement concluded that 'the acidification problem is serious and, even if deposition remains stable, deterioration of soil and water will continue and may increase unless additional control measures are implemented and existing control policies are strengthened'.[37] This Conference also witnessed the vital scientific and political shift of West German positions, related to the domestic media and political 'Waldsterben' uproar.[38] Moreover, Park (1987) maintains that 'by this time (1983/84) ... beyond doubt was the transfrontier character of the problem, in which some countries gained whilst others lost' (p.177). He further states as an example that when the European Parliament Committee on the Environment, Public Health and Consumer Protection held a public hearing on acid deposition in 1983, 'all agreed that the adverse effects of acid rain were clear, and the debate centred *not* on whether or not to reduce emissions but on how it should be done and who should pay for it' (p.174). Studies of the development of national perceptions of the acidification problems also clearly indicate shifting perceptions in countries like the Netherlands, Austria and Switzerland in the wake of the Stockholm Conference and the German change in perceptions and problems.[39]

However, as has been indicated earlier, uncertainty was generally more reduced with regard to SO_2 than to NO_x and VOC emissions. This is of course related to the fact that the sulphur-related problems had a much longer history in terms of scientific and political attention – and that the NO_x and VOC problems were intrinsically more complex. Regarding emission sources, a substantial portion of NO_x emissions stems in many countries from the inland and coastal transport sector, in addition to emissions from power stations and other industry. The VOC emission picture is even more complex. Overall, VOC emissions emanate mainly from three sources: motor traffic; the use of solvents in industrial and household appliances; and oil and gas industries. However, hundreds of compounds qualify as VOCs and they are emitted in a wide range of industrial activities.[40] Still, regime-initiated knowledge improvement processes also led to significant improvements in knowledge on NO_x and VOCs.

With regard to the question of impacts, the picture is complex. On the one hand, the hypothesis that acidification and related fish deaths in Scandinavian lakes can be attributed to transboundary pollution was strengthened and refined through the 1980s.[41] On the other hand, the scientific understanding of forest damage and acidification progressed far less than for surface water acidification.[42] An early hypothesis advanced by the German soil scientist Ulrich maintained that soil acidification related to SO_2 emissions was the underlying cause of forest damage. In the course of time, more complex multiple stress hypotheses seemed to explain the observed patterns of damage better.[43]

From the late 1980s on, the critical loads tool became the main factor.[44] This approach was launched by Swedish scientists and government officials in the early 1980s. As mentioned, the linearity problem and the extent to which reductions in emissions lead to corresponding, witnessed reductions in pollution had for many years complicated the acid rain issue.[45] At the end of the 1980s, developments in the field of modelling – largely within the framework of the ECE/LRTAP – permitted a more precise prediction of the likely effects of reduced acid fallout. This made it possible to provide more precise and specific data about the critical ecological limits and loads for different areas in Europe, and to be more specific about the ecological optimality of the main political solutions like the 30% SO_2 cuts.[46] Within the second sulphur context, it was recognized early in the negotiations that it would be impracticable to reduce sulphur depositions below critical loads by the end of the century. Based on inputs from the 'Regional Acidification Information and Simulation' (RAINS) model developed at the International Institute for Applied Systems Analysis (IIASA), it was instead agreed to reduce by first 50%, then by 60% the gap between current levels of sulphur deposition and critical loads in most of Europe, except for the most acid-sensitive areas. The RAINS model then presented tentative country-specific emission reduction targets. Overall, it has been indicated that this approach has contributed to a change in the fundamental cooperative atmosphere; see, for example, Levy (1995:63): 'The most fundamental effect that critical loads had was to shift the nature of the public debate, both internationally and in many domestic settings, away from determining who the bad guys were, and towards determining how vulnerable each party was to acid rain.' Moreover, it is an outsider's impression that knowledge of the interplay between different substances – and also between these substances and various natural factors – advanced considerably during the 1980s and early 1990s. In summary, these developments led to a more sophisticated and relaxed debate on international air pollution, in both the scientific and political contexts.

Turning to the more specific political development, an overall trend towards a more symmetrical and complex picture can be noted. With regard to the general environmental vulnerability dimension, some important changes occurred in the beginning of the 1980s. *The main change was of course the altered position of the FRG.* After the increased concern over potentially extensive forest damage in 1981/82, the FRG emerged as an important emitter which also perceived itself as seriously affected by these emissions. More or less similar changes occurred in countries like the Netherlands, Switzerland and Austria. In the UK, the situation was mainly unchanged, although some critical voices were making themselves heard. A 1983 report for the Welsh Water Authority maintained that acidification had damaged fish populations in Wales. Moreover, claims by the Ministry of Agriculture, Fisheries and Food (MAFF) that there was no evidence of discernible damage to UK agriculture in general were dismissed in 1984 by the House of Commons Environment Committee as 'complacent and founded upon little other than conjecture'. On the other hand, on the subject of trees, a 1985 survey by the Forestry Commission argued that there was 'no scientific evidence nor any circumstantial evidence in Britain today which points to air pollution causing damage to trees other than locally'.[47] Gradually, however, acid damage to the UK countryside became more visible, although the extent of damage remained disputed throughout the 1980s. For instance, the Forestry Commission stated in 1987: 'There is no sign of the type of damage seen in West Germany occurring in Britain at the moment.'[48]

With regard to aspects related to abatement costs and economic competition, this was of course an important complicating factor through the 1980s and into the 1990s. The shifting of regulatory focus first to NO_x emissions and then to VOC emissions added new political games to the initial sulphur, power station-focused game. An important element in both the NO_x and VOC contexts was the regulation of the transport sector. In a way, increasing focus on this sector contributed to a more complex and less categorical picture in terms of regulatory impact. The transport sector was rather important in all the relevant countries, and most of them experienced regulatory problems in dealing with such emissions. Hence, the asymmetrical sulphur picture was gradually replaced by a more symmetrical one.

In addition, it should be noted that competitive aspects may in some instances not only complicate the cooperative drive, but strengthen it. This is clearly part of the picture in the development of the air pollution issue: when the FRG changed its mind and decided on various types of abatement measures and programmes in the early 1980s, the competitive dimension necessitated an active international effort to harmonize international terms of competition – and the FRG was at least regionally a major actor.[49] On the technological side, there were no major breakthroughs up through the 1980s. Within the sulphur context, flue gas desulphurization (FGD) was the main technological option, generally regarded as a quite expensive one.[50]

With regard to the more specific development of and processes in the beginning of the 1980s within the first sulphur context, the main change in the broad preference picture was of course the more or less dramatic about-turn of West Germany, internationally announced at the Stockholm Conference on Acidification in 1982. Having been a somewhat reluctant signatory of the ECE Convention, it now emerged in support of the Scandinavian call for international action. Interior Minister Baum pledged his government's commitment to a 60% reduction in SO_2 emissions from power stations and large factories by 1993. The background for this change in position was multifarious, with Waldsterben and the emergence of the Green Party as important factors, but there was also a regional political dimension.[51] The change in German policies, from international laggard to leader, has been further confirmed in the ensuing NO_x, VOC and the most recent sulphur negotiations.[52] In my view, the German policy change must be characterized as *the* most important event within the LRTAP context – due to Germany's high score both with regard to basic game power capabilities (being an important emitter) and policy game capabilities (due to Germany's influential position scientifically, economically and politically *vis-à-vis* neighbouring European states).

The UK's official scepticism with regard to the need for international air pollution control did not change much until the late 1980s. The UK chose not to join the 1985 Sulphur Protocol, although allegedly the 30% reduction target was easily within reach.[53] An important change occurred in connection with the final stages of the European Community Large Combustion Plant (LCP) Directive negotiations, although apparently quite reluctantly.[54] Indications of a new policy were further confirmed in 1988, when the UK agreed to both the

EC LCP and Vehicle Emissions Directives, and signed the LRTAP NO_x protocol in November. In this connection, it is fitting to draw attention to the parallel EC and LRTAP acid policy developments and their interplay effects, which can only be hinted at in this context.[55]

Nevertheless, it is important to keep in mind that the NO_x and VOC processes reflected to some extent different problem structures in relation to the sulphur context and hence a more balanced picture with regard to leaders and laggards can be noted in these processes, and also rather different coalitions and lines of conflict. Some main points relevant both for the NO_x and VOC contexts can be noted: first, a quite stable group of leaders can be identified in both processes, comprising countries like Germany, Sweden, the Netherlands, Austria and Switzerland. Hence, the initial, Nordic 'sulphur Mafia' was considerably broadened. Second, Nordic sulphur unity broke down. For instance in the NO_x context, midway through the negotiations, Norway and Finland adopted more intermediary and some would even say laggard positions, as the important role of troublesome transport emissions was gradually clarified.[56] Third, as indicated above, the position of the UK, the important acid emitter and sulphur laggard, became more intermediary and less obstructive in these processes.[57]

Let us then turn to the more recent development of preferences and positions, witnessed in connection with the negotiations on the Second Sulphur Protocol. Scattered evidence confirms that the main political game even in this field has changed a bit.[58] The initial Nordic leader countries were joined not only by Germany, but also by countries like the Netherlands and Austria. Countries which have not experienced a change in the extent to which they are affected by acid rain, like Greece, Italy, Spain and Portugal, formed an uninterested or reluctant group. The EC member states did not adopt a common position in the negotiations and the rifts between some member states during special EC policy coordinating sessions were allegedly difficult to bridge. The UK was not regarded as being in the vanguard of supporters for the Protocol, and was often perceived as obstructive.[59] Hence, old conflict lines had not become totally irrelevant.

In summary, intellectual knowledge about the problems gradually improved, although to a varying extent related to the various substances. From the late 1980s on, the development of the critical loads approach and its subsequent application in the second sulphur context marked an important intellectual and political step ahead within the cooperation. Politically, progress has been somewhat mixed. On the one hand, focus on other problems than sulphur introduced different vulnerability patterns, and more cross-cutting cleavages in terms of national positions and preferences. Hence, the marked initial asymmetrical character of the transboundary air pollution problems was softened somewhat in the course of time and with additional substances added to the regulatory agenda. On the other hand, basic international competitive elements related to domestic abatement programmes clearly remained, as witnessed in the second sulphur process, where old political conflict lines quickly reappeared. In this connection, I find Levy's (1995) emphasis on a radically changed atmosphere after the 'rise' of the critical loads approach interesting, but perhaps exaggerated and clearly debatable.

As a concluding comment, this brief account of the development of problems and preferences further underlines the point about the transboundary air pollution problems as an aggregation of problems with partially different intellectual and political characteristics and structures – but nevertheless with some important inter-linkages. Let us keep this duality in mind when we start our focused institutional discussion.

4.4 THE LRTAP REGIME: MORE 'DISCURSIVE DIPLOMACY' THAN 'DASHING DESIGN'?

4.4.1 Access and Participation: An Open Process of 'Mutual Edification'?

Starting out with the issue of scope of state participation, the ECE and East–West context was deliberately chosen for the regime – both against the background of long-distance transboundary flows of pollutants and a more general ambition to contribute to East–West confidence-building. Article 14 of the convention gave participation rights to ECE member states, to states having consultative status with the ECE, and to regional economic integration organizations. Hence, the inclusion of both Western and Eastern Europe indicates a certain complication in classifying the LRTAP regime as a 'regional' regime, and the additional inclusion of the US and Canada makes the classification in a sense meaningless. On the other hand, the ECE is the Economic Commission for *Europe*, and the European dimension has clearly been dominant within the cooperation.

So, has this broad scope hampered the cooperation in any way – or have the effects been mainly positive, for instance due to a broader financial base? The impression here is that the expansive scope, with the inclusion of the US and Canada, has not been a hampering factor in the work of the Convention, although the picture is obviously somewhat mixed. On the one hand, Canada has been among the driving forces in some processes within the regime, most notably in the VOC negotiations. Moreover, some regime participants point to the benefits of drawing upon American regulatory progress and experiences, especially with regard to the regulation of the traffic and transport sector. Others, however, emphasize that the basic American 'air quality' approach is not always compatible with European regulatory approaches and increasing focus on critical loads; this incompatibility sometimes complicates matters to some extent. Particular positive financial effects are not discernible, as the US and Canada do not contribute much to the EMEP system.[60]

Another special participation dimension concerns the part of the European Community. For instance, in connection with the negotiations on the Convention, political difficulties were noted, caused by the insistence of the EC members that the EC should be accepted as signatory to the Convention.[61] Others have pointed to the obstructive role of the EC concerning the Nordic proposals for a Convention with regulatory teeth: 'As two of the Community's most influential members, the UK and FRG had little difficulty in making their views Community views, even though some member states – notably the Netherlands and Denmark – might have liked to accept the plan.'[62] However, the outcome was that the EC signed the LRTAP Convention in 1979 and became a Party to the Convention in 1982. Moreover, the EC signed the EMEP Protocol in 1984. Due to a continued rupture within the Community with regard to acid rain policies, with the UK, Ireland and Greece forming a reluctant nucleus, the EC did not sign the ensuing 1985 Sulphur Protocol. However, the EC did sign the following NO_x and VOC protocols.[63] With regard to the latest sulphur negotiations, the EC member states did not adopt a common position in the negotiations and the rifts between some member states during special EC policy coordinating sessions were allegedly difficult to bridge.[64] However, the EC did in the end decide to sign this Protocol. Hence, the overall impression is that the EC participation has at times complicated matters somewhat, but nevertheless, the overall direct EC influence on the LRTAP negotiation processes has not been very conspicuous.[65]

With regard to the question of outsiders' access and participation, the LRTAP formal access structure as spelled out in the 1979 Protocol only contained a very general formulation in Article 10, stating that the Executive Body could 'when it deems appropriate, also make use of information from other relevant international organizations'. In practice, the LRTAP meetings have been open to intergovernmental organizations (IGOs), industrial groups and environmental NGOs. Also working group meetings have been open to NGOs – as long as they have 'consultative status' with the ECE. The NGOs have been allowed to participate in discussions, but have seldom used this opportunity. The only 'exclusive' forums within the LRTAP regime have been the unofficial Heads of Delegations meetings during the protocol negotiation processes.[66]

Hence, what has been coined a LRTAP process of 'mutual education'[67] has meant the participation of IGOs like the World Meteorological Organization (important[68]), the World Health Organization (more important over time), the UNEP and the FAO (seldom), the OECD, and the International Energy Association. In addition, European regional organizations like the European

Community have attended regularly.[69] With regard to industrial groups, we have groups such as CONCAWE (Oil Companies European Organization for Environmental and Health Protection). Turning finally to NGOs, active participants have been the British branches of Greenpeace and Friends of the Earth; the International Union for the Conservation of Nature; and the International Council on Environmental Law. The International Institute for Applied Systems Analysis (IIASA) is in a special category, and has played a very important role in connection with the development of the critical loads approach.

Hence, we have a pretty good idea of *who* has participated at the international level more generally. Less is clear with regard to patterns in the specific processes and developments: does inclusiveness vary between the different processes? Has inclusiveness increased in the course of time, and with any effects? Besides, far less is known about the specific effects/impacts of this participation on negotiation outcomes and implementation processes. Levy (1993:86) generally states that 'except for IIASA, none of these groups have much influence over LRTAP decision-making. The influence of NGOs comes mainly via activities inside countries, usually publicizing governmental action within LRTAP'. Gehring's detailed account of the negotiation processes (1994) seems to support such an assessment, with few references to international NGO activity.

So with regard to NGOs, the LRTAP regime has been quite open. Has this hampered work within the regime in any way? What about different types of actors – have the main target groups like industry and the energy sector participated in an active way – or have such groups exercised decisive pressure at the domestic level, while environmental NGOs have dominated the international forum? With regard to openness, this has apparently mainly functioned positively. According to Norwegian regime participants, the chief exception is the NO_x process, in which real give and take processes could not be started before the NGOs had been 'expelled'.[70] However, the parties have also consciously chosen to keep Heads of Delegations meetings aimed at concluding negotiations closed for non-state actors. Regarding target group participation, the impression is definitely that these important actors largely ignore the international forum, and concentrate most of their energy on influencing national political processes.

What about the question of high-level and ministerial inputs to main regime meetings? First, due to the recurring protocol negotiations at quite regular intervals (around 3–4 years), the LRTAP cooperation has been marked by an interplay between bureaucratic or lower profile and political or high profile processes. Still, the LRTAP process was probably infused with more high-level political energy in the early phases of the cooperative process than in the more recent phases, due to closely related high-level meetings like the Stockholm

Conference in 1982 and the Munich and Ottawa meetings in 1984. This was probably a reflection of growing concern over acidification problems at the time, and also a heightened interest in getting a sharper international regulatory instrument in place.

Concluding this section, overall the inclusive and open access structure seems to have functioned positively. The East–West dimension was to some extent structurally given by the mutual transboundary fluxes of pollutants. The North American link seems less natural, but has provided both moderate benefits and drawbacks. NGOs have participated constructively, but not very actively, in the international forum – perhaps except for the final phases of the NO_x negotiations. Their participation has taken place within certain limits: most importantly, they have been barred from Heads of Delegations meetings during negotiation processes. Regarding the level of proceedings, due to the recurring protocol negotiations at quite regular intervals, LRTAP cooperation has been marked by a regular interplay between bureaucratic or lower profile and political or high profile processes.

On the whole, interesting questions remain to be clarified about more factual matters (like for instance the composition of delegations) and causal impact questions. Not least interesting is the interplay between international access and participation, and national pressure politics. For instance: what has participation in international scientific and political bodies meant for the ability to influence domestic processes for scientists, NGOs and administrators? How has open international access been utilized domestically by various domestic forces, like industry and environmentalists?

4.4.2 Decision-Making Rules: A Flexible Consensus

As a point of departure, Article 12 in the 1979 Convention stated that amendments to the Convention should be adopted by consensus, and enter into force 'for the Contracting Parties which have accepted it on the ninetieth day after the date on which two-thirds of the Contracting Parties have deposited their instruments of acceptance with the depositary'. This was later specified so that the Convention required 16 ratifications for protocols to enter into force, out of the 33 signatories at the time. According to Levy (1993:86), negotiators settled on 16 as a number that was small enough to prevent small groups from blocking protocol enforcement, but large enough to ensure that the aggregate effect was meaningful.

A natural assumption is that the consensus requirement obviously has reduced the strength of the protocols and hence the course of the cooperation. However, closer scrutiny raises questions on such a thesis. First, consensus has been practised with flexibility. Informally, a liberal norm has developed, opening up ways to establish protocols without the consent of all convention parties. For instance, in connection with the establishment of the 1985 Sulphur Protocol, the majority of the parties secured formal acceptance from the reluctant UK.[71] Second, regime participants indicate that the consensus requirement has also changed a bit in the course of time, with greater willingness recently to push reluctants harder. This may then be looked upon as another sign of a flexible application of the basic consensus requirement. Still, the formal consensus approach is seen as an integral element in the whole functioning of the cooperation, rooted in the initial East–West confidence-building dimension of the regime. Hence, more formal changes seem very unlikely.[72]

However, would regulatory strength and possibly regime effectiveness necessarily have been higher with majority voting procedures? This question is perhaps not as obvious as it may seem at first glance. For instance, it is questionable if in *any* of the negotiation processes carried out so far there has been a majority for a much stronger output. To my knowledge, in connection with the 1985 sulphur negotiations, there were never any serious discussions about a more ambitious 50 or 60% cut. A 30% cut became quite early a 'focal point' in the negotiations. In the NO_x negotiations, there was possibly an initial majority behind a 30% cut, roughly similar to the target adopted in the preceding sulphur context. However, when the final stage of the negotiations started, this possible majority was long gone. This was clearly demonstrated by the support for the political, more ambitious declaration adopted in connection with the formal negotiations. Even with a longer time span, more flexible base year and a less binding status, the declaration was only signed by 12 countries, some of them reluctantly.[73]

In summary, rooted in the initial East–West confidence-building dimension of the regime, the decision-making approach is a consensual one, though practised with flexibility. One or a few reluctant parties have not hindered the adoption of protocols, but a general acceptance from such reluctants has been secured. Given the constellation of interests in the various negotiation processes, with a substantial number of reluctants, it is highly questionable if majority voting procedures alone would have resulted in stronger protocols.

4.4.3 The Role of the Secretariat: A Stage-Hand at the Mercy of the UN?

Compared to other international regimes with specifically established administrative units, like for instance the International Whaling Commission Secretariat,[74] the LRTAP Secretariat is a rather different formal entity. Related to the initial choice of ECE as the basic cooperative context, the LRTAP Secretariat functions have been provided by the Air Pollution Section of the ECE Environment and Human Settlements Division, with technical support from the ECE Secretariat. Hence, the LRTAP Secretariat functions were added to an existing institution's agenda. In terms of resources, given the broad regional context with a substantial number of parties with poor domestic administrative resources for environmental issues, the LRTAP Secretariat staff can hardly be characterized as over-sized and over-endowed with resources.[75] The Air Pollution Section has long had five professional staff members, with two support staff members. The costs of meetings, documentation and Secretariat services have been covered by the regular budget of UN/ECE.[76] Hence, the Secretariat is not financed directly by the parties, but is dependent on the wider ECE resource situation. As stated by participants in the cooperation, 'we are entirely at the mercy of the ECE'.[77] Against the background of the general financial crisis in the UN, the ECE financial situation has not developed positively either.

Perhaps to a greater extent than many other international environmental regimes, the LRTAP Secretariat is weak by design. The reluctance of the parties with regard to giving the regime organizational clout was symbolized for instance by their unwillingness in 1983 to allocate resources to uphold the one post financed so far by the UNEP. The argument was formal: Article 11 of the Convention requested the Executive Secretary of the ECE to carry out secretarial functions – and so be it.[78] Proposals for an improved resource situation for the Secretariat have several times been put forward by the Nordic countries, but have been rejected. Hence, one may wonder if the initial definitely beneficial ECE link and setting – related to the important East–West dimension throughout the cooperation – has become more of an impediment than an asset for at least this administrative part of the cooperation.

Given the modest resource situation and no mandate for activism from the parties, the role of the Secretariat has become very much that of a stage-hand, arranging meetings within the various scientific and political bodies within the regime and collecting an increasing amount of emission and compliance information. With the scientific–political complex to serve having become considerably complex, this contributes to a practical restriction of issues and tasks that can practically be addressed.

A more recent additional task is related to the servicing of the 1994 Sulphur Protocol Implementation Committee (see section 4.4.6). Hence, the resource situation of the LRTAP Secretariat seems to have developed unfavourably over the years, as servicing functions related to new protocols have successively been added to the workload – and the administrative capacity has remained more or less constant. Still, the impression is that the Secretariat has done a good job, despite limited resources.[79] Have the limited resources really seriously hampered the cooperative process so far? Could a larger Secretariat do a better job, for instance for those countries within the cooperation that have less administrative and financial resources? Regime participants indicate that the UN economic crisis has of course not had a positive effect. However, it is emphasized that much administrative back-up work for the cooperation is carried out in connection with many of the other bodies within the cooperation – working groups and task forces. This means that the total administrative and secretariat picture is not as bad as a narrow Geneva Secretariat focus could indicate. Thus, a certain scepticism is noted with regard to the vision of a much stronger Secretariat, if this would mean reduced importance for the other bodies mentioned above. However, an improved travel budget could make it easier for the Secretariat to keep in touch with the various subsidiary bodies, and hence strengthen the coherence of the system.[80]

In summary, there seems to be little doubt that the ECE/UN-related LRTAP Secretariat falls clearly into the stage-hand category – and even a relatively weak one, resource-wise. This is what a majority of the parties have wanted, but it is also related to the general financial crisis within the UN. However, the Secretariat has functioned effectively inside these structural constraints, and administrative back-up has been carried out by other bodies within the system. Hence, although the role of the Secretariat has apparently been no large asset for the development of the regime, it has not been an impediment either.

4.4.4 The Role of the Agenda: The Triumph of Sequential Decision-Making?

As a point of departure, the basically loose and open-ended agenda laid out in the LRTAP Convention should be noted. As indicated, the Convention did not specify any pollutants, but stated that monitoring activity and information exchange should start with sulphur dioxide. Moreover, the issue of a future establishment of more specific protocols was *not* explicitly mentioned in the Convention.

This basic openness and issue flexibility has been pointed to as an institutional strength. Although the LRTAP was created primarily in response to sulphur emissions and acidification of Scandinavian lakes, it has developed into a forum for coordinating research and policies concerning a variety of pollutants and air pollution problems.[81] Based on progress so far, the development of the LRTAP agenda and regulatory process may definitely be termed 'sequential', with an initial focus on sulphur, turning thereafter to the NO_x problem, and then on to the VOC problem, before the parties returned to sulphur in 1991 – and are presently struggling to treat the NO_x and VOC issues in combination.[82] On the one hand, this can of course be seen as a rational ability to break down a complex transboundary air pollution problem into several, more manageable problems – dealt with gradually, as knowledge has improved. Hence, the sulphur issue has evidently had a much longer scientific and political history than the other relevant substances, since the first protocol negotiations started in the beginning of the 1980s. Moreover, the NO_x issue gained increasing attention during the course of the sulphur negotiations, so it is only natural that the negotiators turned their attention to NO_x as soon as the sulphur process was finished.

On the other hand, the single-substance and in a sense narrow regulatory approach may also have something to do with interest politics, at several stages in the development of the regime. For instance a Central European proposal in 1983 to extend the proposed sulphur regime to cover NO_x emissions as well (due to assumed forest damage linkages) was rejected first and foremost by the Nordic countries, long concerned with sulphur emissions and lake acidification problems. Moreover, a German suggestion in 1986 to negotiate a combined NO_x and VOC protocol was also rejected.[83]

However, as knowledge of the considerable degree of interplay between the various pollutants (into 'acid cocktails') has increased in the course of time, the ongoing round of LRTAP negotiations – which 'naturally' according to practice so far, would be on a new NO_x protocol – is partly concerned with a protocol targeting *both* NO_x and VOC emissions. This can of course be interpreted as an expression of a certain frustration with regard to a sequential, narrow approach among the parties – given the various points of environmental and regulatory interconnectedness. However, on the whole, it seems right to say that the parties so far seem to have regarded this more narrow negotiating approach, focusing on one group of substances at a time, as the most effective one in this context – given the state of knowledge in the early phases of the cooperative process.

In addition, an intricate structure of scientific, technical, economic and political working groups has broken down the definitely comprehensive agenda – as further elaborated in the next section. In this connection, as additional indications of the merits of flexibility, the LRTAP has also used smaller, more informal workshops focusing on lesser parts of the problems.

In conclusion, the LRTAP Convention laid out a loose and open-ended agenda, with a basic issue flexibility which turned out to be an institutional strength. Moreover, the development of the LRTAP agenda may definitely be termed sequential, with an initial focus on SO_2, turning thereafter to the NO_x problem, and then on to the VOC problem, before the parties returned to SO_2 in 1991. The fact that the parties are now considering broader and more combined approaches seems primarily to be the result of increased knowledge about the interplay of various substances and the need for regulatory approaches to match such interactive effects. Hence, the structuring of the agenda seems to have been a moderate asset for regime development so far.

4.4.5 The Organization of the Science–Politics Interface: A Flexible and Complex Basis for 'Discursive Diplomacy'?

Let us first briefly describe the evolution of the institutional setup. A first thing to note is that one part of the LRTAP scientific–political complex remained from pre-Convention days – the 'Working Party on Air Pollution Problems' (WPAP). The WPAP was initially under the ECE body 'Senior Advisers to ECE Governments on Environmental and Water Problems'. Other parts of the scientific–political complex grew out of the aforementioned OECD monitoring programme, namely the EMEP ('Cooperative Programme for Monitoring and Evaluation of Long-Range Transmissions of Air Pollutants in Europe') programme. The rest of the complex was established in connection with the Convention, with sub-groups gradually being added to the structure. The EMEP has been financed by mandatory contributions from the parties, according to a specific Protocol established in 1984. The costs related to other scientific bodies under the Convention have been covered by voluntary contributions from the parties.

Until 1991, the structure was roughly as follows: on the administrative and political side, the main bodies have been the 'Executive Body' (EB) of the Convention, with the parties meeting annually since 1983, and the 'Working Group on Abatement Strategies' (WGAS), an important forum for continuous negotiations (established in 1989). On the scientific and technical side, subsidiary bodies under the EB have successively been added to the institutional structure. Hence, during the first sulphur process, the EMEP Steering Body; the 'Group of Economic Experts on Air Pollution' (GEAP); the 'Working Group on Effects' (WGE); and the aforementioned 'Working Party on Air Pollution Problems' (WPAP) were all established. The Working Group on NO_x was established in 1985, and the Working Group on VOCs (WGV) in 1988. Under these bodies, several 'International Cooperative Programmes' (ICPs) and task forces have been in operation. For instance, related to the development of the critical loads approach, a Task Force on Mapping was established in 1988 (led by West Germany). At the same time, a Task Force on Integrated Assessment Modelling (led by the Netherlands) was established, and soon identified the 'Regional Acidification Information and Simulation' (RAINS) model at the Institute of Applied Systems Analysis (IIASA) in Vienna as the most promising.[84]

This organizational setup was reorganized in November 1991. The current organizational structure is somewhat simpler: on the administrative and political side, in addition to the EB, there is now a 'Working Group on Strategies' (WGS). On the scientific and technical side, in addition to the 'Working Group on Effects' (WGE) and the EMEP Steering Body, there is now a 'Working Group on Technology' (WGT). Current International

Cooperative Programmes under the WGE are forests (led by Germany), freshwater (Norway), materials (Sweden), crops (UK), and integrated monitoring (Sweden – see Figure 4.1).

The EMEP monitoring programme warrants some specific comments. It was initiated by the ECE in cooperation with the United Nations Environment Programme (UNEP) and the World Meteorological Organization (WMO) as part of UNEP's 'Global Environment Monitoring System' (GEMS). The main objective of EMEP has been to provide governments with information on the deposition and concentration of pollutants, along with data on the quantity and significance of long-range transmission of pollutants. The programme has three main elements: emissions data, measurements of air and precipitation quality, and atmospheric dispersion models. The EMEP sampling network consists of some 100 stations in 33 countries, and the work has been coordinated by three international centres, two in Oslo and one in Moscow. As mentioned, a specific EMEP financing protocol was established in 1984. Funding is now provided by all parties to the EMEP Protocol, according to a cost-sharing agreement developed by the parties to the Convention on the basis of the UN 'assessment scale' (based on GNP, population and geographic criteria).[85] The 1995 EMEP budget was around 1.9 million dollars.[86]

So, has this organizational model been a successful one? First, related to what was mentioned in section 4.4.4 on the agenda, the basic flexibility of the system must be declared a success. As noted by Levy (1993), the fact that the LRTAP has been 'consistently science– and ecosystem–driven' means that working groups have progressively been organized around potential environmental damages, and permitted transfrontier pollutants to enter the diplomatic agenda, namely: 'This accounts for the ease with which VOCs entered the agenda, as well as for the current investigations into mercury and persistent organic compounds.'[87] Second, the formally advanced (for example, with financing based on a separate, specific protocol) and well-functioning EMEP system has represented a strong scientific foundation and 'core' in the development of the regime. A third interesting element in the LRTAP model is the establishment of a permanent negotiating forum, in the Working Group on Strategies (WGS). This body may be seen as a mediating buffer between science and politics – a 'not too formal' meeting-place for scientists and administrators, allowing the building of consensual knowledge on both scientific and political strategic matters. Regime participants emphasize the flexibility in frequency of meetings and generally much less time-consuming formalities as an advantage of the WGS style of functioning compared to the Executive Body meetings.[88] Hence, the functioning of the WGS should be an interesting topic for further comparative study – in order to further delineate the uniqueness of, and success related to, the LRTAP institutional approach. Finally, regime participants also emphasize that the personal component should not be disregarded in this connection, as the LRTAP scientific–political complex has been blessed with key persons combining scientific and political perspectives.[89]

In conclusion, in line with several others, my impression is that the scientific and technical cooperation organized by the LRTAP has been one of the regime's main assets. But looking more carefully into this, one may ask whether this really has anything to do with a successful organizational design. All international environmental regimes have scientific and technical advisory groups. Is the LRTAP in any way special? Well, the strong scientific core represented by the EMEP monitoring programme must be emphasized; and the flexible adding of new substances and bodies to the evolving institutional structure; along with the role of the Working Group of Strategies as a coordinating and mediating body between science and politics. This organizational structure has created a well-functioning backdrop for 'discursive diplomacy', resulting in successive learning and confidence-building.

4.4.6 Verification and Compliance Mechanisms: a Unique Verification Capacity not Further Utilized?

An important point of departure here is that monitoring of state performance has been mainly based on the parties' annual reports to the Secretariat on emissions and procedures adopted for the abatement of emissions and the measurement of acid precipitation. A general call for information exchange was expressed in Article 4 of the 1979 Convention, followed up by more specific commitments regarding emissions reporting in the subsequent protocols. In addition to the annual reports, there is a more comprehensive review of national abatement strategies and policies every four years. The most recent one was carried out in 1994, so the next one should be in 1998. However, what makes LRTAP rather different is a limited capacity for additional, 'independent' verification of emission figures. This capacity stems from the EMEP monitoring system, based on emissions data, measurements of air and precipitation quality, and atmospheric distribution models. Referring to the periodic reviews and the EMEP system, Sand (1990B:259) maintains: 'Few other international agreements can be said to come equipped with verification instruments of this calibre.' However, the EMEP reports are also partly based on national reports;[90] moreover, some countries have failed to report emissions; and monitoring coverage in Southern Europe is seen by EMEP itself as insufficient.[91] On balance, the impression is that the EMEP system in theory does provide additional verification capacity, although less than could easily be envisaged.[92]

Nevertheless, the *practical* compliance control potential has so far not been utilized much. Critical compliance discussions have been non-existent, as there have been no provisions in the convention or the protocols until quite recently that authorize the Executive Body to examine critically the data provided in the national reports.[93] At the most, countries have made oral clarifying statements at EB meetings.[94] Again, this must of course be seen partly in light of the East–West non-confrontational dimension prevalent in the regime. Does all this mean that the verification instruments 'even of this calibre' have been without importance for state policies? My guess would be that the very existence of EMEP data has contributed somewhat to reporting soberness in the West and hence general confidence-building within this group of countries, but not as a very important aspect in the process. However, this remains to be investigated further.

Still, the LRTAP compliance regime sharpened its teeth in connection with the 1994 Sulphur Protocol. A specific implementation committee was established, with a mandate of reviewing implementation and compliance, and including decisions on 'action to bring about full compliance with the protocol'.[95] It is composed of eight legal experts from the parties. An interesting question is whether these experts will rely solely on information from the parties themselves, or whether information and reports from, for instance, environmental NGOs will also be systematically collected and assessed. It is difficult to find a precedent for such independent inputs in the functioning of international environmental regimes so far. Still, LRTAP has been an institutional forerunner several times before. The establishment of such a committee is at least an important *symbolic* step, communicating a greater will of the parties to take compliance and implementation more seriously. But the more specific practical implications are hard to evaluate. Within environmental politics, the institutional model was the implementation committee established within the ozone-layer regime.[96] However, that committee has not functioned long enough to draw many practical conclusions (see Chapter 5). Apart from 'institutional diffusion' from the ozone regime, the most important background factor for tougher compliance procedures is probably the fundamental changes in the East–West relationship and greater openness in the East. These changes provide a much more beneficial setting for critical follow-up discussions, both at the international and national level, than was the case in the 1970s and 1980s. In addition, the increased regulatory sophistication over time has created an increased need for improved institutional procedures.

One may ask: would effectiveness have been higher with a tougher compliance regime in place earlier? As compliance with the protocols has been generally good, and very good in the sulphur case, the talk of tough compliance mechanisms seems simply not relevant for LRTAP so far. The main problem has not been lacking compliance; rather that the protocol requirements have fallen far short of what is needed to deal effectively with the air pollution problems.

Let us then wind up with some reflections on the issue of 'positive' incentive aspects. LRTAP has not developed any mechanisms for financial transfers from West to East so far. This has been characterized as one of the biggest failures of the LRTAP regime.[97] However, the Working Group on Strategies began discussions on the matter in 1992. The establishment of some sort of financial mechanism, facilitating burden-sharing in connection with the possible additional abatement costs envisaged for meeting 'critical loads' in different parts of Europe, has been discussed. Three main options have been proposed: (1) an acidification fund; (2) joint implementation projects, where high marginal abatement cost countries could meet part of their reductions commitments by financing reductions in lower cost countries; (3) a tradable permits scheme. Still, crucial clarifications of the political and practical feasibility of the various options still remain.[98]

Summing up, the monitoring of state performance has been mainly based on the parties' annual reports to the Secretariat, on emissions and procedures adopted for the abatement of emissions, together with a more comprehensive review of national abatement strategies and policies every four years. What sets LRTAP a little bit apart is a limited, potential capacity for additional, 'independent' verification, stemming from the EMEP monitoring system. However, the reports of EMEP are partly based on national self-reports, and the capacity for independent verification has never been systematically utilized. Critical compliance discussions were until quite recently not on the agenda, mainly due to East–West considerations. However, the establishment of a specific implementation committee in connection with the 1994 Sulphur Protocol, with a mandate for reviewing implementation and compliance, and including decisions on 'action to bring about full compliance with the protocol', signals a less lenient line with regard to reporting and follow-up. Hence, there will be a delicate balancing challenge: being tougher, but preserving the basic non-confrontational character of the regime.

4.5 CONCLUDING COMMENTS: MORE 'DISCURSIVE DIPLOMACY' THAN 'DASHING DESIGN'?

The LRTAP regime was of course to some extent 'designed for weakness'. In the regime formation process, important emitter states like the UK and Germany were quite negative, and many countries were indifferent. None of these states had experienced any significant domestic acid damage at this early stage. Eastern European countries were not very eager either. Hence, a Framework Convention and much weight given to knowledge improvement and general confidence-building are understandable elements in the regime formation outcome. Overall, it is important to keep in mind the general East–West confidence building dimension underlying this regime from the very start. Still, this soft start grew into a style of operation that proved quite effective. However, for understanding the degree of success the LRTAP regime has after all achieved, with reduced emissions as a visible but somewhat spurious measure, the catalytic event is indisputably Germany's about-turn in 1982, related to the domestic 'Waldsterben' uproar. Germany's shift from laggard to leader represented a crucial and symbolic lasting shift in the overall power balance between laggards and leaders within the regime. An aspect also possibly contributing to LRTAP effectiveness is the very much parallel EC policy processes in this field in the 1980s and 1990s. The EC–LRTAP interplay effects both with regard to international regulatory processes and domestic implementation efforts, are interesting issues for further study.

Although emissions have been stabilized, reduced and often 'over-reduced' in relation to international commitments, LRTAP can only be given moderate direct credit for this. In the first sulphur and NO_x contexts, although the picture varies between countries, much behavioural change would seemingly have happened 'anyway' – due to energy policy changes, unrelated economic and industrial changes, European Community processes and so on. However, both the VOC process's awareness-raising and knowledge improvement and the second Sulphur Protocol's development and application of the critical loads approach indicate that there is a *process* dimension to regime effectiveness that a strict focus on 'behavioural impact so far' may ignore.

In terms of the environmental and problem-solving dimensions to the effectiveness debate, the evolving match between scientific notions about ecologically optimal solutions and actual policies adopted must be characterized as moderate with regard to the three first protocols within the regime. Although clear-cut, consensual and precise scientific advice pointing towards much more ambitious targets was lacking, there was seemingly a widespread feeling in the scientific community that the targets agreed upon were ecologically ineffective, but still steps in the right direction. The 1994 Sulphur Protocol is an important step forward also in this regard, both in terms of sharpening the scientific input with regard to critical limits in the environment, and also in terms of formulating policies explicitly related to the aim of closing the gap to the optimal conditions. However, despite substantially reduced emissions and lagged environmental improvements, even the 1994 Protocol does not imply a closure of the gap between emissions and critical limits in the environment in the near future.

Hence, the overall assessment of the LRTAP regime must be 'only moderately effective' in terms of behavioural impact and measured against crude notions of ecologically optimal policies, but more effective in a more diffuse and even less measurable awareness raising process perspective.

LRTAP's moderate performance in terms of behavioural impact has much to do with a basically *hard case* to deal with: societally important emitter activities related to:

- energy production and consumption, and industrial processes and transport, with related powerful target groups to deal with for regulators;
- coal availability and cheapness in important emitter countries, and hence with employment implications related to regulations;
- technologically complicated and quite expensive abatement options, and lack of technological breakthroughs;
- asymmetrical transboundary flows of pollutants, with some nations being net importers and some net exporters; and
- asymmetrical vulnerability to air pollutants, with unfortunate combinations like the cases of Norway and Sweden, being both high/net importers and having particularly vulnerable soil characteristics.

So what about the more precise role of the LRTAP regime's design in all this? Has the organization of the LRTAP regime been an asset, an impediment, or irrelevant for effectiveness so far? Although a complex question, the suggested answer would be that the arena function of LRTAP seems to have been far more important than the actor functions, and hence that specific design does not seem to have mattered very much so far. However, both some positive and negative organizational elements can be noted. On the positive side, the steady and sequential regulatory development should be noted, implying a constructive interplay between administrative, lower-key phases and briefer high-profile, ministerial interventions, infusing additional political energy into the processes. Moreover, an important asset seems to be the organization of the scientific–political complex. Here, the strong scientific core represented by the EMEP monitoring programme must be emphasized; in addition, the flexible adding of new substances and bodies to the evolving institutional structure; along with the role of the Working Group on Strategies as a coordinating and mediative body between science and politics. This dense organizational structure has created a well-functioning backdrop for 'discursive diplomacy' to take place, resulting in gradual learning and confidence-building.

On the negative side, a resource-starved Secretariat must be noted, related to a natural and beneficial ECE and UN affiliation in the initial 'détente' phases of the cooperation, which over time may have become something of an inflexible shell. Compliance mechanisms can be characterized as both weak, under-utilized (namely the potential EMEP check) and some would say under-developed (namely no progress on an East–West financial transfer mechanism).

However, just as in many other aspects of this regime, the marked non-confrontational design of the compliance system is related to the East–West dimension, and hence the development towards a tougher compliance regime symbolized by the establishment of a specific implementation committee in connection with the 1994 Sulphur Protocol will be faced with a delicate balance challenge: being tougher, but preserving the basic non-confrontational character of the regime.

Moreover, as already indicated, I have much sympathy for the perspective that even if the specific design of the process may have been largely irrelevant, the sum of the parts is definitely not irrelevant and in a way one may say that the 'process itself' has mattered. In this connection, Marc Levy's (1993) concept of 'toteboard diplomacy' is interesting. According to Levy, although LRTAP regulatory rules were weak, they were not irrelevant. 'They served a vital role in magnifying pressure on recalcitrant states, in keeping the consensus-building activities high on governments' agendas, and in assisting domestic environmental proponents of action' (p.77). Hence, the 'toteboard' perspective points toward a complex interplay picture, with various types of interactions between 'endogenous' and 'exogenous' causal factors. The regime *process* matters – yes – but making precise causal measurements of the contributions of the various factors in such a situation is quite challenging, and calls for more detailed, national research than has been carried out so far. As has been indicated, I have suggested the term 'discursive diplomacy' as a general concept, referring to the diffuse effects of regular meetings and related dissemination of various types of knowledge – both of a professional and personal kind. Is *this* the most important institutional effect? Maybe talk is not so cheap after all?

NOTES

1. Oden (1968).
2. For more information on these 'formative' years, see for instance Chossudovsky (1989).
3. Nordberg (1993).
4. Wettestad (1995C).
5. The 'transboundary fluxes' element was primarily relevant for geographically large states like the Soviet Union and the United States, with major emission sources that had no transboundary impact on the ECE region beyond the national territory. See for instance Gehring (1994:156).
6. These 12 countries were Austria, Belgium, Denmark, Finland, France, West Germany, Italy, Liechtenstein, the Netherlands, Norway, Sweden, and Switzerland.
7. Among the signatories, 15 countries and the EC committed themselves to the regular 30% reduction; four chose the freeze option; and three chose the TOMA option. See Gehring (1994:180).
8. *Yearbook of International Co-operation on Environment and Development* (YBICED) 1998/99, pp.68-69.

9.   For an analysis of the negotiations and content of the 1994 Sulphur Protocol, see for example, Gehring (1994:185.93); and Churchill, Kutting and Warren (1995).
10. *Yearbook of International Co-operation on Environment and Development* 1998/99, pp.68-69.
11. This section is mainly based upon the most recent LRTAP comprehensive progress report, published in 1995 (ECE/LRTAP, 'Strategies and Policies for Air Pollution Abatement').
12. See Table 17 of the report (ibid.:137) for a complete sulphur compliance overview.
13. See Table 18 of the report (ibid.:138) for a complete NO_x compliance overview.
14. Wettestad (1996).
15. The science–politics relationship within LRTAP is more fully discussed in Wettestad (1995C; and forthcoming 1999B).
16. Haigh (1989).
17. Bakken (1989:202).
18. Wettestad (1995B).
19. This approach was launched by Swedish scientists and government officials in the early 1980s. See for instance Levy (1995:61–64).
20. For example, the Norwegian Environment Minister Thorbjørn Berntsen called his British counterpart a 'shitbag'...
21. Summary of the 1996 report from the Norwegian Institute for Nature Research, in the Norwegian newspaper 'Dagbladet', 24 September 1996.
22. Regarding the EC's air pollution policies and their relationship to LRTAP, see for instance Haigh (1987; 1989); Boehmer-Christiansen and Skea (1991); Liberatore (1993).
23. According to Levy (1993:126), 'the sulfur protocol probably had significant effects on the emission reductions in seven countries, including the largest and fourth-largest emitters in Europe (USSR and United Kingdom). A protocol that affects only these seven probably counts as a success'.
24. Communication with Oran Young, October 1997.
25. See for instance Park (1987).
26. Interview with Harald Dovland, Norwegian Institute for Air Research, May 1989.
27. As for instance stated by McCormick (1989:69): 'pollution control is expensive – no one seriously questions this basic proposition'.
28. As stated by Boehmer-Christiansen and Skea (1991:4): 'While Germany, at the heart of Europe, shares its atmosphere with many neighbours, some relatively clean, others to the east decidedly not, Britain is a wind-swept off-shore island little affected by atmospheric pollution originating abroad. However, the UK and FR Germany are themselves the largest polluters in Western Europe and winds spread the SO_2 and NO_x originating from German chimneys over a wide continental area'.
29. See for instance Hajer (1995).
30. Miller (1989:41).
31. See for instance Wetstone and Rosencrantz (1983); Chossudovsky (1989); and Gehring (1994) for detailed accounts of the negotiation process.
32. According for instance to Wetstone and Rosencrantz (1983:142), 'British scientists recognized Scandinavia's acidification problems, but questioned whether sulphur dioxide discharged by Britain's power plants was to blame'.
33. Wetstone (1987:179).
34. Wetstone and Rosencrantz (1983:206).
35. Readers more interested in the details of the various processes are advised to consult sources like Gehring (1994).
36. As stated by Sand (1990B:247): '(EMEP) has produced voluminous and increasingly reliable evidence that sulphur and nitrogen compounds emitted by a wide range of stationary and mobile pollution sources are dispersed through the atmosphere over thousands of miles ... EMEP results – annually reviewed, updated, and approved by an intergovernmental steering body – make it possible to quantify the pollutant depositions in each country that can be attributed to emissions in other countries'.
37. Cited in Wetstone (1987:186).

38. See for instance Boehmer-Christiansen and Skea (1991: ch.10).
39. See for instance Hajer (1995) on the shift in Dutch perceptions.
40. Levy (1995:68). He further notes that 'their life span in the atmosphere, the distances they travel, and the amount of ozone they are responsible for are all subjects of scientific controversy'.
41. In brief, fish deaths seemed to be more related to the release of aluminium than to the acidification itself. Moreover, Gunnar Abrahamsen (1988) writes: 'In the 1960's and 1970's, fish kills and water acidification were considered the most important puzzles in relation to the acid rain problem. Within the scientific community, the fish kills were generally agreed to be caused by factors related to freshwater acidity. However, one reason for the increased acidity was intensively discussed and two fronts were established: one with the view that the water acidification was entirely caused by the deposition of acid from the atmosphere, and the other which considered the acidification to be due mainly to factors such as afforestation, reduced grazing etc. Today, I feel it is correct to say that both sides were partly right, although it is probably true that the recent rather abrupt acidification is mainly due to atmospheric input', (p.2).
42. See for instance Boehmer-Christiansen and Skea (1991:38–40).
43. As noted by Boehmer-Christiansen and Skea: 'While forest damage is far from being completely understood, a consensus is emerging that air pollution may be but one factor among many contributing to a complex set of damage syndromes' (1991:40).
44. As indicated, a 'critical load' can be defined as a 'quantitative estimate of an exposure to one or more pollutants below which significant harmful effects on specified sensitive elements of the environment do not occur according to present knowledge'. See for instance Boehmer-Christiansen and Skea (1991:29).
45. See for instance Park (1987: ch.3).
46. An accepted element of the approach is the generation of so-called 'target loads' from critical loads, target loads taking into account economic factors especially, but also considering technological, social and political factors. More specifically, to use the critical loads approach, the following information is needed: (1) inventories of current emissions and projections of future emission rates; (2) estimates of the potential for and costs of emission reduction; (3) long-range transport models; (4) maps of critical loads and target loads; (5) integrated assessment modelling. See for instance Nordberg (1993).
47. McCormick (1989:96).
48. Cited in Waterton (1993:83–86).
49. This dynamic became even clearer in the more EC related context of vehicle emissions regulation, namely: 'For the car industry, German policy priorities were to protect export markets, contain Japanese imports and maintain a reputation of well-engineered, high-performance cars. These challenges were perceived to be best met by moving over as rapidly as possible to clean cars equipped with three-way catalytic convertors. Trade and investment implications favoured higher environmental standards' (Boehmer-Christiansen and Skea, 1991:279).
50. See for instance McCormick (1989:99).
51. Commenting upon the 'Waldsterben'/Green Party thesis, Boehmer-Christiansen and Skea (1987:3) maintain: 'However, this explanation, although not incorrect, is insufficient. From a German perspective, broader social movements had succeeded in affecting party political as well as regional considerations which in turn helped to tip the balance of interest in a long-standing debate in favour of strict, federally mandated emission controls'.
52. As documented by Gehring's detailed account of the negotiation processes (1994: ch.4).
53. See for instance McCormick (1989:85).
54. As indicated by Boehmer-Christiansen and Skea (1991:245): 'A strong political desire both to avoid European isolation and to clarify emission abatement requirements produced a broader flexibility and a willingness to compromise'.
55. Within the EC, political forces led by Germany put pressure on the UK. First, there were the Large Combustion Plant (LCP) negotiations, started in 1984. In June 1988, the UK agreed to cut its sulphur emissions from existing combustion plants by 20% (1993); 40% (1998); and

60% (2003), with 1980 levels as baseline. Second, the negotiations on the Vehicle Emissions Directive were initiated by Germany in 1984. FRG's aim was the US vehicle standards for new vehicle types, meaning in practice catalytic converters for all new vehicles. The UK opposed this idea vigorously, due to the commitment to 'lean-burn' technology by the nationally owned British Leyland and Ford Europe. In brief, the ensuing battle between governments, the car industry and environmentalists ended in the 'Luxembourg (compromise) package' in 1987, requiring only cars with engines above 2 litres to have catalytic converters, affecting only 10% of the cars manufactured in the UK (see for instance Boehmer-Christiansen and Skea, 1991: ch.12; Waterton, 1993:34–35). These negotiations were conducted simultaneously with the LRTAP NO_x protocol negotiations, and it seems reasonable to assume a certain interplay between the two processes.

56. See for instance Stenstadvold (1991:104).
57. See for instance Wettestad (1998) for a discussion of the different political game for the UK in the NO_x context, compared to the sulphur context.
58. See Levy (1995) and Churchill, Kutting and Warren (1995).
59. See for instance Churchill, Kutting and Warren (1995:182)
60. Norwegian interviews, autumn 1995.
61. Jackson (1990:225).
62. Wetstone (1987:179).
63. For more information on EC acid rain politics and the relationship to LRTAP, see for instance Haigh (1987); Boehmer-Christiansen and Skea (1991); Liberatore (1993).
64. Churchill, Kutting and Warren (1995:182).
65. However, over time, the parallel EC and LRTAP policy processes complicate assessments of the 'real' LRTAP impacts and effectiveness. But that is another story...
66. Interview with Lars Nordberg, LRTAP Secretariat, May 1996.
67. Sand (1990B:256).
68. This assessment and the following ones are based on information from LRTAP Secretary Nordberg, provided in May 1996.
69. Levy (1993:86).
70. Norwegian interviews, autumn 1995.
71. Interview with Per Bakken, Norwegian Ministry of Environment, 1991.
72. Norwegian interviews, autumn 1995.
73. For instance Norway signed very reluctantly. See for instance Laugen (1995) and Wettestad (1998).
74. See for instance Andresen (1993).
75. For instance Levy (1993:84) has characterized the Secretariat as 'small, overworked and underfunded'.
76. *Green Globe Yearbook* (1996:86).
77. Norwegian interviews, autumn 1995.
78. See Gehring (1994:138).
79. Norwegian interviews, autumn 1995.
80. Ibid.
81. As stated by Marc Levy (1993:110): 'As a result, although LRTAP was created primarily because of a political crisis over Scandinavian lakes and sulfur, it has evolved into a forum for coordinating research and policies toward a variety of pollutants (many thought not to present transboundary problems in 1979) which threaten a variety of receptors also not thought to be at risk in 1979'. See also Sand (1990B:257).
82. See June 1997, 'Facing problems' Acid News, 2, June 1997, p. 6.
83. See Gehring (1994), pp.142–144 ('sulphur rejection'); p.172 ('NO_x rejection').
84. Gehring (1994:182–183).
85. Dovland (1987); personal communication with Lars Nordberg, LRTAP Secretariat.
86. Lars Nordberg, personal communication, autumn 1995.
87. Levy (1993:111).
88. Norwegian interviews, autumn 1995.
89. Ibid.

90. Harald Dovland, personal communication, 1991.
91. Levy (1993:89).
92. In this connection, see also di Primio (1996).
93. Szell (1995).
94. As stated by Levy (1993:91): 'Strategy and policy reviews are not interpreted; they are simply collated and published. There is no effort to ascertain whose measures place them in compliance with either specific protocols or broader norms ... Although no one is ever "cross-examined", states frequently make oral statements offering clarifications and emphasizing major points at EB meetings'.
95. Article 7 in the 1994 Protocol.
96. Norwegian interviews, autumn 1995.
97. Levy (1995:65–66).
98. As noted by Levy (1995:66).

5. A Triumph for Institutional Incentives and Flexible Design? The Vienna Convention and Montreal Protocol on Ozone Layer Depletion[1]

5.1 INTRODUCTION: INSTITUTIONAL OVERVIEW

The stratospheric ozone layer shields life on Earth from potentially disastrous levels of ultraviolet radiation. Depletion of the ozone layer as a potential environmental problem appeared for the first time on the international agenda at the United Nations Conference on the Human Environment in Stockholm in 1972. The Conference called for research on stratospheric transport (SST) and distribution of ozone. Then, in 1974, based on the work of two American groups of scientists – Stolarski/Cicerone and Molina/Rowland – the theory was launched that a group of man-made chemicals called chlorofluorocarbons (CFCs) could destroy the ozone-layer.[2] CFCs are a family of chemical compounds containing chlorine, fluorine and carbon. Being non-toxic, non-carcinogenic and non-flammable, CFCs were widely used in refrigeration and air conditioning, as blowing agents and aerosol propellants and in solvents for cleaning electronic parts. The disturbing ozone layer depletion theory led to the establishment of research and monitoring programmes, conducted mainly by the United States in the mid-1970s. By the late 1970s, the ozone depletion issue was placed on the agenda of international environmental and scientific organizations like the World Meteorological Organization (WMO) and the United Nations Environment Programme (UNEP). In 1977 UNEP created a 'Coordinating Committee on the Ozone Layer' (CCOL) and adopted a plan of action. Negotiations on a binding international political instrument were started in 1981/82.[3] In 1985, the Vienna Convention on the Protection of the Ozone Layer was signed by 20 countries plus the European Community (EC).[4] Although the Convention contained 21 articles and technical annexes, it did not include any specific emissions control measures. However, UNEP was empowered to convene negotiations on a follow-up protocol. Then, in 1987, in the context of among other things the discovery of the Antarctic 'ozone hole',

24 countries and the EC agreed on the important Montreal Protocol. This Protocol introduced specific measures for the regulation of CFCs and halons, the latter being another important group of ozone-depleting substances (ODS).[5] The next major regulatory round took place in London in June 1990, in the context of increasing scientific evidence and technological development. Here, the parties to the Montreal Protocol agreed to increase the regulatory scope of the Montreal Protocol in terms of substances, to accelerate CFC phase-out, and to phase out halons by the year 2000.[6] Furthermore, at the fourth Meeting of the Montreal Parties in Copenhagen in November 1992, a new accelerated phase-out was agreed on, and the parties further increased the regulatory scope.[7] In addition, meetings in 1995 and 1997 have specified and further elaborated the regulations (see section 5.2.1).

The 'structural' institutional setup has of course developed over time, and more details are provided in section 5.4. However, a condensed 'snap-shot' summary looks like this: on the scientific side, the Conference of Parties to the Vienna Convention established a Meeting of Ozone Research Managers, which meets every three years (every two years until 1993), composed of government experts on atmospheric research. This group reviews ongoing national and international research and monitoring programmes and produces a report to the Conference of the Parties (CoP). Moreover, the Montreal Protocol has established three panels of experts, to be convened at least one year before each assessment: a Scientific Assessment Panel; a Technology and Economics Assessment Panel; and an Environmental Effects Panel. In addition, ad hoc groups on data reporting and destruction technologies have been in operation. On the political side, there is also a formal dual structure. The Conference of the Parties related to the Vienna Convention is held every three years (every two years until 1993). The Montreal Protocol has an annual Meeting of the Parties (MOP). There is also a separate implementation committee, with representatives of ten parties, which was established in 1990. In addition, the Open-Ended Working Group of the Parties and the Bureau of the Montreal Protocol meet inter-sessionally to develop and negotiate recommendations for the MOP on protocol revisions and implementation issues. Secretarial functions are carried out by a Secretariat at the UNEP headquarters in Nairobi which serve both the Convention and the Protocol. In 1990, a Multilateral Fund was established, financed by developed countries, to support phase-outs in developing countries. The Fund is governed by a 14-party Executive Committee and has its own Secretariat in Montreal.

Figure 5.1   The ozone regime: organizational setup

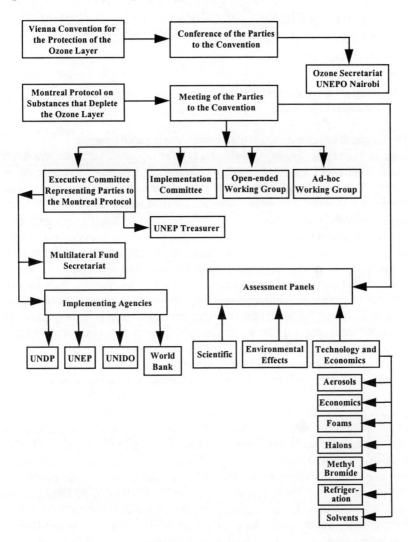

5.2 THE TRICKY EFFECTIVENESS QUESTION: RAPID INTERNATIONAL PROGRESS, BUT WHAT ABOUT THE NATIONAL 'PROOFS OF THE PUDDING'

5.2.1 Political Effectiveness: Swift International Progress and Fair National Follow-Up

The strength of regime regulations: weak start; rapid progress
Turning first to the question of the strength of regime regulations, the word which most easily springs to mind with regard to regulatory development is 'rapid'. The 1985 initial Vienna Convention was a 'classic' loose framework convention. Article 2 contained the general obligations on the parties. The first section described the main goal of the Convention: 'The Parties shall take appropriate measures ... to protect human health and the environment against adverse effects resulting or likely to result from human activities which modify or are likely to modify the ozone layer'. The principal means to achieve this end included cooperation by means of systematic observations, research and information exchange; and adoption of appropriate legislative or administrative measures. Hence, in itself, the Convention failed to specify any concrete measures which implied changes in the behaviour of any state compared to a situation without the Vienna Convention.[8] The most specific functions lay in the obligations concerning scientific cooperation.

The 1987 Montreal Protocol was a giant step forward with regard to ambitiousness, bindingness and not least specificity. The Protocol included specific measures and timetables for reducing the production and consumption of ozone-depleting substances. Article 2 of the Protocol distinguished between the so-called 'Group I' substances (fully halogenated CFCs: 11, 12, 113, 114, 115), the production and consumption of which were basically to be halved by the year 1999; and the so-called 'Group II' substances (halons), the production and consumption of which were to be stabilized at 1986 levels by 1993. Halons were primarily used for firefighting purposes. In addition, Article 5 dealt with the 'special situation of developing countries'. Here, 'low-consuming' developing countries acquired a ten-year implementation lag in relation to the obligations laid out in Article 2 – hence the term 'Article 5 countries' later used in connection with developing countries.[9] Although being a definite step forward in comparison to the Vienna convention, it must be pointed out that the special treatment of the developing countries implied a potential increase in their CFC use. Hence, regulatory flexibility definitely had two sides here: on the one hand, it clearly reduced the overall 'bite' and strength of the measures agreed on; on the other hand, without these regulatory loopholes, several key countries (key especially if one looks some years ahead) might have chosen to stay out of this process completely.

The London 1990 and Copenhagen 1992 amendments accelerated and specified these obligations in several ways. The London meeting agreed to increase the regulatory scope of the Montreal Protocol by deciding to include several gases not covered by the 1987 agreement (several CFCs, carbon tetrachloride used in the manufacture of CFCs, and methyl chloroform used as a cleansing agent); to accelerate CFC phase-out (50% cut by 1995 and 100% by 2000); and to phase out halons by the year 2000. Developing countries retained their ten-year grace period for all obligations. In addition, a specific financial and technological assessment mechanism was established. The same development was seen at the Copenhagen meeting: a new accelerated phase-out was agreed on: a 100% phase-out by 1996 for CFCs, and by 1994 for halons.[10] In addition, the parties further increased the regulatory scope to include HCFCs used as substitutes for CFCs (a consumption peak beginning in 1996, and a gradual phase-out between 1996 and 2030) and methyl bromide used for agricultural purposes (freeze at 1991 levels by 1995). It should be noted here that developing countries refused to accept obligations regarding these new substances.

The Vienna 1995 and Montreal 1997 meetings resulted in more moderate further regulatory development. More specifically, the 1995 seventh meeting of the Montreal Parties defined and elaborated the HCFC regulation – with a developed country production and consumption phase-out by 2020, and a developing country stabilization by 2016 and phase-out by 2040. Methyl bromide was to be phased out in developed countries by 2010 (with a 25% reduction by 2001 and 50% reduction by 2005). Developing countries were to stabilize their consumption of methyl bromide at present levels by 2002. Overall, developed countries pledged more money to the Multilateral Fund.[11] Finally, celebrating the Montreal Protocol's 10th Anniversary in that very same city, the 1997 Montreal meeting strengthened the methyl bromide regulations by advancing the developed countries' phase-out to 2005 and introducing a 2015 phase-out date for developing countries. Moreover, an import/export licensing system for the prevention of illegal trade in controlled substances was adopted as a special amendment.[12] This development is summed up in Table 5.1.

All in all, given the loose 1985 Vienna Convention baseline, the international regulatory situation changed quite drastically over a seven year time period – which, actually, is roughly the same time span that the acid rain/LRTAP participants used to come up with the first Sulphur Protocol. Still, what has this swift international process led to in terms of national behavioural changes – the 'proof of the effectiveness pudding'?

Table 5.1   Overview of regulatory development

Substances (Base-line)	Montreal 1987	London 1990	Copenhagen 1992	Vienna 1995	Montreal 1997
CFCs 11, 12, 113, 114, 115 (1986)	mid 1989: freeze mid 1993: -20% mid 1998: -50%	mid 1989: freeze 1995: -50% 1997: -85% 2000: -100%	mid 1989: freeze 1994: -75% 1996: -100%	no change	no change
Halons 1211, 1301, 2402 (1986)	1992: freeze	1992: freeze 1995: -50% 2000: -100%	1992: freeze 1994: - 100%	no change	no change
10 other CFCs (1989)		1993: -20% 1997: -85% 2000: -100%	1993: -20% 1994: -75% 1996: -100%	no change	no change
Carbon tetrachloride (1989)		1995 : -85% 2000 : -100%	1995 : -85% 1996 : -100%	no change	no change
Methyl chloroform (1989)		1993: freeze 1995: -30% 2000: -70% 2005: -100%	1993: freeze 1994: -50% 1996: -100%	no change	no change
HCFCs (1989 plus 3,1% of CFC consumption in 1989)			1996: freeze 2004: -35% 2010: -65% 2015: -90% 2020: -99.5% 2030: -100%	baseline: 1989 plus 2.8% of CFC consumption in 1989	no change
H-BFCs			1996: -100%		no change
Methyl bromide (1991)			1995: freeze	1995: freeze 2001: -25% 2005: -50% 2010: -100%	1995 : freeze 1999: -25% 2001: -50% 2003 : -70% 2005:-100%

Note: In relation to these requirements, the developing countries generally have a ten-year grace period in terms of implementation. (*Source*: Gehring (1994) and Oberthur (1997B))

Compliance and behavioural change: overall progress, but regional differences

Turning to the compliance picture, progress is on the whole satisfactory.[13] The global production and consumption of CFCs, halons, other fully halogenated CFCs, methyl chloroform, and carbon tetrachloride had by 1995 been reduced by about 75% from 1986 baseline levels – with the best data available on the two first groups of substances.[14] However, although the data are shaky, the global production and consumption of HCFCs seem to have increased three-fold from the 1989 baseline level. With regard to methyl bromide, the data are even more uncertain, and reporting obligations are of a quite recent nature. With this caveat, reported data show a slowly declining trend, while estimates suggest a slight increase.

In relation to this overview picture, there are marked regional differences. Compliance in the industrialized countries is overall very good, despite slow progress with regard to HCFCs and methyl bromide and some scattered instances of non-compliance. The situation in the 'countries with economies in transition' (CEIT) is far more problematic. Several countries, and most importantly Russia, have been unable to meet the CFC and halon phase-out targets of the industrialized countries. In fact, they have themselves invoked the regime's non-compliance procedure, and a 'package' including revised targets and Global Environment Facility (GEF) assistance has been established.[15] Russia has also been involved in illegal CFC production and smuggling to the West.[16] Production and consumption in the developing countries have increased substantially. In 1995, for instance, developing country CFC consumption was nearly 40% higher than in 1986, and the general consumption of ozone-depleting substances was larger than in industrialized countries. Moreover, production and consumption have been particularly dynamic in the Asian newly industrialized countries. China alone accounts for half of the developing countries' consumption and even more of the production. However, the developing countries are of course in a special situation as they were given a ten-year grace period in the Montreal Protocol.[17] Still, as the activity of the Multilateral Fund has apparently had moderate influence on this increasing trend so far,[18] the uncertainty related to the further development of implementation efforts in developing countries is the main 'black cloud' on the ozone regime horizon.

How, then, can we interpret the many positive developments so far, especially in the industrialized countries? Do we have convincing evidence that the reported behavioural changes have been caused by the developing ozone regime – or would they have happened anyway? Although there is so far a general lack of detailed national implementation and regime influence studies, the following factors point toward the tentative conclusion that the ozone regime can be credited for a substantial portion of the reported behavioural changes, at least with regard to CFCs.[19] First, no 'natural' phase-out due to general economic development could be expected from the late 1980s on, as the CFC production trend from 1960 to 1985 was steadily increasing, although with some natural market variations.[20] Second, successful unilateralism either by the US or the EC seems unlikely; unilateral measures adopted by the US in

1978 and the EC had limited effects (in fact, CFC production increased from 1980 to 1985). Moreover, it is not plausible that the US could unilaterally provide (billion dollar) incentives to persuade the rest of the world to adopt its regulations. In addition, US commitment to international CFC control was highly uneven.[21] Third, and not least important, without binding international measures, there would have been less incentive to look for substitutes for the ozone-depleting substances; in other words, the Montreal measures and later amendments radically accelerated the industry's search for substitutes. After having received the crucial international regulatory signals, market forces pretty much drove the implementation processes.[22] A fourth factor is the regime's contribution to general knowledge improvement and related national reassessments of the economic importance of the targeted ozone-depleting substances.

In summary, international regulatory development has been impressive, and available national compliance data indicate that the required behavioural changes are overall being implemented by the industrialized countries, apparently substantially influenced by the international process. However, less impressive follow-up in the East and South and general reporting problems add notes of soberness and caution to this otherwise convincing success picture.

5.2.2 The Environmental and Problem-Solving Dimensions: Moves in the Right Direction

First, what can be said about the developing match between scientific knowledge and advice and the international policy measures taken in response? Even if the agreed measures have failed to solve the problem, were they 'the best possible', given the knowledge situation at the time? Although of course a complex assessment to make, an overall picture of high correspondence over time emerges.[23] Scientific progress and reduced uncertainty were steadily followed by increasingly stringent political decisions within a short time span. For instance, the 1987 Montreal Protocol can clearly be interpreted as a response to the discovery of the 1985 Antarctic 'ozone hole' and alarming results from a comprehensive WMO/NASA research programme. Moreover, the 1990 London revisions were decided upon on the basis of confirmations by the Ozone Trends Panel of the 'ozone hole' and 'strong indications' that man-made chlorine compounds were primarily responsible for the observed reduction in ozone. In addition, a 1989 synthesis report from the scientific assessment panels concluded that a complete phase-out of all major ozone-depleting substances was 'of paramount importance in protecting the ozone-layer'.[24] Similarly, the 1992 Copenhagen amendments were based on conclusions from both the scientific and not least the economic and technological assessment panels.[25] As can be noted in this brief overview, the regime played an increasingly important role over time as the main framework for knowledge improvement.

What about the current picture, then: is there an imminent solution to the ozone depletion problems? Like most other environmental problems, there are substantial time lags between reductions in ozone-depleting substance emissions and ozone-layer effects. Unlike most other gases, ozone-depleting substances are not chemically broken down or rained out in the lower atmosphere, but due to their exceptionally stable chemical structure, persist and migrate slowly up to the stratosphere. Recent research indicates, for instance, that it takes three to five years for CFCs to reach the stratosphere. A consensus view is now that chlorine released in the stratosphere unleashes a complicated chemical process which continues to destroy ozone for several decades. Depending on their individual structure, different CFCs may remain intact for many decades; the lifetime of CFC-11, for instance, is estimated to be 50 years.[26] Because of such long lifetimes, nine-tenths of all CFCs ever emitted are still in the atmosphere.[27]

So what is the general picture? Reductions in ozone abundance of about 4–5% per decade at mid-latitudes in the Northern and Southern Hemispheres have been suggested by both ground-based and satellite monitoring instruments. Moreover, the Antarctic 'ozone holes' of 1992 and 1993 were the most severe on record, and a substantial 'hole' is expected to occur each spring for many decades to come because stratospheric chlorine and bromine abundances will very gradually approach the levels of the late-1970s (prior to the Antarctic 'ozone hole') during the next century. According to scientific assessment reports released in 1994, if countries stuck to their commitments under the Montreal Protocol, ozone depletion would continue to worsen until the end of this century. The peak total chlorine and bromine load in the troposphere was expected in 1994, with a stratospheric peak lag of about 3–5 years.[28] However, more recent information about higher consumption of ozone-depleting substances in developing countries than expected may mean a delay in this development.[29] Meanwhile, the first indications of effective regulations can already be detected: there are declining growth rates in the atmospheric concentrations of controlled substances. Data from recent years clearly show declining growth rates of CFCs and halons. The abundance of carbon tetrachloride is actually decreasing.[30] Moreover, the observations of declines in growth rates from several monitoring networks worldwide are consistent (except for carbon tetrachloride) with forecasts based on recent emission reductions.[31] In 1995, American scientists reported growth rates close to zero for CFCs, and decreasing concentrations of methyl chloroform.[32] Reports from the 1996 Ozone Symposium indicate that the trend has now actually changed from one of continued ozone loss to a gradual increase in ozone levels.[33] Still, as already indicated, it must be kept in mind that continued ozone layer restoration is heavily dependent on the implementation of regulations that have been agreed on, not least by the developing countries.

5.2.3 Summing Up

Despite reporting problems and a lack of national knowledge, the overall impression is that the international regulatory development has been impressive, and available data indicate that the required behavioural changes are largely being implemented by the industrialized countries, apparently greatly influenced by the international process. However, less impressive follow-up in the East and South must be noted. In terms of environmental problem-solving, the mutual match between evolving knowledge and international policy responses has been significant, and the first atmospheric signs of effective regulations can be detected. Addressing implementation failures in the CEIT and increasing the production and consumption of ODS in developing countries are the main challenges for upholding regime effectiveness in the years ahead.

How, then, has this development come about?

5.3 ACCOUNTING FOR HIGH EFFECTIVENESS: MODERATELY MALIGN PROBLEMS BECOMING MORE BENIGN?

5.3.1 The Background for a Loose Framework Convention: High Uncertainty and Hesitant States[34]

How can the ozone depletion problems be characterized in the mid-1980s, in terms of knowledge and principal interests? And how can these initial problem characteristics shed light on the regime creation phase and the establishment of the Vienna framework convention?

In terms of knowledge and 'intellectual' problem characteristics, the overall picture is one of high complexity. As mentioned in the introduction, an essential element of the current knowledge on ozone depletion is the theory launched in the mid-1970s that CFCs (chlorofluorocarbons) could destroy the ozone layer, based on the work of two American groups of scientists – Stolarski/Cicerone (S/C) and Rowland/Molina (R/M). S/C indicated that chlorine released from space rockets could destroy ozone; R/M suggested that CFCs were not broken down in the lower atmosphere, but drifted slowly up through the atmosphere, where they reacted with ozone molecules, broke them down, and consequently depleted the ozone layer. This theory was refined over the years, but the ozone depletion problems must overall be characterized as intellectually extremely complex and not well understood by chemists and atmospheric scientists.[35] Moreover, and definitely important, the situation in the mid-1980s was still one of lacking empirical proof. Measurements of ozone levels had been carried out for 30 years, but had not yet demonstrated any statistically significant loss of total ozone. Evidence concerning the harmful effects of ozone modification was also sparse. Hence, despite widespread US acceptance, some scientists and the chemical industries questioned the validity of the basic theory. Efforts from the late 1970s on to establish an international consensus by organizations like the World Meteorological Organization (WMO), the United Nations Environment Programme (UNEP) and the International Council of Scientific Unions (ICSU) were multiple. A comprehensive international research programme was launched in 1984, including 150 scientists from 11 countries. However, by 1985, an international consensus had failed to emerge. Technologically, experience from the 1978 spray can ban in the US and the industry's own research indicated that development of alternatives to CFCs was largely a question of the right market incentives, as several chief alternative gases had been identified. But no technological breakthrough was announced before 1985.

In terms of interests, as all states would be negatively affected by increased ultraviolet radiation (although the degree of vulnerability might vary somewhat), no nations could perceive any benefits from ozone depletion. Hence, with regard to environmental vulnerability, concepts like 'winners'/'losers' and 'pollution exporters'/'importers' were less relevant in this case. Moreover, on the regulatory side, CFCs were not critically important for industrial and economic development, either country-wise or industry-wise. As already mentioned, CFCs were primarily used in refrigeration and air conditioning, as blowing agents and aerosol propellants, and in solvents for cleaning electronic parts. For instance, CFCs accounted for only 2% of the important American CFC manufacturer Du Pont's revenues in 1987 and a slightly higher percentage of its profits. Furthermore, promising substitutes were in the pipeline. Production and consumption were at this stage concentrated mainly in the industrialized countries, with the US and the EC together producing about 70% of all CFCs and consuming about 60%. Hence, at this initial stage, the ozone depletion problems must overall be characterized as somewhat malign. This was largely because the situation was one of substantial intellectual uncertainty and complexity. Although CFCs were not critically important for industrial and economic development, there were potential competitive effects related to regulatory development, primarily between American and European producers of ozone-depleting substances.

In terms of major participants and their preferences, they were in this initial phase the Toronto Group, the US and the EC. In addition, the USSR and Japan should also be mentioned. The Toronto Group was formed in 1983 by Canada,

Finland, Sweden, Norway and Switzerland; and joined later that year by the US. This group sought CFC reductions and a ban on nonessential use of CFCs in spray cans. However, the EC was somewhat of a laggard in much of this regime creation phase, together with the USSR and Japan. The role of the EC was due to several factors.[36] First, EC production and export of CFCs were increasing in the late 1970s and early 1980s, while the US market share was decreasing. Second, the ozone depletion problem was discovered by Americans, and the scientific work was still US-dominated. In addition, major European countries were more concerned with issues like acid rain (compare the 'Waldsterben' debate in Germany in the early 1980s). However, it should be noted that the EC countries were divided on this issue. Belgium, Denmark, West Germany and the Netherlands were increasingly inclined towards strong CFC controls (with only West Germany being a major producer). The UK, France, Italy, and Spain, all rather large producers, resisted stringent measures.[37] In the US, the ozone depletion problem had been a hot issue since the beginning of the 1970s. Still, the US also experienced domestic political problems on this issue, as the anti-regulatory Reagan government took office in 1981, and the new Environmental Protection Agency (EPA) administrator downplayed the ozone depletion problems – complicating the US negotiating position. Hence, during the beginning of the 1980s, although being a definite scientific leader, the US must still be characterized as something of a political laggard. This changed in 1983/84, due among other things to a change of leadership in the EPA.[38]

Against a background of scientific uncertainty and lack of empirical evidence, the factors briefly outlined above give us an idea of why the preferences among the main actors, the US and the EC, can perhaps best be described as somewhat hesitant at the time of the establishment of the Vienna Convention.

5.3.2 The Background for Rapid Regime Development: Reduced Uncertainty, Technological Progress and Converging Preferences in the North[39]

The regime heyday: late 1980s and early 1990s
Overall, uncertainty was gradually reduced from 1985 on. Two months after the adoption of the Vienna Convention, Joe Farman and his research team from the British Antarctic Survey published their *Nature* paper on the Antarctic 'ozone hole' – the first empirical indication that the theories launched might be correct. Under Dr Bob Watson's leadership, the already mentioned 1986 WMO/NASA report was clearly important in terms of consensus building. The report indicated, among other things, that continued emissions of CFCs 11 and 12 at the 1980 rate could reduce the ozone layer by about 9% by the last half of

the 21st century. Moreover, the ozone layer was not only threatened by CFCs 11 and 12 but also by other fully halogenated alkanes and halons, used for firefighting purposes. However, the main breakthrough in terms of empirical evidence came shortly *after* the adoption of the Montreal Protocol. In March 1988, the Ozone Trend Panel released the results of a 16 month comprehensive scientific exercise. The panel concluded that the evidence 'strongly indicates that man-made chlorine species are primarily responsible for the observed decrease in ozone'.[40] In addition, the 1989 Synthesis report continued to add more elements to the picture, and led to the recommendation from nearly 500 scientists to phase out completely all major ozone-depleting substances.

On the technological side, things developed quite quickly after the adoption of the Montreal Protocol. Four months after Montreal, several hundred industry representatives met in Washington to exchange information and stimulate research on alternatives to CFCs.[41] Moreover, on the basis of Article 6 in the Montreal Protocol, a technology review panel was appointed, consisting of over 100 international experts. The panel's 1989 Synthesis Report concluded that, based on the current state of technology, the five controlled CFCs could be reduced by over 95% by the year 2000. Moreover, the economic panel's part of this report concluded that the monetary value of the benefits would undoubtedly be much greater than the costs of CFC and halon reductions. But it was also acknowledged that developing countries would be less able to invest in this effort due to more immediate concerns such as food supply and economic development.[42] Hence, a drastic cut in CFCs and halons seemed both technologically feasible and economically reasonable within a short period after the Montreal Conference.

Related to this development, perceptions of the magnitude of the problems changed. Mounting evidence suggested that increased ultraviolet radiation, related to ozone layer depletion, induced skin cancer, cataracts, suppression of the human immune response system and the development of some cutaneous infections such as herpes. Plants reacted adversely and aquatic organisms would be negatively affected by increased UV-B radiation. This meant that potential regulatory benefits got increasingly specific, while costs were reduced in line with rapid technological progress. Hence, it has been argued that intellectual progress towards the end of the 1980s indicated that at least the industrialized countries in many ways faced a relatively benign cost-efficiency problem, where the main challenge was coordination and information perfection.[43]

Still, this does not mean that the process leading up to the important Montreal Protocol breakthrough was uncomplicated. After a domestic US administrative battle between, on the one hand, the Office of Management and Budget and the Departments of Commerce and Energy, and on the other the EPA and the State Department, the latter coalition got support from the Senate, which passed a resolution calling for a 50% reduction and eventual phase-out.

This was approved by President Reagan in the summer of 1987, and gained strong support from Canada and the Nordic countries, among others. Overall, the US played an important part in the process leading up to Montreal, founded on threats of unilateral action and persuasion with a basis in US scientific, diplomatic and political strength.[44] Meanwhile, discussions continued within the EC, with Germany gradually moving towards the US position, but with the two other main CFC producers in the EC, France and the UK, holding back. Only threats of a complete collapse of the Montreal negotiations and skilful entrepreneurial diplomatic efforts, especially by the UNEP leader Mostafa Tolba, made the EC Commission give in.[45]

After the Montreal Protocol and alarming signals from the Ozone Trends Panel, and following Du Pont's announcement of a CFC and halon manufac-turing stop by the end of the century, the US in March 1989 called for a complete phase-out of CFCs by the year 2000. Within the EC, the UK stance was softening, due to pressure from environmental groups and the UK Parliament, and because ICI (the UK's biggest CFC producer) began to take a more positive position towards strengthened regulations. At a meeting hosted by a 'greened' Prime Minister Margaret Thatcher in March 1989, France gave in, and the EC was able to support the US by declaring that it would eliminate CFCs completely by the end of the century. Hence, 15 months after Montreal, the main discrepancies between the US and the EC had vanished. Moreover, although the developing countries at this stage were dissatisfied with distributional/financial and technology transfer issues, they supported the ultimate objective of a total elimination of CFCs and halons.

The more recent, less dynamic period
The process of knowledge improvement has continued. Two subsequent rounds of assessment panels have been carried out: in 1991 to advise the 1992 Copenhagen meeting, and in 1994 to advise the 1995 Vienna meeting. The 1991 report pointed to continued observations of ozone loss, including the first observations of temperate latitude losses in summer in addition to the increasing intensity of the Antarctic ozone hole. Moreover, the report indicated for the first time that methyl bromide emissions resulting from human activities were contributing significantly to ozone loss. The 1994 report indicated continued ozone losses, but also, as already mentioned, the first indications that the Protocol was working: growth rates in the atmospheric concentrations of controlled substances were declining.[46] Overall, models have become more powerful, more substances have been identified, and there is growing empirical evidence, for example in the form of ozone loss seasonally observed over Antarctica.

However, despite the development of such a general level of consensus, ozone politics in the 1990s have not developed without strife and conflict. In connection with the 1992 Copenhagen meeting, there was little disagreement concerning an accelerated phase-out of already controlled substances.[47] However, there was more conflict over the regulation of additional substances: HCFCs and especially methyl bromide. Due to the role of this latter substance in agriculture (soil fumigation), the EC and especially its Mediterranean members could not accept a US proposal for a complete phase-out by the year 2000. Moreover, fierce protests came from Israel, 'whose delegation was almost entirely composed of representatives from the interested industry that makes Israel a major producer and exporter of methyl bromide',[48] and several developing countries. In addition to these substantial conflicts, there was a more general North–South division over matters related to the special treatment of developing countries and the operation of the Multilateral Fund established at the London 1990 meeting. Both the size and status of the Fund in the following years was debated, with the major donor countries being reluctant with regard to specific long-term financial commitments.

In general, then, the issue of developing countries and their needs has complicated the picture in the 1990s. During the late 1980s, these countries produced and consumed only a small fraction (less than 10%) of the ozone-depleting substances compared to the OECD countries. Although there are variations also within the developing country group, these countries envisioned future substantial increases in the production and use of the relatively cheap CFCs, and production and consumption limits could be perceived as potential barriers to their own economic growth, at least in a short-term perspective. Importing countries could face higher prices for substitutes, and CFC-producing developing countries could face problems with access to new technologies and patent rights. The OECD countries consumed about 88% of the CFCs with less than 25% of the world's population.[49] Some figures can illustrate the altered situation: as touched upon earlier, production of CFCs in developing countries increased by 87% between 1986 and 1993, and exports increased seventeen-fold. While the consumption of CFCs dropped by 74% in industrialized countries during the same period, it increased by more than 40% in the developing countries.[50]

With regard to the Vienna 1995 'tenth anniversary' meeting, developing countries remained reluctant to contemplate tighter controls on HCFCs and methyl bromide. The US argued for a 'no change' policy with regard to HCFCs and a year 2001 phase-out date for methyl bromide, and the EC Environmental Commissioner put forward a similar EC position on methyl bromide.[51] The outcome on HCFCs entailed only minor adjustments, which prompted a group of 25 parties to sign a political call for stronger action ('The Vienna Declaration on HCFCs'). Somewhat more progress was made with regard to methyl bromide, with the decision to ban the substance in developed countries by 2010 (with a 25% reduction by 2001 and a 50% reduction by 2005). Developing countries were to stabilize their consumption of methyl bromide at present levels by 2002. However, this decision also prompted a political declaration by more impatient parties. Regarding CFCs, developing countries succeeded in establishing the more 'lenient' London 1990 amendments as their regulatory baseline and not the stricter 1992 Copenhagen amendment.[52] At the 1997 Montreal meeting, the main issues and conflict lines were quite similar to the Vienna 1995 meeting.[53] The issue of methyl bromide saw a conflict, first, within the group of industrialized countries – with the 'impatient' US and Canada pitted against the 'reluctant' Southern European countries. Moreover, there was a conflict between a relatively 'impatient' North and a more 'reluctant' South, with the latter pointing to the need for additional funding from the Multilateral Fund and technology transfer in order to agree to and implement stricter regulations. With regard to HCFCs, the discussions were primarily related to the industrialized countries and the picture was somewhat reversed, with the 'reluctant' US and Canada arguing that their office air conditioning systems needed HCFCs for a long time and the 'impatient' EC suggesting available substitutes.

5.3.3 Some Brief Notes on Entrepreneurial Leadership: Strong Initially; Less Marked over Time?

In general, entrepreneurial leadership was strong in the crucial first regime development phase from 1985 to 1990.[54] Several types of leadership can be discerned, both on the intellectual and political side. Intellectually, the American leadership in the ozone depletion issue had its roots back in the mid-1970s. NASA played an important part in the 'Coordinating Committee on the Ozone Layer' (CCOL) established in 1977. In 1984, a large international research programme was launched by WMO and NASA, including 150 scientists from 11 countries. From the mid-1980s, several sources point to Bob Watson as a leading American figure within the scientific community engaged in ozone research. He had a keen awareness of the need to balance the complicated requirements of the scientific venture in terms of national and industrial legitimacy, with scientific integrity and not least political usability.[55]

Politically, with regard to national efforts in the negotiations, again the American efforts stand out in a field that also includes the Nordic countries. The US provided strong leadership from early 1986 on.[56] Over 60 US embassies were utilized in an information and influence strategy; diplomatic initiatives were closely coordinated with like-minded countries like Canada, New Zealand, Switzerland, and the Nordics; and the chief US negotiator Benedick led several missions to European capitals.[57] Moreover, the role of UNEP and its leader at the time, Mostafa Tolba, of course warrants some special attention. UNEP played an important part as an arena for ozone negotiations from the early 1980s on. Tolba entered the negotiating scene in spring 1987, soon exerting considerable influence.[58] He could draw upon at least three power sources: first, he was the head of the host organization; second, given the scientific and technological complexities of the ozone issue, he was himself a scientist; and third, he was clearly a charismatic person. Tolba utilized various leadership and negotiation strategies: institutional changes through small, shielded meetings of key delegations, as well as direct confrontations and 'midnight theatrics'.[59] After Montreal, he continued to influence the process at least until the 1990 London meeting.

In the 1990s, the leadership question has become more diffuse. There was probably a less pronounced need for strong leadership as the regulatory process acquired a stronger momentum of its own and, at least temporarily, entered more cooperative waters.[60] As indicated in the previous section, depending on the issue, the US, the EC, and the Nordic delegations have generally been leading actors.[61]

5.3.4 Summing up: From 'Moderately Malign' To 'Relatively Benign' Characteristics?

Although starting out and remaining an intellectually complex problem, with a high reliance on computer models and scarce and long-term empirical effects, consensus and certainty have increased quite rapidly, largely due to a broad-based international research effort. This alone indicates that the issue of interplay between the development of problem characteristics and the activity of international institutions is important to clarify. Due to the global, indivisible character of the radiation-shielding ozone layer, all states would be negatively affected by increased ultraviolet radiation (although the degree of vulnerability might vary somewhat), and no nations could perceive any benefits from ozone layer depletion. Moreover, the causes of the problem lie in a relatively small group of substances (though larger than initially realized), at first produced mainly by the US and some European countries (though with a rapidly growing participation of developing countries both in terms of production and consumption); they are utilized primarily in refrigeration and cooling, which may be regarded as only moderately important societal activities (though important in warm climates). In a positive interplay with international regulatory development, significantly enhanced by various forms of entrepreneurial leadership, technological progress has been steady. However, the latent fundamental asymmetry in every global regulatory effort has gradually been uncovered: between the rich countries of the North who can afford greener, more expensive alternative substances and the poorer countries of the South who would prefer to keep present and, in particular, future development costs at a minimum.

These problem characteristics and trends have been reflected in preferences which at the beginning of the 1990s had converged significantly among the industrialized countries, and this picture also included the developing countries at a very general level. However, subsequent events have increasingly opened up more specific sub-conflicts, both within the group of developed countries and between North and South over regulatory development and financial and technological transfers related to the follow-up of regulations agreed on. Overall, there is little doubt that this improvement in the characterization of problems, preferences and capabilities – from being 'moderately malign' to 'relatively benign' – can throw substantial light over the rather high effectiveness of the ozone regime so far. Based on this general account, let us proceed to the focused institutional questions.

5.4 THE INSTITUTIONAL DESIGN OF THE OZONE LAYER REGIME: NOT ONLY 'INCREASINGLY BENIGN' PROBLEMS, BUT ALSO AN EXTRAORDINARILY POWERFUL DESIGN?

5.4.1 Access and Participation: Lucky Circumstances and Successful Design Elements

Starting with procedural matters, according to Article 6 of the Vienna Convention and Article 11 of the Montreal Protocol, any state could participate, and any national or international body could be represented as an observer unless one-third of the parties objected. Hence, both Meetings of the Parties and meetings of the Open-Ended Working Group of the Parties have been open to all governments, whether or not they are parties to the regime, as well as to observers from international agencies and NGOs. States that have been neither parties nor observers have had no voting rights.[62]

Turning then to the important question of state participation, the regime has over time developed into a truly global one, matching the global scope of the ozone layer depletion problem. However, the initial political game was mainly within the OECD group, largely reflecting the fact that countries within this group were the dominant initial producers and consumers of the focused substances. Due to lucky circumstances, this meant that a small group of industrialized countries obtained a brief, though crucial period in which the agenda was dominated by the concerns of these countries and companies – before the game and the agenda were broadened to include the crucial, complex issue of the special needs and concerns of the developing countries. The truly global character of the regime has increased over time, in step with the growing importance of actual and potential ODS production and use in other parts of the world. Hence, aided by specific institutional mechanisms, the match between state participation and problem-creating activities has over time become quite good. On the production side, the match has been favourable all along, with the main producing countries among the 45 nations participating at the Vienna negotiations, and these countries have also signed and ratified the subsequent protocol and amendments. Bringing in the consumption side automatically activates the question of developing country participation, and the overall picture here is that this participation has increased substantially over time. Sixteen developing countries participated in Vienna; more than 30 in Montreal; and by 1992, 55 developing countries had ratified the Montreal Protocol.[63] However, important developing countries like China and India held out until 1990, related of course to complicated questions of global equity and the willingness of developed countries to provide financial and technological assistance.[64] India and China have since ratified both the Convention, the Protocol, and the London amendments.[65] There have been several specific institutional mechanisms to increase participation. First, there was the establishment of the Multilateral Fund and the issue of financial and technological assistance to developing countries (further elaborated in section 5.4.6). Moreover, there was also the issue of restrictions on trade with non-parties, in order to prevent non-participating countries from gaining competitive advantages. Such trade sanctions are based on Article 4 of the Montreal Protocol ('Control of Trade with Non-Parties'), and apply to both imports and exports. According to several sources, these clauses have worked effectively in terms of increasing state participation.[66]

Turning to the question of outsiders' access and participation, and especially the role of industrial and environmental NGOs,[67] the overall inclusive model utilized had its origins in the 'Coordinating Committee on the Ozone Layer' (CCOL) process, initiated in the 1970s.[68] The main task of the CCOL was to coordinate research undertaken by national and international agencies, and bring together scientists from governments, industry, universities, and international agencies to assess the risks of ozone-layer depletion. According to Gehring (1994:204), 'the principal body to be established under the convention ... was not designed as a gathering of a limited club of international guards of the ozone-layer ... Instead, it envisaged comprehensive meetings combining all kinds of knowledge and interests relevant to the issue-area'. The following brief quantitative overview of the development is illustrative: in 1985, representatives from 45 nations, three industry organizations (observers) and non-governmental groups met in Vienna. At the second meeting of the parties in London in 1990, 95 governments and more than 40 NGOs were present. Close to 50 NGOs were present at the Copenhagen meeting, and around 60 NGOs attended the 1995 Vienna meeting. More specifically, the NGOs have participated at both working group and plenary levels, with the right to speak during deliberations. Both analysts, regime participants and the Secretariat generally emphasize the positive contribution of the environmental NGOs.[69] For instance, according to Benedick (1991:205), 'the proponents of ozone layer protection generally avoided invoking apocalypse and resisted temptations to overstate their case in order to capture public attention'.

However, this basically open access and broad participation has not been entirely positive and unproblematic. The use of smaller, 'explicitly informal' workshops and groups at several points in these processes can be interpreted as a way of avoiding some of the inflexibility and rhetoric inherent in large, media-scrutinized forums. Benedick's (1991) seminal account of regime negotiations and development up to and including the 1990 London meeting contains several references to this dimension of the access issue. In the process leading up to the Montreal Protocol, smaller workshops were organized. These workshops included governmental representatives, UN officials, academics, industrialists and environmentalists – all acting in their private capacities. According to Benedick (1991:47), 'the process was characterized by breaking down the problems into smaller components, developing consensus by incremental stages, and, as important as any other factor, establishing a degree of rapport and mutual confidence among future participants in the diplomatic negotiations'. Moreover, describing the several negotiating rounds leading up to the final Montreal Protocol: 'Tolba then (at the April 1987 session) convened his informal consultative group of 10 delegations heads, *meeting out of the limelight and away from the crowds of industry and environmental observers*' (ibid.:85; my italics). In addition, as a general lesson, he states: 'The informal fact-finding efforts during 1985 and 1986 and again during 1989 and 1990 – workshops, conferences, consultations – established an environment conducive to building personal relationships and generating creative ideas, and thereby facilitated the formal negotiations. During the negotiations themselves, the use of small working groups and a single basic "chairman's text" aided in the gradual emergence of consensus' (ibid.:207). Norwegian participants also emphasize the importance of these informal and rather exclusive gatherings of people hand-picked by Tolba.[70] Hence, in order to make political progress at crucial initial stages of the regime's development, the inclusive approach has been abandoned and a quite exclusive approach has been utilized – excluding not only various 'outsider' groups, but also most of the nation states. More recently, a rather exclusive model has been utilized for meetings within the Implementation Committee (IC), for instance in connection with the case of possible Russian and Eastern European non-compliance. Hence, environmental NGOs have been barred from participation in the IC meetings.[71]

Turning then to the question of level of proceedings and especially the issue of ministerial participation, the ozone process was first characterized by substantial ministerial-level involvement, especially in the crucial and dynamic first phase of the regime. For instance, in Montreal, 16 out of 24 nations were represented at ministerial or deputy ministerial level. In addition, several presidents and prime ministers were personally involved in the negotiation process. In London, 'evidencing the importance accorded this meeting, nearly all the parties were represented at ministerial or equivalent level'.[72] Moreover, both at the 1992 Copenhagen and the 1995 Vienna meetings concluding ministerial sessions have been an important ingredient in the negotiation process. Second, the system of regular meetings in the Open-Ended Working Group of the Parties[73] has ensured a systematic and continuous participation of the relevant national bureaucratic personnel with various types of broader issue-specific knowledge.

Let us then round off with some concluding reflections. First, the ozone access and participation model was deliberately designed to be open and inclusive, closely linked to central problem characteristics. Given the fundamental global effects of ozone layer depletion, more or less global consumption of destructive substances, high scientific uncertainty, and technological substitution opportunities, there was little to lose and much to gain from actively including a more or less global group of states as well as a broad range of societal actors, including scientists, industrialists, and environmental NGOs. Overall, this model secured inputs and ideas from a wide spectrum of actors. However, general openness was combined with selective inclusiveness throughout this process, in the form of smaller and more informal workshops, meetings and working groups. It seems reasonable to assume that this 'generally inclusive-temporarily exclusive' approach chosen within the ozone regime contributed positively to the general development of the regime. Moreover, due to lucky circumstances, the initially limited number of important producers and consumers signified an initial regulatory arrangement that was more manageable and far from global. In terms of more specific impact on regime development and effectiveness, two key institutional issues stand out within the access and participation context. First, institutional density, both in terms of many meetings within a rather short time span and substantial high-level and ministerial participation probably contributed to the rapid progress in the late 1980s and early 1990s. Moreover, specific institutional mechanisms in the form of prospects of financial and technological assistance and fears of trade sanctions served to increase the regulatory scope and bite of the regime and hence enhance the legitimacy and robustness of the regime.

5.4.2 Decision-Making Rules: Formally Beyond Consensus, but What About Practice?

Generally, the issue of decision-making rules and practice must be seen in the basic ozone decision-making context, characterized by the balancing of different interests and concerns both within the group of developed countries and between North and South. Not surprisingly, the Vienna Convention generally emphasized consensus. Still, it should be noted that Article 9 of the Vienna Convention opened up opportunities for a qualified majority rule in connection with amendments to the Convention and Protocols. Paragraph 3 reads: 'The Parties shall make every effort to reach agreement on any proposed amendment to this Convention by consensus. If all efforts at consensus have been exhausted, and no agreement reached, the amendment shall as a last resort be adopted by a three-fourths majority vote of the Parties present and voting at the meeting, and shall be submitted by the Depository to all Parties for ratification, approval or acceptance'. With regard to amendments to protocols, a two-thirds majority should suffice for their adoption.[74] Moreover, Article 9(5) of the Convention established a basic right of reservation.[75]

The balancing of different interests and concerns came more to the forefront in connection with the Montreal Protocol negotiations. The US had different interests in this connection; on the one hand, it feared that countries with strong interests in an issue could be overwhelmed by a majority vote. Hence, it launched the idea of a two-step or qualified majority. This implied that actions could only be taken if they had support from a certain number of countries representing a specific proportion of total CFC consumption. On the other hand, being an overall 'progressive' force in this context, the US wished to see the regulative process continuing smoothly. Hence, together with like-minded countries like Canada and the Nordic countries, the US favoured a flexible adjustment procedure based on the decisions of the Meeting of the Parties, while more reluctant actors at the time, like the EC and the Soviet Union, favoured a traditional international treaty amendment and national ratification procedures. The result was a compromise: with regard to substances already subject to control measures, the Meeting of the Parties could make a decision, if possible by consensus. The minimum requirement was, however, only a two-thirds majority of the parties present and voting, which had to represent at least 50% of the combined consumption of the parties.[76] As commented by Benedick (1991:90): 'Thus, if a sufficiently large consensus developed for reductions beyond 50%, neither the United States nor the EC alone could block it, although both together could. The protocol was so designed that such future changes in the stringency and timing of reductions of already controlled substances would be considered "adjustments" to the provisions and therefore binding on *all* parties, even those who had not voted with the majority'.[77] All other changes, including decisions on new substances and related control measures, would require the regular treaty-amendment procedure stipulated in the Vienna Convention. Hence, the question of right of reservation became quite complex, at least in theory; allowed in cases of new protocols or amendments; not allowed in cases of regulatory 'adjustments' related to substances already controlled.[78] The qualified majority approach was also reflected in the procedures governing entry into force of the Protocol; the requirement here was ratification by at least 11 parties, together constituting at least two-thirds of estimated global consumption of controlled substances as of 1986.[79]

So, what about the practical effects, then? Although the decision-making machinery established has been hailed by legal experts as a 'great novelty in international environmental law',[80] no votes have ever been taken at the Meetings of the Parties. Does this automatically mean that this 'novelty' has meant little or nothing in practice? Not necessarily, although evidence is scarce. According to some analysts, 'undoubtedly ... the fact that reluctant countries knew they would be outvoted heavily influenced their decisions (in 1990 and 1992)'.[81] In addition, it is also reasonable to assume that the complicated decision-making procedures have had important symbolic and integrative effects, functioning as formal, codified expressions of power balancing and considerations for the interests of important actors and groups of actors within the regime. Not necessarily contradicting the aspects above, Norwegian process participants generally emphasize the practical spirit of consensus and willingness to seek pragmatic solutions. Instead of seeking immediate and optimum solutions, the most ambitious actors have generally opted for an incremental process approach: first make substances part of the formal regulatory machinery in a generally acceptable way, and then work for gradually tougher commitments.[82] Moreover, the emphasis on consensus is also expressed by the Secretariat. The global character of the problem and the need for global participation point toward a generally consensual approach.[83] However, as clarified at the 1995 Vienna meeting, a sort of flexible consensus has been utilized. When only one party has objected, the decision has still 'been carried by consensus', and the position of the dissenting party has been 'clearly reflected' in the report of the meeting.[84]

In summary, although considerable weight is also formally given to the principle of consensus, decision-making rules contain the possibility of decisions to be made by a three-fourths (Convention) or two-thirds (Montreal Protocol) majority; and even to be binding for possible outvoted minorities. However, in practice, a kind of flexible consensus has been utilized at meetings within the regime, not allowing one single party to block the whole process. Hence, the practical effects of the majority voting clauses could stem from their symbolic and integrative functions, and/or their 'hidden stick' functions. Both effects need further investigation.

5.4.3 The Role of the Secretariat(s): Stage-hand(s) with Powerful Connections?

As indicated earlier, UNEP was clearly one of the leading international organizations that focused on the depletion of the ozone layer issue in the late 1970s and early 1980s. This was natural, given the global character of the issue. UNEP launched its 'world plan of action on the ozone layer' in 1977 and the same year established the 'Coordinating Committee on the Ozone Layer' (CCOL). In 1981, UNEP's Governing Council approved a Swedish initiative to establish a working group to start negotiations on an international convention on the ozone layer. Hence, UNEP carried out the secretarial functions *de facto* from the early 1980s on. However, at the 1985 Vienna conference, disagreement arose on the secretarial issue, with scientists largely favouring WMO and diplomats and administrators favouring UNEP. Hence, the formal assignment was deferred to the first Meeting of the Parties.[85] At this meeting, the secretarial question was formally settled in favour of UNEP, in fact *after* UNEP had been assigned secretarial functions related to the follow-up of the Montreal Protocol. Thus, secretarial functions were formally divided between the Convention and the Protocol, but in practice the two Secretariats have cooperated closely and shared employees.[86]

In terms of resources, UNEP as an organization is of course in a totally different league from what is common for international environmental regimes. However, the size of the Ozone Secretariat itself has not been so remarkable. The number of staff by March 1998 was five professionals and eight support staff. Turning to the financial situation, with regard to the Convention, the annual budget has increased from around $300 000 in 1994 to around $1 300 000 for 1999; regarding the Protocol, the annual budget for the most recent years has been of the order of $3 million; and the administrative budget for the Multilateral Fund has been around $9 million.[87] Hence, the importance of the UNEP connection lies probably primarily in potential organizational back-up. Given the many tales of UNEP leader Tolba's entrepreneurial importance, can the Ozone Secretariat be characterized as an especially active Secretariat? On the one hand, initial ideas put forward by the Nordic countries in the regime creation process of an 'activist' Secretariat – 'a semi-autonomous entity with an independent responsibility to further the policy of the regime' – were clearly rejected. The Secretariat was 'reduced from an agent facilitating the regime process to a mere servicing body'.[88] On the other hand, there are some observations that indicate a rather active profile. First, it seems to have played an active role in convening informal and formal meetings in the first crucial, complicated phases of the regime's development. Moreover, UNEP has been able to offer the negotiating nations a Secretariat that is technically experienced in atmospheric science and treaty-making.[89] Hence, the UNEP Secretariat produced early drafts of both the Vienna Convention and the Montreal Protocol. Third, as noted by Parson (1993:67), the Secretariat's authority to convene review panels and to call Meetings of the Parties to review their results, gives it considerable power to force the agenda. Hence, Parson states: 'There is a delicate balance between the procedural, agenda-forcing power spun off to expert groups and the secretariat, and the substantive power that remains in the Parties. That balance is in part maintained by frequent meetings of the Parties' (p. 67). In addition, the Secretariat has also come to play an important role in connection with the parties' implementation reporting and in the cases of non-compliance, in cooperation with the Implementation Committee.[90] A matter clearly in the grey zone between institutions and procedural leadership is UNEP's secretarial and 'guiding' function at the Montreal negotiations, which provided the formal platform for UNEP director Tolba's entrepreneurial contributions to the Montreal process. More generally, participants in the cooperative process emphasize the crucial interplay between Tolba and the Secretariat, with the Secretariat acting as a kind of executive and implementing committee.[91] However, more information is clearly needed to settle this 'secretariat versus personal leadership' matter more conclusively.

Altogether, despite limited resources and staffing, the Ozone Secretariat has in several ways contributed to the progress within the regime, and perhaps more so than envisioned in the regime creation phase. The Secretariat has handled informal and formal meetings of the parties, provided treaty text drafts, convened review panels, and increasingly played a role in matters of reporting and compliance issues. More generally, the UNEP connection has obviously been a strength, especially in the early phases of the regime development. However, it must still be maintained that several aspects of the actual role of the Ozone Secretariat lie in the dark so far. We have heard much about the entrepreneurial leadership carried out by UNEP's leader Tolba in the initial phases of the regime. We know less about the interplay and relative importance of organizational and personal factors in this initial phase, and not least, we also have only scattered knowledge about the more recent functioning of the Secretariat. A reasonable interpretation is that the main functions and role of the Secretariat have changed somewhat – from the more entrepreneurial role in the crucial, initial Montreal days to a still important, though lower-key and more 'technical' role in more recent years.

5.4.4 The Ozone Agenda: Designed Flexibility or a Lucky, Gradual Development?

In the Vienna Convention, no specific activities or substances were mentioned, and hence the formal agenda was defined quite loosely. However, a resolution was adopted at the Vienna Conference, calling for negotiations on a future protocol on CFC production, emissions and use.[92] Moreover, as there had already been an unsuccessful effort to establish a CFC protocol in Vienna, an informal agenda targeting these substances as well as halons quickly formed. According to accounts of the regime development process, the organization of the agenda in this pre-negotiation phase was very successful.[93] Several informal workshops broke the problems down into smaller components, developed consensus by incremental stages, and established personal relationships and mutual confidence among the future participants in the diplomatic negotiations. Moreover, at the 1985 Leesburg workshop, the idea of an 'interim protocol' was first launched, implying that a treaty could be designed with periodic reassessments of the evolving science, and with built-in mechanisms for revisions of control measures.[94] This basic agenda and regulatory flexibility was later built into the Montreal Protocol. The Protocol stated that the parties were to meet in 1990 and at least every fourth year thereafter to determine if the control measures were to be changed (Article 6). Other accounts of the regime development process have indicated that institutional factors have primarily been important after 1987, and among them the structuring of the agenda.[95] Edward Parson (1993) pinpoints the establishment of the various review panels. These panels moved a broader set of questions out of the negotiating forum – including the feasibility of different phase-out schedules as well as their consequences for the stratosphere – and made the whole process more manageable. In other words, Parson indicates that it is also possible to see the establishment of scientific and technological advisory groups – which are definitely not an institutional device invented in connection with the ozone regime – in an 'agenda-relieving' perspective.

Due to both lucky circumstances and institutional contributions, the agenda has developed gradually. Two main trends can be discerned in this regard: first, gradual development of knowledge and technology has added new substances to the negotiating process in phases. From an initial focus on some CFCs and halons in Montreal, several other CFCs and substances like carbon tetrachloride and methyl chloroform were added in London, and HCFCs and methyl bromide were added to the agenda and regulatory focus in Copenhagen. This gradual development of knowledge has of course to some extent happened as a result of deliberate research initiatives and research coordination. Although the main side of this gradual development has been positive, regime participants state that more knowledge on 'ozone depleting potentials' and a broader regulatory focus from the very beginning would have increased the size of the regulatory 'basket' and made more comprehensive solutions possible.[96] Second, with the benefit of hindsight, it was beneficial for the process that the issue of the developing countries' situation, and the regulatory and financial mechanisms needed to address their special concerns, increased only gradually in importance. As noted by Benedick (1991:148): 'The nations of the South, most of which had been onlookers in the ozone negotiations through 1987 as the rich countries argued over chemicals scarcely used in the developing world, moved to centre stage in 1989 and claimed a major role in revising the protocol'. Hence, as has been discussed earlier, the industrialized countries obtained a brief, though crucial period in which the agenda was dominated by the complicated and complex concerns of these countries and companies – before the agenda and the game were truly globalized.

In summary, both designed flexibility and fortunate circumstances have been significant in this connection. On the design side, the agenda has been 'relieved' of scientifically and technologically complicating issues through the establishment of the review panels. Moreover, a scientific/technological knowledge development process has been initiated to support the successive development of the regime. In addition, a flexible agenda has been adopted as a formal principle. More due to uncontrollable processes and luck, a consecutive adding of new substances and complex issues like the special needs of the developing countries, have permitted a beneficial institutional adaptation and assimilation. Hence, the ozone case lends support to the benefits of sequencing and picking relatively easy subjects first, but this development can only to a modest degree be credited to the ozone negotiators.

5.4.5 The Organization of the Science–Politics Interface: Well Adapted to the Circumstances, but are there any General Lessons?

Given the high scientific uncertainty and complexity, and the strong technological dimension characterizing this issue-area in the mid-1980s, the regime could clearly play a potentially important role through the more systematic coordination and organization of scientific and technological activities. The initial scientific process was dominated by US scientific agencies, and most of the research was initiated, conducted and carried out by US scientific institutions, with NASA serving as a driving force. The organization history of the science–politics interface in this issue-area goes back to the late 1970s, with the establishment of the Coordinating Committee on the Ozone Layer (CCOL) as an important step in 1977. The main task of the CCOL was to coordinate research undertaken by national and international agencies, and bring together scientists from governments, industry, universities, and international agencies to assess the risks of ozone layer depletion,[97] hence providing an arena for a science–politics dialogue.[98] In 1984, a large international research programme was launched by WMO and NASA, including 150 scientists from 11 countries. A three-volume report was published in 1986, characterized as particularly important in shaping consensus in this field.[99] Hence, before 1988, the ozone regime had a rather loose scientific–political structure, more in the form of a network.[100] However, as noted by Skodvin (1994:85), the network was quite firmly connected. Throughout the process, many of the same scientific institutions and even the same scientists were mainly responsible for initiating and coordinating research, with the US of course as a dominant actor. Pursuant to Article 6 of the Montreal Protocol, in 1988 the scientific–political complex was institutionalized in four Assessment Panels: scientific, environmental, technological, and economic; and an integrated synthesis report was presented in 1989. According to Article 6, the panels were to produce assessments at least every four years. Moreover, 'at least before each assessment, the parties shall convene appropriate panels of experts qualified in the (relevant) fields and determine the composition and terms of reference of such panels'. Hence, at least formally, the ozone regime does not have standing scientific and technical bodies like most other international environmental regimes. In later rounds, the number of panels has been cut down to three main ones. The first is a Scientific Assessment Panel, composed of government experts and others, reviewing the development of scientific knowledge related to the needs of the parties; the second is a Technology and Economics Assessment Panel, which includes many industrial and NGO representatives. This panel assesses technical options and costs related to the limitation in use of ozone-depleting substances, and questions related to technology transfer and the needs of developing countries. Finally, the Environmental Effects Panel surveys the state of knowledge of the impacts on health and environment of the altered ozone levels. In addition, there are *ad hoc* groups on data reporting and destruction technologies.[101]

The establishment of the panels implied broader participation and served to reduce the earlier marked American bias and to increase the general geo-political representativeness of the process.[102] For instance, 110 experts from 22 countries contributed to the technology panel's report in 1988–89, and an even greater number, including several from additional countries, reviewed it.[103] Moreover, the panels also served to broaden the area of research by including issue areas that had not been covered in a systematic manner earlier, for instance the economic issues. In this respect, the ozone regime has been something of an exception in international environmental politics. With regard to recruitment of the panels, panel chairmen are elected at Meetings of the Parties, and these chairmen then put together the panels on the basis of principles adopted by the parties. On the one hand, the recruitment policy places great weight on scholarly merits and peer review procedures; on the other, the ozone policy also emphasizes 'the widest possible geographical balance' in the selection of experts.[104] Overall, the main impression seems to be one of internationally guaranteed objectivity and authoritativeness.[105] It should also be noted that there is a separate advisory body related to the Vienna Convention part of the ozone regime – the Meeting of Ozone Research Managers – convening every three years. This body is composed of government experts on atmospheric research, and health and environmental effects related to ozone layer depletion. Working in close cooperation with WMO, the meeting reviews and reports to the Conference of the Parties on international and national research and monitoring programmes, to ensure proper coordination and to identify gaps that need to be addressed.[106]

What about the specifically focused buffer question? Before 1988, CCOL can reasonably be seen as a buffer between the scientific and political processes. In 1988, the Meeting of the Parties established an Open-Ended Working Group for the consideration of the panel reports and their integration into one synthesis report.[107] The Working Group was open to all parties to the Montreal Protocol, as well as governmental and non-governmental observers. Hence, an *intergovernmental* body reviewed and synthesized knowledge from panels composed of experts working in a *personal* capacity. As commented by Gehring (1994:270), 'this second step (the intergovernmental review) was designed to make information prepared by experts acceptable by governments that would have to make coordinated policy choices. Results would be apt to provide a secure and commonly agreed upon foundation for ensuing political negotiations'. This buffer function of the Open-Ended Working Group has been confirmed by the Secretariat; the Working Group discusses all technical findings from the Assessment Panels and makes recommendations to the Meeting of the Parties.[108] In addition to the functions carried out by the Working Group, in the early phases of the regime, a more 'personal' communication function carried out by UNEP's leader Tolba can also be noted. For instance in his opening statement to the first meeting of the Open-Ended Working Group in 1989, on the basis of the panel reports, he made several specific recommendations for adjustments and amendments to the Montreal Protocol for consideration by the participants.[109]

So, how should we assess the ozone science–politics model? First, the impression is definitely that the ozone scientific–political complex has achieved a rather effective way of functioning in a short period of time – like many other aspects of this regime development. Second, it is not easy to say how much of the apparently well-functioning science–politics dialogue can be credited to the organizational model *per se*. As the panels have been regarded as forums 'with the stamp of international objectivity and authoritativeness',[110] international institutional design seems to have mattered at least a bit. Moreover, effective two-way communication between the panels and the Meetings of the Parties seems to have been achieved, partly with the Open-Ended Working Group as mediator. Hence, it has been indicated that after 1987, with institutionalization of scientists' roles in the assessment panels, scientists' influence over the negotiations has advanced their previous agenda-setting role to the exercise of substantial influence over certain aspects of the negotiated decisions.[111] Referring to the process leading up to the London 1990 meeting, Gehring (1994:277) maintains that 'never before in the decade-long process of development of the international regime for the protection of the ozone-layer had the scientific and technical knowledge necessary as a foundation for political negotiations been prepared with similar care'. Hence, and in conclusion, the ozone model has developed over time, with the formal establishment of a review panel process in 1988 as an important watershed event. The organizational model has functioned well, and may be an important institutional contributing factor in shedding light on the rather high effectiveness achieved so far.

5.4.6 Verification and Compliance Mechanisms: Innovative Sticks; Complicated Carrots?

In terms of institutional verification and compliance challenges, the ozone depletion issue area was initially characterized by both 'benign' and more 'malign' aspects. The initial limited number of major producers and consumer countries and industries was of course a positive aspect. On the more complicating side, the importance of industrial and technological substance substitution as well as the trade component gave topical interest to concerns over industrial secrecy and competitiveness. The Vienna Convention, related to its lack of specific, regulatory components, only contained a general paragraph on the transmission of information; 'in such form and at such intervals as the meetings of the parties to the relevant instruments may determine' (Article 6). In line with the regulatory development and specification in the Montreal Protocol, a more specific compliance regime began to take form. In Article 7, the parties were required to provide annual data on production, imports and exports of all controlled substances. Moreover, Article 8 called for the development of a non-compliance regime, to be adopted at the first Meeting of the Parties. However, the development of such a regime took time, due to the new, complex and in certain respects sensitive character of the issue.[112] Hence, it was not before the parties' fourth meeting in Copenhagen in 1992 that such a regime was adopted.[113] Before continuing on this subject, let us dwell a bit on the reporting requirements and practical experiences.

The data reporting part of the ozone regime is based on two main pillars.[114] First, reports from the parties are required concerning the production, export and destruction of ozone-depleting substances, both with regard to 1986 baseline data and annual data thereafter.[115] Second, the Secretariat receives these reports; processes and analyses them; and produces summary compliance reports (which are public) to the Implementation Committee as well as the Meetings of the Parties. In terms of reporting practice, recent reports and reviews indicate serious reporting problems.[116] To mention some of these problems: many countries do not report on time: for instance, with regard to the 136 parties due to report for 1994, only 57 parties (42%) had reported by October 1995.[117] Moreover, many reports have been 'consistently incomplete': of the 126 parties due to report for 1993, only 69 parties (54%) had reported complete data by October 1995.[118] In addition, baseline data (1986 or 1989) have been missing for a number of countries. In general, as reporting capacity is higher in the industrialized countries than in the developing countries and the CEIT, reporting practice has been better in the former than in the last two groups of countries.[119] Related to the issue characteristics indicated at the beginning of this section, there is also a confidentiality dimension surrounding these reports.[120] Nearly all data involved are confidential, and only total national production and consumption of regulated substances are reported publicly. Due to commercial considerations, only broad groups of chemicals are reported, and exports and imports are not reported as separate categories. An additional issue in this context is the refusal of the EC countries to provide data on the national level, making it impossible to assess the compliance of individual European states. EC countries only report to the EC Commission, and these reports remain confidential. Overall, then, given these problems, is the reporting system a failure? According to Norwegian regime participants, reporting must overall be regarded as surprisingly good, given global participation and substantial variation in administrative capacities. The will to report is clearly there.[121] Other sources support this picture of a steadily improving system, despite deficiencies, not least due to the fine job done by the Secretariat.[122] The question of success or failure is of course also a relative one.

Let us then return to the broader compliance issue and first take a closer look at the more specific Montreal Protocol non-compliance procedures. The idea of developing such a mechanism was put forward by the US during the 1987 Montreal negotiations, but took several years to put into practice.[123] The main principles were adopted at the 1992 Copenhagen meeting.[124] The procedure included a general aim to avoid complexity: to be non-confrontational (although an investigative process could be initiated either by other parties or the Secretariat); to be transparent; and to leave the decision-making to the Meeting of the Parties. As a very interesting institutional innovation, a specific Implementation Committee was established in 1990.[125] The Committee was composed of ten parties, two from each of the five main geographical regions of the world, elected for a two-year period. The Committee's main formal functions were to consider and report on any complaint from, or reference by, a party; to consider and report on the annual report of the Secretariat; to request, where necessary, further information on cases before it; to undertake, 'upon the invitation of the Party concerned', data compilation inside the territory of that party; and to exchange information with the financial mechanism of the Montreal Protocol.[126] Moreover, the Committee could decide to present cases of potential non-compliance to the Meeting of the Parties. Formally, the outcome of this process could be trade sanctions against states unwilling to sign the agreement or abide by its provisions. Up to 1994, the Committee's work mainly focused on reporting problems, especially related to baseline data, in close cooperation with the Secretariat. 'Mild' forms of pressure and technical assistance from the Committee contributed to increased reporting.[127] In 1995, the Non-Compliance Procedure was invoked for the first time, related to the looming non-compliance of five countries with economies in transition (Belarus, Bulgaria, Poland, Russia, and Ukraine).[128] Initially, this case was handled by the Secretariat and the Technology and Economics Assessment Panel, indicating a fine-tuned institutional balance between several bodies within the regime. Without going into the details of this complex case, it can be concluded that the approach taken within the Implementation Committee has been a basically cooperative one (in line with the general principles summed up above), with an emphasis on various forms of assistance to secure compliance – however *not* offering extensions or adjustments of the regulatory obligations undertaken. This has been characterized as important in principle.[129] Generally, the development of the work of the Implementation Committee – from 'milder' reporting problems to tougher non-compliance issues – is of course a reflection of the generally rougher political terrain which the ozone regime is now entering.

The main 'positive' compliance-strengthening element in the ozone regime is undoubtedly the establishment of the Multilateral Fund, financed by developed countries, in order to pay for developing countries' incremental costs inherent in meeting control obligations, and some technology transfer provisions.[130] The idea of a fund arose in the process leading up to the 1990 London Conference, related to the stricter phase-out control measures in the pipeline. After complicated negotiations, characterized as the most difficult issue in the entire 1990 treaty revision process,[131] a compromise financial mechanism was laid out in Article 10 in the London Revisions. The Multilateral Fund, financed by the industrialized countries and based on the principle of additionality, was to be overseen by an Executive Committee with a balanced 14-member North–South representation, in cooperation with the World Bank, UNEP and the United Nations Development Programme (UNDP). The Executive Committee has a Secretariat in Montreal, with a three-year operating budget of $7.6 million (drawn from the fund), and nine professional staff. The first three-year budget of the interim Multilateral Fund was stipulated to be 'up to' \$240 million, with a 25% contribution from the US and nearly 35% from the EC (based on the UN assessment scale).[132] At the eighth Meeting of the Parties, a replenishment of the Multilateral Fund at a level of 540 million dollars was decided for the period 1997–99.[133]

In terms of practice, the initial phase of the Fund was slow, and encountered problems like staffing delays and turf battles between involved agencies. The voluntary contributions from the industrialized countries have so far been inadequate, and this goes especially for the CEIT. At the 1996 eighth Meeting of the Parties, as in the preceding period, a shortfall of \$74 million was realized for the 1994–1996 period.[134] Still, by 1996, 76 country programmes had been approved, and the coverage of the Fund's activities had been expanded to over 99 countries. Moreover, by October 1996, 12 612 tonnes of CFCs had been phased out, from a projected 75 300 tonnes phase-out.[135] As already noted, this has in no way been enough to stem the tide of rising ODS production and consumption in the developing countries. This touches upon what has been termed a fundamental 'contractual difficulty' within the regime, as 'Article 5 countries are allowed to increase their consumption of ODS during the Period that the Fund is paying for projects to phase out their ODS use' (DeSombre and Kaufman, 1996:125). Hence, some progress has been made, but important bureaucratic and strategic problems remain. It has for instance been indicated that the World Bank is ill-suited for these types of projects, and as indicated above, the job may in itself be characterized as ambiguous and lacking focus and direction.[136] Lacking progress in this regard may lead to reduced willingness from the developing countries to take on new obligations and implement existing ones. Hence, there is a complicated interplay of factors, and both 'vicious circles' and 'positive circles' are imaginable.

Summing up, on the procedural side, the ozone regime must be characterized as quite advanced (reflected for instance in the attention given to this regime by international law experts). This is related first and foremost to its non-compliance regime, which includes a specific implementation committee, and to the establishment of a special Multilateral Fund to aid developing countries' implementation efforts. In practice, the ozone regime has so far experienced serious reporting problems, and the Fund has not functioned as expected, although there has been some improvement. Hence, overall, despite problems, procedural and practical verification and compliance improvements *may* have contributed to more recent regime development and effectiveness,[137] but only the establishment and functioning of the Fund can be regarded as more fundamental causal factors. It is very probable that without this accommodation of developing countries' interests, global collaboration on ozone-layer politics could have broken down entirely in the 1990s.

5.5 CONCLUDING COMMENTS: IS THE OZONE INSTITUTIONAL MODEL AN ESPECIALLY POWERFUL ONE?

Overall, the first decade of the ozone regime must be characterized as quite effective. The international regulatory development has clearly been impressive. Despite reporting problems and a lack of national knowledge, available national data indicate that the required behavioural changes are largely being implemented, although more easily and fully in the North than in the East and South – and clearly influenced by the international process. In terms of the environmental and problem-solving dimension, the match between evolving knowledge and international policy responses has been high, and the first atmospheric signs of effective regulations can be detected. Hence, addressing implementation failures in the East and not least the increasing production and consumption of ODS in the South are the main challenges for upholding regime effectiveness in the years ahead. These issues make it more uncertain whether the next decade of the ozone regime will prove equally effective.

But what does 'clearly influenced by the international process' mean, more specifically? As far as I can see, there are only a few specific institutional design candidates capable of shedding light on the relatively high effectiveness achieved so far. One is the issue of varied and 'dense' participation. 'Dense' refers especially to the critical first five years of the regime's functioning, which saw several major conferences and more regular meetings of the actual and potential parties. This is partly related to the two-tier development of the regime, with a parallel Vienna Convention and Montreal Protocol meeting system. These many meeting points are of course a reflection of the priority given to this issue by the parties, but the multitude of meetings in turn also contributed to scientific and political knowledge and confidence-building among the parties. Hence, as in several other instances, a complex interplay between 'exogenous' and 'endogenous' institutional factors may be noted. Varied participation refers to the fact that a constructive balance seems to have evolved both with regard to outsiders' access and the level of participation. With regard to NGO access, overall openness has been combined with selective inclusiveness throughout this process, in the form of smaller and more informal workshops, meetings and working groups. With regard to level of participation, extensive ministerial participation at crucial points in the regime's development has added important political weight to the more continuous bureaucrat- and scientist-driven process in the multitude of regime bodies.

Second, two specific institutional mechanisms are salient. There is the issue of restrictions on trade with non-parties, in order to prevent non-participating countries from gaining competitive advantages. According to several sources, these clauses have worked effectively in terms of increasing state participation. Also, the establishment of the Multilateral Fund must of course also be noted, as an innovative way of dealing with the special needs of the South related to these issues. Without the Fund, the further participation of important developing countries like India and China could have been uncertain, with important symbolic effects for other developing countries. However, given the fact that the financing and functioning of the Fund have been problematic so far, the actual causal significance seems modest. Still, given the important future role of developing country action, the Fund is one of the most important institutional factors for continued regime progress.

Third, a constructive, evolving interaction between the Secretariat, the Advisory Panels, the Open-Ended Working Group of the Parties, and the Implementation Committee must be noted as a clear institutional strength. Although only the Implementation Committee can be regarded as an institutional innovation in itself, the evolving interaction of these bodies in terms of research coordination and synthesis/'translation', reporting improvements and non-compliance issues has given the regime parties a substantial international administrative back-up.

Finally, on the institutional side, some readers have no doubt missed an analysis of the role of regime regulation design in the preceding discussion. Without opening up this discussion too far, an important prominent aspect is the basic flexibility built into the regime. This is evident both in terms of an explicit acknowledgement of the need to review regime regulations in light of evolving scientific evidence at periodic intervals, and the 'adjustment' procedure for substances already controlled, preventing a complicated ratification process for at least *some* of the decisions made within the regime.

Still, as indicated earlier, the impression is clearly that the change in characteristics describing problems, preferences and capabilities – from 'moderately malign' to 'relatively benign' – can shed considerable light over the effectiveness of the ozone regime so far. Although starting out as an intellectually complex problem, relying heavily on computer models and dealing with uncertain long-term effects, consensus and certainty have increased quite rapidly; largely due to a broad-based international research effort. This alone indicates that the issue of *interplay* between the development of problem characteristics and the activity of international institutions is an important one. Due to the global, indivisible character of the radiation-shielding ozone layer, all states would be negatively affected by increased ultraviolet radiation (although the degree of vulnerability might vary somewhat), and no nations could perceive any benefits from ozone layer depletion. Moreover, the causes of the problem lie in a relatively small group of substances (though larger than initially realized), at first produced mainly by the US and some

European countries (though with the rapidly growing participation of developing countries both in terms of production and consumption), and utilized primarily in refrigeration and cooling, which may be regarded as only moderately important societal activities. In a positive interaction with international regulatory development, significantly enhanced by various forms of entrepreneurial leadership, technological progress has been steady. However, the latent fundamental asymmetry in every global regulatory effort has gradually been uncovered: between the rich countries of the North who can afford greener, more expensive alternative substances and the poorer countries of the South, who wish to keep present and in particular future development costs at a minimum. The basic problem structure may thus be changing again, in a more malign direction. This is due to the fact that the issues that can ensure further progress, like for instance methyl bromide, touch upon politically sensitive interests like agriculture, and also increasingly affect broader interest clashes between the North and the South.

Overall, a rough explanatory balance between 'endogenous' regime factors and 'exogenous' problem and interest factors may be suggested, with an interesting interplay issue to be clarified by further research. One obvious key to such clarification is to divide the more detailed assessment of the interaction between institutional and problems/preferences into clearly defined *phases* – to capture better the dynamics of the process.[138] For instance, the role of the Secretariat was probably quite different in the dynamic, Tolba-influenced Montreal days from the more recent, generally more grey and complicated days. However, that remains to be substantiated.

NOTES

1. In this case, interviews focusing especially on institutional issues were conducted in December 1995 with Per M. Bakken, Norwegian Ministry of Environment, and Ivar S. Isaksen, University of Oslo. In addition, I draw upon a written response to a selected list of institutional questions provided by G.M. Bankobeza, Programme Officer/Lawyer with the Ozone Secretariat, dated 6 November 1995. Thanks to Georg Børsting, Norwegian Ministry of Environment; Sebastian Oberthur, Ecologic; and Jon B. Skjærseth, FNI, for helpful comments.
2. The work of Stolarski and Cicerone suggested that chlorine atoms destroyed thousands of ozone molecules in the stratosphere, while the work of Molina and Rowlands focused on CFCs and the release of large quantities of chlorine in the upper atmosphere. See for instance Morisette (1989).
3. For further information on the regime creation process, see for instance Gehring (1994:221–234) and Parson (1993:34–40).
4. As of 1 March 1998, the Vienna Convention has been ratified by 166 parties, including the EC. See *Yearbook of International Co-operation on Environment and Development* (1998/99), pp. 78–79.
5. The Montreal Protocol entered into force in January 1989, and as of 1 March 1998, has been ratified by 165 parties including the EC (Ibid.).

6. The London amendment has as of 1 March 1998, been ratified by 120 parties including the EC (ibid.).
7. The Copenhagen amendment has as of 1 March 1998, been ratified by 81 parties including the EC (ibid.).
8. As pinpointed by Skjærseth (1992A:10).
9. 'Low-consuming' developing countries were those whose annual calculated level of consumption of the controlled substances was less than 0.3 kilograms per capita.
10. For a summary of the Copenhagen meeting, see for instance Environmental Policy and Law (1993).
11. See for instance ENDS Report (1995A) and Environmental Policy and Law (1996:66–71), for summaries of the Vienna meeting.
12. This is for instance described in International Environment Reporter (1997B and C).
13. This section is primarily based on Oberthur (1997A and B).
14. Data availability and verification and compliance issues are further discussed in section 5.4.6.
15. See for instance Greene (1996).
16. Ibid.
17. However, the Montreal Protocol's Article 5 stated that developing countries' consumption should 'not exceed an annual calculated level of consumption of 0.3 kilograms per capita'.
18. This is further discussed in section 5.4.6.
19. This section draws heavily on Skjærseth (1992A) and Parson (1993).
20. See for example, Benedick (1991:27).
21. Parson (1993:70–71) identifies at least three crucial stages where US support for the international process was threatened by a domestic backlash: 1985; 1987; and 1990. He maintains: 'For the United States, and indeed for all activists, a continuing international process provided the momentum needed to smooth over uneven commitment and attention at the national level'.
22. See Parson (1996:24–25).
23. For instance, according to Skjærseth (1991), the correspondence was 'remarkable'. Oberthur (1997 B:6) states that 'the political decisions of the Parties have always been very close to the options that appeared to be preferred in the reports of the assessment panels'. See also Skodvin (1994; forthcoming 1999).
24. Benedick (1991: 110, 133).
25. Gehring (1994:307–313).
26. NOAA et al. (1994:10).
27. Benedick (1991:10–11).
28. NOAA et al. (1994:7–8).
29. Oberthur (1997A:66–67).
30. Parson (1996).
31. NOAA et al. (1994:7, 13).
32. International Environment Reporter (1995C).
33. International Environment Reporter (1996).
34. See for instance Skjærseth (1992A); Gehring (1994); and Rowlands (1995) for general overviews of these issues.
35. See for instance Morisette et al. (1990:11).
36. See for instance Jachtenfuchs (1990) and Benedick (1991).
37. Benedick (1991:35).
38. Parson (1993:38).
39. It should be noted here that the following brief sections cover a period of ten years of complex knowledge and political development. It goes almost without saying that the following account is a broad overview and that readers interested in more specific detail with regard to scientific development, national positions, international negotiation processes and so on are advised to consult sources like Benedick (1991); Gehring (1994); Litfin (1994); and Parson and Greene (1995).
40. Cited in Benedick (1991:110).
41. Benedick (1991:104)

42. Gehring (1994:276–277); Skjærseth (1992A:34).
43. See Skjærseth (1992A:35).
44. See for instance Parson (1993:60); Benedick (1991: ch.6).
45. See for instance Benedick (1991: ch.7).
46. Parson and Greene (1995:20,35).
47. Gehring (1994).
48. Gehring (1994:9).
49. Benedick (1991:148).
50. Brown et al. (1996:68).
51. International Environment Reporter (1995D).
52. Environmental Policy and Law (1996).
53. International Environment Reporter (1997B and C).
54. See for instance Benedick (1991); Gehring (1994); Oberthur (1997B).
55. See for instance Skjærseth (1992A:46–47), building upon an interview with Bob Watson in *New Scientist*, 29 April 1989, pp. 69–70.
56. See for instance Benedick (1991: ch.5); Parson (1993:60); Gehring (1994: ch.6).
57. Benedick (1991:55–59).
58. See for instance Benedick (1991: ch.7).
59. Benedick (1991:75).
60. See for instance Skjærseth (1992A:46).
61. See Gehring (1994) and Oberthur (1997 B); the latter especially with regard to EC positions in the 1990s. For instance, the US had problems with the HCFCs issue, and the EC had problems with the methyl bromide issue.
62. *Green Globe Yearbook* (1997:97).
63. Benedick (1991); Gehring (1994:9).
64. See for example Benedick (1991: ch.12).
65. *Green Globe Yearbook* (1997:95–96).
66. See Ulfstein (1996:106), based on information from the Secretariat; and Brack (1996).
67. See Barrat-Brown (1991) for a critical discussion of NGO access to the work under the Convention and the Protocol.
68. Norwegian interviews, autumn 1995.
69. Norwegian interviews, autumn 1995.
70. Norwegian interviews, autumn 1995.
71. Greene (1996). For contributions that generally argue for extensive participation of NGOs in the various regime bodies, see Barrat-Brown (1991) and somewhat more reluctantly Victor (1995).
72. Benedick (1991:169).
73. By July 1998, 17 meetings of the Open-Ended Working Group had been held.
74. Article 9.4 in the Vienna Convention.
75. As stated in Article 9(5): 'Amendments ... shall enter into force between parties having accepted them'.
76. Montreal Protocol, Article 8c. For a summary of this discussion, see Gehring (1994:255).
77. With regard to the question of 'adjustments' and commitment here, see Montreal Protocol Article 2.9.D.
78. According to Szell (1996:213), this unusual exception to the rule that decisions taken by less than unanimity do not automatically bind the outvoted minority had its background in the fact that, at the time, 'all prospective Parties knew that the trend of the instrument was in the direction of eventual total elimination of production and consumption of all the controlled substances ... leaving open for further discussion and decision merely the secondary matter of the timing of the phase-out schedule'.
79. Montreal Protocol, Article 16.
80. J.G. Lammers; referred to by Benedick (1991:90).
81. French (1994:62).
82. Norwegian interviews, autumn 1995.
83. Communications with the Secretariat, autumn 1995.

84. UNEP/Ozl.Pro.7/12, Seventh Meeting of the Parties to the Montreal Protocol on Substances that Deplete the Ozone Layer, p.53.
85. Parson (1993:40).
86. Gehring (1994:258).
87. *Green Globe Yearbook* (1997:93–97).
88. Gehring (1994:209).
89. See Szell (1993:40–41).
90. Greene (1996).
91. Norwegian interviews, autumn 1995. See also Szell (1993:39).
92. Gehring (1994:234).
93. See Benedick (1991).
94. Benedick (1991:49,50).
95. Parson (1993).
96. Norwegian interviews, autumn 1995.
97. Benedick (1991:40).
98. Skodvin (1994:86). For a more recent general discussion of the science–politics interface within the ozone regime, see Skodvin (forthcoming 1999).
99. Morisette et al. (1990:11).
100. According to P. Haas, the ozone regime is a clear example of a case where an 'epistemic community' operated and influenced the development of the regime. See for instance Haas (1990A).
101. *Green Globe Yearbook* (1997:97).
102. See Skodvin (1994:87).
103. Gehring (1994:274).
104. UNEP/Ozl.Pro1/L.1/add. May 1989. Referred to in Skodvin (1994:87).
105. Parson (1993:61).
106. *Green Globe Yearbook* (1996:108).
107. Gehring (1994:270).
108. Communication with the Secretariat, November 1995.
109. See UNEP /Ozl.Pro.WG.I(2)/4, 4 September 1989. Pinpointed in Skodvin (1994:89).
110. Parson (1993:61).
111. Ibid.
112. Szell (1995:99).
113. For a discussion of the Montreal Protocols' non-compliance regime from a legal perspective, see Koskenniemi (1992).
114. See Oberthur (1997A).
115. With regard to consumption, information is derived from reports on production, imports and exports, and substances destroyed. Communication with Sebastian Oberthur 5 May 1997.
116. For more general discussions, see for instance Parson and Greene (1995); Parson (1996); Oberthur (1997 A).
117. *Green Globe Yearbook* (1996:107).
118. *Green Globe Yearbook* (1996).
119. Oberthur (1997A:11).
120. See Parson and Greene (1995:37–38).
121. Norwegian interviews, autumn 1995.
122. Oberthur (1997A:61) states: 'As a result of recent improvements, there is in most cases a comparatively good fit between global production and consumption data at least in the case of the major ODS (CFCs and halons in particular)'.
123. See Szell (1995:99–103).
124. Gehring (1994:315–319); Szell (1995).
125. For more details on the functioning of the Implementation Committee, see Victor (1995); Parson and Greene (1995); Greene (1996).
126. Environmental Policy and Law (1989).
127. Parson and Greene (1995); Victor (1995).
128. Victor (1995).

129. See Greene (1996) for a more detailed discussion of this case.
130. For more general discussions of the functioning of the Fund, see for instance Parson and Greene (1995); DeSombre and Kaufman (1996); and Biermann (1997).
131. Benedick (1991:152).
132. Skjærseth (1992A:43–44); Parson (1993:50–51).
133. *Green Globe Yearbook* (1997:95).
134. *Global Environmental Change Report* (1996).
135. *Green Globe Yearbook* (1997:95).
136. In addition to DeSombre and Kaufman (1996), see also Parson and Greene (1995:38–41) and Parson (1996).
137. For instance, according to Victor (1995:5), 'perhaps only ten percent of the improved data reporting can be traced to the activities of the Implementation Committee'. This may well be 'no mean accomplishment' as stated by Victor, but such assessments are clouded by various uncertainties, especially as the background for the 10% assessment is not provided.
138. Parson (1993) contains interesting institutional pieces to such a more dynamic puzzle; see for instance pp.64–68.

6. Combining Comparative and Case Study Evidence: Institutional Findings

6.1 INTRODUCTION

After the case-by-case presentations in the previous chapters, the natural next step is a more comprehensive analytical effort. Hence, this chapter has as an important ingredient a comparative analysis, taking into account however the challenging nature of such a venture. The first section takes on the first and in many ways fundamental comparative challenge, related to the effectiveness scores of the respective regimes. Are there clear differences in effectiveness between the regimes? The following section addresses important elements in the simplifying notion of 'all other things being equal' as utilized in connection with the institutional and organizational assumptions. How similar are the focused regimes with regard to various control factors? The third and main section contains the institutional discussion. The focused institutional factors and developments from the different cases are briefly summed up in comparative tables, followed by discussions of case-specific and comparative evidence related to each institutional factor.

But let us first turn to the crucial and complex question of possible differences in effectiveness.

6.2 ARE THERE DIFFERENCES IN EFFECTIVENESS BETWEEN THE REGIMES?

Let us first briefly consider the effectiveness assessments related to each of our four cases. Beginning with the closely related OSCON and PARCON regimes, let me first sum up the relatively straightforward OSCON development. It seems reasonable to divide the development of this regime into two main phases, with the 1987 London North Sea Conference (NSC) as a symbolic turning point. Before 1987, the most important dumping problems – dumping of industrial waste, contaminated sewage sludge, incineration at sea, and dredge spoil – were regulated by convention provisions and recommendations adopted in the Commission to control dumping. National behavioural change seemed marginal. In the wake of the 1987 NSC, a process started that implied a shift from 'dumping control' to a gradual phasing out of all dumping. By 1990, it had been decided to phase out incineration in the north-east Atlantic by 1991, industrial waste by 1996 (1989 in the North Sea), and sewage sludge at the latest by 1998. Accordingly, national behavioural changes and a significant decline in dumping took place. Given the development sketched above, it seems pretty clear that both dumping-related marine pollution policies and problems would have been quite different without the decisions taken within the Oslo Commission (OSCOM) and the related North Sea Conference forum. Another matter is whether it is equally effective if transaction costs and questions of broader resource priorities are included in the picture, but this will not be pursued further in this connection. Hence, it makes sense tentatively to give the OSCON regime a *high* effectiveness score.

Turning to the PARCON regime, this case has both similarities and differences compared with OSCON. A similar feature is that the 1987 North Sea Conference had much of the same 'watershed' effect on this cooperation – also splitting its history into two parts. Regarding the early phase of PARCON, judged on the basis of the nature of the international regulations agreed upon (that is, few and general) and available knowledge on national processes in the UK, Netherlands and Norway, it seems reasonable to assume a low degree of behavioural effectiveness. Much points in the direction of a significant increase in political effectiveness in the wake of the 1987 NSC, related to a complex interplay between the North Sea Conference and PARCON processes. Not least on the basis of the more easily measured NSC implementation processes, significant behavioural change has definitely taken place – although in several respects not sufficient to fulfil international targets. National evidence from the UK, the Netherlands and Norway indicates that land-based marine pollution policies in the area would clearly have been different without PARCON, but less different than in the case of OSCON and dumping.

With regard to the different and tricky environmental and problem-solving dimensions: although the relationship between science and politics has been clarified over time and the match improved, it seems highly questionable whether the measures undertaken so far have meant much more than a rough upholding of the status quo. Hence, based on current knowledge, it makes sense to give PARCON tentatively a somewhat lower effectiveness score than OSCON, which points towards a roughly *medium* score.

Let us then move on to a regime covering a much wider region than the two above: the LRTAP regime, dealing with acid rain and air pollution. The formal development of this regime is somewhat different from the two foregoing, as regulatory development has taken place in the form of several protocols related to specific substances. Data on emissions reductions and behavioural changes related to the substance that has been given most regulatory attention so far –

sulphur dioxide, SO_2 – indicate that substantial behavioural changes have taken place. Compared to the formal 30% reduction target, considerable 'over-compliance' can be found in several of the countries, and all signatories end up as compliers. Regarding the NO_x protocol, compliance evidence indicates that a majority of the parties reached the stabilization target. Hence, some behavioural change seems to have taken place. With regard to VOCs, some limited action seems to have occurred. However, on the one hand, a substantial part of the behavioural changes undertaken in relation to protocols established so far seems to have little or nothing at least *directly* to do with the LRTAP regime. On the other hand, symbolized by several additional protocol negotiation processes recently concluded or in progress, the LRTAP regime has undoubtedly changed the national perceptions and agendas with regard to air pollution problems and politics. Hence, a counterfactual assessment points to a quite similar tentative conclusion to that for PARCON: without LRTAP, air pollution policies would clearly have been different, but at least in some countries, not necessarily drastically different. In terms of the environmental and problem-solving dimensions, the transboundary acidification and air pollution problems have been reduced, but 'solution' and getting below 'critical loads' in both the rural and urban environment are partly related to the implementation of more newly established regulations and to the revision of established regulations and to the consideration of various new substances and sub-problems. In reality, this is a venture extending well into the next century. Hence, overall, it makes sense in this case also to characterize effectiveness tentatively as roughly *medium*.

We now move on to the final regime, which is global and 'atmospheric': the ozone regime (Vienna Convention/Montreal Protocol). Regulatory development within this regime has evolved in a slightly different manner from the regimes discussed so far: although it too started out with a loose framework convention in 1985, the regulatory grip was tightened considerably with the 1987 Montreal Protocol, and has been gradually tightened further through several rounds of revisions in 1990, 1992 and to some degree 1995 and 1997. This regulatory development has been accompanied and underpinned by an organized, collaborative scientific effort, and has represented a clear international driving force for the technological development of substitute substances. Moreover, despite reporting problems and a lack of national knowledge, available national data indicate that the required behavioural changes are largely being implemented, although more faithfully in the North than in the East and South. Hence, at least in the industrialized countries, the ozone-depleting substances are well on their way to being phased out, production- and consumption-wise. These measures will not immediately solve the problem, as already-emitted gases will continue their attack on the ozone layer for several decades. However, in the most crucial regulatory period in the last part of the 1980s and the first part of the 1990s, there seems to have been a remarkable match between science and politics. The evolution of science and consequent reduction of uncertainty were steadily followed by more and more radical political decisions within a short time span. The crucial counterfactual assessment here turns out then to be quite similar to the case of OSCON: one definitely get the feeling that the ozone policies and problems, and especially perspectives (as time lags are substantial) would have been much worse without the international regulatory process. However, there are several signals that we are entering rougher territory, witnessed for instance in implementation failures in the East and rapidly increasing production and consumption of ODS in the South. Still, it makes sense to characterize effectiveness as quite *high* so far.

This rough overview indicates that the synchronic comparative venture in this context involves two quite effective regimes and two regimes with a more medium, intermediate effectiveness score. It seems pretty clear that OSCON and the ozone regime must be regarded as more effective than the two other regimes in this sample. With regard to OSCON, behaviourally, a virtual phase-out of dumping has been decided upon, and is being implemented. This development must also be regarded as a quite effective solution to this particular north-east Atlantic marine pollution problem complex. True, the OSCON regime had a substantial and not very effective 'warm-up' period where little happened, but this is more or less the case with all the regimes we are dealing with here. In fact, given the complex nature of international collaboration in general, and the high degree of various types of uncertainty related to environmental and pollution issues in particular, generally speaking it does not seem reasonable to expect a very high degree of effectiveness in the first, formative years of such regimes. Regarding the ozone regime, international regulatory action has been comparatively very rapid, and international measures which will lead to rough problem-solving have been decided upon and are well on their way to being implemented – although implementation problems in the East and not least production and consumption developments in the South cast a sinister shadow over this picture.

Although it makes a lot of sense to rank the two other regimes – PARCON and LRTAP – as somewhat less effective than the two above, they are indeed very hard to rank in relation to one another. Both regimes have seemingly spurred some emissions reductions and behavioural change, and it may very well be that PARCON, clearly inspired and aided by the North Sea Conference processes in the 1990s, has achieved more than LRTAP. On the other hand, zooming in on regulative development, it may be argued that the development of the 'critical loads' approach within LRTAP and the significant role played by this approach in the establishment of the revised Sulphur Protocol and the several new and advanced protocols underway, are more significant achievements in a more long-term perspective than the recent policy development within PARCON. Hence, ranking these regimes more precisely in relation to one another involves among other things a tricky balancing act between achievements so far and regulatory development and future implications. However, in addition to this synchronic comparative opportunity, there are clearly diachronic analytical possibilities related to all the regimes. Most marked in this respect are the closely related OSCON and PARCON regimes. As these regimes contain a much more marked watershed event than the other cases – the 1987 North Sea Conference decisions – they are especially singled out in the ensuing analysis.

Summing up, we are basically left with one important diachronic option and two synchronic comparative options. The focused diachronic comparative effort involves the closely related OSCON and PARCON regimes, where the main question becomes: is the marked shift in effectiveness over time within these regimes caused by changes in institutional design? The focused synchronic comparative options involve the two most effective regimes – OSCON and ozone – versus the two more moderately effective regimes – PARCON and LRTAP. The main question here is whether the two most effective regimes are marked by a similar and particularly effective institutional design compared to the less effective regimes.

However, before we can start the focused institutional and organizational comparison and discussion, the comparative foundation has to be refined a bit more. In line with traditional comparative logic, the simplifying premise of 'all other things being equal' was introduced in Chapter 2. The pertinent question is then to what extent this premise matches the empirical realities in the cases discussed here.

6.3 ARE 'ALL OTHER THINGS EQUAL'? SOME NOTES ON COMPARATIVE FEASIBILITY

Although there are definitely some similarities in problem characteristics and process-related leadership between some of these regimes, there are also a number of differences. This represents a considerable challenge to the comparative venture. That is also why an important method for assessing the importance of institutional factors is more detailed case analysis and efforts at tracing important causal pathways. However, in order to draw out as much as possible of the diachronic and synchronic comparative potential inherent in our cases, it is important to be aware of differences in problem features and process-related leadership which may contribute to spurious conclusions. As indicated above, we have one especially focused diachronic option involving the closely related OSCON and PARCON regimes, and two main synchronic comparative options involving the two most effective regimes – OSCON and ozone – versus the two more moderately effective regimes – PARCON and LRTAP. Hence, as a structuring device for this brief discussion of the basic comparability of the regimes, let us first sum up the basic problem and process similarity and development of OSCON and PARCON; then add ozone to the OSCON picture in order to get a notion of the two most effective regimes' problem and process similarity; and then finally add LRTAP to the PARCON picture in order to get a notion of the two less effective regimes' problem and process similarity.

Let us first turn to a very brief account of problem development related to OSCON and PARCON. With regard to general similarity, they have both been dealing with marine pollution within the same regional context. Moreover, much of the same political dynamic in terms of leadership may roughly be discerned in the two regimes. An interplay between the Nordic countries and the Netherlands can be discerned in both regimes, although the role of the Dutch was probably more important within PARCON than within OSCON. But there are also obvious differences between the regimes. First and foremost, PARCON has undoubtedly been dealing with a more malign problem than OSCON. The dumping problems addressed by OSCON were initially surrounded by a high degree of ecological, technological and economic uncertainty. There were also marked differences in vulnerability and abatement costs among the participants. Regarding the land-based pollution problems addressed by PARCON, uncertainty was initially high, both with regard to inputs, concentrations and effects. Compared to the dumping activities, the industries and activities contributing to land-based pollution problems were in general far more important for most of the states, and international competitive effects related to abatement measures were highly relevant. But in addition to initial differences in malignity, there is little doubt that the dumping problems over time developed in a more benign way. For instance, important countries unilaterally ended dumping in the North Sea, and problems like incineration at sea developed from a malign incentive problem to a more benign coordination problem. The land-based problems changed less drastically. Scientific uncertainty was reduced and communicated better to decision-makers through the work of the North Sea Task Force. But the basic competitive aspects related to abatement measures pretty much remained. Hence, summing up the OSCON–PARCON picture: *although there are several contextual similarities, the dumping problems were less important and malign than the land-based problems at the outset. Over time, the dumping problems also developed in a more benign way than the land-based problems.*

Turning then to the most effective regimes, OSCON and ozone, the basic features and development of the dumping problems have already been described. The ozone problem was initially a complex problem, marked by high uncertainty and low consensus, although with some politically advantageous features like the fact that no countries had anything to gain from ozone layer depletion and all states would be negatively affected by such depletion. However, the knowledge situation improved considerably over a fairly short time-span, and not least, it became clear that societal benefits related to the phasing out of important ozone depleting substances like the CFCs clearly outweighed costs. Moreover, conflicts over substitution costs and competitive effects turned out to be manageable, at least in the North. In addition, a basic point is of course that both the production and consumption of ozone-depleting substances were and are not crucially important for the economic development of states. Also, the activities were relatively few in number and easy to pin down, compared for instance to the numerous emission types and myriad of emission sources contributing to land-based marine pollution. However, in a comparative perspective, there are of course some very important differences between the North Sea dumping and global ozone problems and processes. The one that most immediately springs to mind is the fact that the OSCON dumping problems involve and affect a limited number of states within perhaps the comparatively richest region in the world; while the ozone depletion problems affect the whole globe, and production facilities and trade have also increasingly become globalized. Moreover, in terms of process-related leadership, there seem to be marked differences, with heavies politically on the world stage such as the US and the EC in turn carrying the regulatory torch within the ozone regime. As indicated earlier, process-related leadership seems to have been far less marked within the dumping regime. Hence, summing up the OSCON-ozone picture: *both these problems have several benign features, with the relatively limited economic importance of the problem-creating activities as a central aspect. And both developed in a benign way in terms of knowledge and cost–benefit calculations. But ozone depletion is a global problem with many and heterogeneous actors, while dumping has been a regional problem involving quite homogeneous actors. On the other hand, there has been much heavier leadership in the ozone case.*

Finally, a very brief summary of the somewhat less effective PARCON and LRTAP regimes' problem features and processes, which in some respects in fact may be more similar than OSCON and PARCON. First and foremost, this applies to the basic malignity and development of problems. As can be recalled, regarding the land-based pollution problems addressed by PARCON, uncertainty was characterized as high, both with regard to inputs, concentrations and effects. The industries and activities contributing to land-based pollution problems were important for the states, and international competitive effects related to abatement measures were probable. Switching then to the transboundary air pollution problems addressed by LRTAP, initial uncertainty was also high, and the basic transboundary transport thesis was disputed. As in the case of marine pollution, abatement measures would affect the international competitive situation of important industrial branches. With regard to the development of these two problems, there are rough similarities. There has been a marked knowledge improvement process in both regimes, but probably most advanced within the acid rain regime, symbolized by the identification of environmental 'critical loads', on which regulations may roughly be built. With regard to the political development of these regimes, this is of course a multifaceted issue, and both similarities and differences exist. Some broad similarities can be noted: for instance, none of the problems developed in a very benign fashion. In both regimes, the pollution problems considered were gradually seen as more complex and involving more substances – and a probable interplay between these substances was increasingly realized. Both regimes contained a basic regulatory clash between the UK and most of the other participants, this was the important conflict line in substantial time periods in both regimes, but it gradually decreased. However, the transboundary air pollution problems of course contained an important East–West dimension, which increased the cooperative challenge in several ways. With regard to process-related leadership, it was definitely carried out within both regimes, but by various and changing actors over time. Hence, summing up the PARCON–LRTAP picture: *there are also here several similarities between the problems, but also obvious differences, perhaps most marked in the East–West broader problem scope within the LRTAP regime.*

Hence, this overview of basic comparative similarity indicates that although there are differences in problem characteristics between the two rather effective ozone and dumping regimes and between the two somewhat less effective marine land-based and transboundary air pollution regimes, the overall picture provided by these cases is roughly in line with the hypothesis that high effectiveness is caused by more benign problems and low effectiveness is caused by more malign problems.[1] But this does in no way rule out institutional contributions. First, the diachronic case of OSCON and PARCON developments indicated marked increases in effectiveness in spite of substantial problem stability. Moreover, more generally, problems seldom develop in a more benign way 'on their own', and regime contributions, for instance in the form of the coordination and organization of knowledge production processes, is a very relevant causal candidate. In this context, let us turn to the more detailed institutional scrutiny.

6.4 THE RELEVANCE OF THE INSTITUTIONAL FACTORS: COMBINING CASE EVIDENCE AND COMPARATIVE CLUES

6.4.1 The Multifaceted Issues of Access and Participation: Scope, Outsiders' Access and Level of Participation

Let us first briefly repeat the focused dimensions and the suggested fundamental assumptions guiding the analytical work conducted. The obvious dimension to focus on first has to do with the fundamental scope of the cooperation, with the most relevant distinction being between a regional and global scope. This distinction is of course closely related to important problem characteristics, but there are also regional, more limited options related to global problems. Anyway, the basic assumption here was that, in a short-term perspective, regimes with few and homogeneous participants tend to be more effective than regimes with many and heterogeneous participants, regardless of the true problem scope. However, in the longer-term perspective, it is more doubtful whether regimes not covering all major contributors to the environmental and resource problems addressed can remain effective. Given that at the regional level it is easier to achieve both a good match between problem scope and participation, and benefit from smaller group dynamics, it seems reasonable to assume that regional regimes tend to be more effective than global ones, irrespective of the time perspective.

The next dimension shifted attention away from states and formal parties towards the question of various types of interested, non-state actors' access to and participation in regime activities like meetings of the parties. This cluster of issues raises important questions of balance between the need for legitimate, broad-based international activities and the need for effective decision-making. These are questions of the balancing of different considerations and different needs in different phases, and if seen as an inclusiveness continuum, it seems reasonable to assume that regimes with a generally inclusive access and participation profile tend to be more effective than regimes with a more exclusive profile.

The final dimension shifted the attention again back somewhat towards the state level and focused on the question of the type of state representatives. A central distinction here is between administrative level, 'bureaucratic' participants and higher level 'political' participants like ministers. Given the need for regular political 'vitalization' of regime activities, the basic assumption in this connection goes like this: regimes with regular higher-level political participation in regime activities tend to be more effective than regimes which do not have, or have only rarely, such 'political' participation. Let us then turn to an overview of the case evidence.

Table 6.1   Access and participation: the overview picture

	OSCON	PARCON	North Sea Conferences	LRTAP	OZONE
Partici-patory scope	The broader north-east Atlantic region. Important change in 1988; 'differentiated' decisions and actual decoupling of reluctant states outside the nucleus group of North Sea states.	The broader north-east Atlantic region. Same 'differen-tiation' change in 1988 as OSCON, and much of the same effects.	The narrower and more homo-geneous North Sea region.	Regional European 'plus'; with East–West and North American dimensions. Some variation with regard to actual partici-pation in the various protocols.	In principle global, as problem scope is global. In practice, over time, all important producer and consumer countries of ozone-depleting substances have come to partici-pate in the regime, partly induced by 'positive' and 'negative' incentives.
Outsiders' access and partici-pation	Restricted and limited access and partici-pation up to 1990; more inclusive after 1990.	Same as OSCON.	Quite inclusive from the 1987 Conference and onwards.	Overall quite inclusive all along, both with regard to industrial and environmen-tal groups. Exclusive concluding phases of negotiation processes.	Overall inclusive; in order to com-bine different types of relevant knowledge and interests. Frequent use of smaller workshops. Also more exclusive forums and phases.
Ministerial versus adminis-trative partici-pation	First decade administratively dominated; recent decade regular minis-terial inputs through the NSCs in 1987, 1990, 1993 and 1995; in addi-tion the 1992 Ministerial OSPARCOM meeting.	Same as OSCON.	Ministerial conferences; visible political fights attracting media and NGO attention.	Due to the regular proto-col negotiations (around 3–4 years), inter-play between bureaucratic/ lower profile and political/high profile processes.	Fairly frequent high ministerial-level involve-ment. Several presidents and prime ministers have been person-ally involved in the negotia-tion processes. Most marked in early phase.

Summing up the development over time of OSCON, PARCON, and the closely related North Sea Conferences (NSCs), can we point to developments in terms of issues related to access and participation that may throw light over the marked increase in effectiveness? As indicated in Table 6.1, several access and participation changes may throw light on the marked increase in OSCON and PARCON effectiveness from the late 1980s on. First, the 1988 introduction of differentiated decisions within OSCON and PARCON, explicitly justified by differing geographical, hydrological and ecological conditions within the convention area, allowed the decoupling of less ambitious parties like Spain and Portugal. Second, the OSPARCON system changed in a more inclusive direction from 1990 on. Third, the continuous closely related higher profile North Sea Conference process – with four conferences in the years 1987–1995 – meant generally higher involvement of NGOs, media and politicians in the cooperative process in this latter period. Still, it should definitely be noted that the political NSC process can and must build upon and feed its results into the continuous, legally binding and systematic work within the Commissions and their related bodies. Hence, there are interesting interplay effects and complementarity of functions at work here.

Comparing then OSCON and ozone, do they represent opposite approaches? Even if OSCON and ozone have roughly similar effectiveness scores, access and participation scores seem to differ a bit. As a general comment, the inclusive approach chosen within the ozone regime is closely related to central problem characteristics and has contributed positively to the development of the regime. In terms of the more specific impact on regime development and effectiveness, two key institutional issues stand out. First, institutional density, both in terms of many meetings within a quite short time period and substantial high-level and ministerial participation, contributed to the rapid progress in the late 1980s and early 1990s. Moreover, *specific institutional mechanisms* in the form of prospects of financial and technological assistance and fears of trade sanctions as a regime non-member served to increase the regulatory scope and bite of the regime and to enhance regime legitimacy and robustness over time. The OSCON development path is quite different, but the development of a more inclusive policy-making style in this context has also had positive and vitalizing effects. However, both cases contain an interesting interplay between more secluded phases and forums and more inclusive and high-profile processes.

Finally, comparing PARCON and LRTAP, are there both similarities and differences? Even if PARCON and LRTAP have roughly similar effectiveness scores, the access and participation profiles of the regimes exhibit both differences and similarities. Overall, the most striking participatory difference between the two regimes lies in the state participatory scope, where LRTAP contains a wider scope of participants than PARCON – despite a basic

European, regional focus. Hence, compared for instance to the more effective and 'narrower' dumping regime, this aspect is a potential candidate with regard to factors which may throw light on LRTAP's moderate effectiveness score. There have also been some initial differences in outsiders' access and participation, but these are probably of less practical importance. Both regimes have benefited from a fruitful interplay between bureaucratic/lower profile and political/high profile processes, which is one of the interesting candidates with regard to effectiveness enhancing factors and hence counterbalancing forces to other, more complicating organizational factors.

The assumptions examined: access and participation matter, but nuanced thinking necessary

Overall, the case studies indicate that international access procedures and related participation patterns matter under certain conditions, and can in some instances even be quite decisive factors. Let us take a closer look at the three focused dimensions.

Regarding the access and participation issue, the basic point of departure in the scope of state participation dimension was the assumption that, in a short-term perspective, regimes with few and homogeneous participants tend to be more effective than regimes with many and heterogeneous participants, regardless of the true problem scope.[2] However, in the longer-term perspective, it was seen as more doubtful whether regimes not covering all major contributors to the environmental and resource problems addressed can remain effective. Given that at the regional level it is easier to achieve both a good match between problem scope and participation, and benefit from smaller group dynamics, it also seemed reasonable to assume that regional regimes tend to be more effective than global ones, irrespective of time perspective. At first glance, then, the ozone case study does not fit the suggested pattern. Given various benign problem features and strong scientific and political leadership, the contradictory weight of this case should, however, not be exaggerated. The development of OSCON and PARCON, with the smaller and more homogeneous North Sea Conference forum as an important motor, supports the basic logic here. Moreover, also highly relevant in this context is the differentiation within the ozone regime between industrialized countries as a more limited 'ozone motor' and the 'Article 5' developing countries with a ten-year implementation delay. In a way, this differentiation downplayed more short-term problem-solving effectiveness in return for increased long-term political effectiveness and regime legitimacy – and hopefully increased long-term problem-solving effectiveness. The LRTAP development may also contain elements of this logic, both in the somewhat varying scope of the protocols compared to the all-encompassing convention, and the establishment of the smaller and more ambitious NO_x Declaration group in relation to the broader and less ambitious group of countries signing the formal NO_x Protocol. Hence, in practice, all these regimes have found ways to, so to speak, transcend the requirements for rather broad state participation (be it global or regional) set by problem scopes and long-term legitimacy, by combining broader forums with narrower and politically effective institutional contexts. However, this may indicate that *both* the global and regional contexts may be too broad to combine political and problem-solving effectiveness over time; it is necessary to develop smaller and more homogeneous 'clubs'.

Turning then to the international design question often given most attention, the inclusiveness of various types of non-state actors, the basic assumption was that, although there is clearly a question of balancing different considerations and different needs in different phases, regimes with a generally inclusive access and participation profile tend to be more effective than regimes with a more exclusive profile. However, the rough comparative analysis does not unambiguously give support to the logic suggested here. For instance, both the effective ozone regime and the less effective LRTAP have had quite open access structures all along. Hence, nuanced thinking is clearly necessary. To start with the easy part: the development over time within these regimes has definitely been towards more open access and increased participation. This is most clearly witnessed within the OSCON and PARCON regimes, which have developed from more or less 'bureaucratic clubs' with little outside interest, via the much more media- and NGO-dominated North Sea Conferences to a new comprehensive OSPAR Convention with more open access rules written into it and a number of organizations participating. The background for this is diverse. Partly, it has to do with environmental politics growing more complex and affecting new groups of public and private groups and organizations. Environmental politics has become too important to be left to the environmental authorities alone. But it also has to do with environmental NGOs growing stronger and more self-assured, being able to point to a general green trend from the mid-1980s as a legitimizing basis for their claims for easier access. Moreover, the ozone regime is probably the case where open access and broad participation has been most explicitly hailed as a driving force behind the results achieved by the ozone regime. However, closer study reveals that none of the cases studied here has been 'purely' inclusive or exclusive. The 'open' ozone regime utilized more secluded workshops and meetings, and the 'secluded' PARCON regime has been closely linked to the more public and open North Sea Conferences, before opening itself up. Hence, the seemingly different approaches chosen are not so different after all: over time, all the regimes have found ways to combine the wide spectrum of inputs and political energy related to the open model with the intimacy and overview more easily achieved in more secluded forums. Judging from these cases, somewhat similar to findings related to the scope of participating states, *differentiated* access seems to be the keyword, at least with regard to negotiation processes on regime regulations. A general model increasingly utilized is one with open access to plenary meetings and preparatory stages, and more restricted access to meetings on details and fine print, and final stages.

Finally, with regard to the question of ministerial and high-level political inputs, the basic assumption was that regimes with frequent high-level meetings and infusion of political energy tend to be more effective than regimes with more moderate high-level and political contributions. Turning to the case evidence, the development over time of the OSCON and PARCON regimes clearly supports this logic. Going from an administrative, 'shielded' setting to a more high-level political setting may have been *the* decisive factor within the wider north-east Atlantic marine pollution setting. This functioned both in the more malign PARCON and more benign OSCON context. However, evidence from the cases also point to a need for refinement of the suggested thesis. There is an important interplay between solid administrative groundwork and spectacular ministerial gatherings. On the one hand, the implementation problems witnessed in both the North Sea and the NO_x and acid rain cases indicate the importance of having a solid bureaucratic and scientific foundation for important and necessary 'political take-offs' at ministerial gatherings. On the other hand, the slow progress of the pre-North Sea Conference OSCON and PARCON work indicates the dangers of not having any political take-offs at all. Hence, there is an important balance to be struck, and an 'optimal' degree of politicization to be found; probably dependent on the more specific history of, and problem visibility in, each case. A general rule of thumb could be that regimes regulating low visibility activities need more high profile and regular political input than regimes regulating more visible and specific activities more suited for general political attention and public campaigns.

6.4.2 Decision-Making Rules: Formal Differences; Practical Similarities

The analytical point of departure here was that the decision rules of unanimity and consensus tend to lead to less effective regimes than (qualified) majority voting rules. However, a moderating distinction was made with regard to effects in different phases. Although majority voting rules have at least the capacity to lead to more environmentally ambitious rules (though it cannot be taken for granted that the majority is always on the 'progressive' side), the implications for implementation performance are more uncertain. It is easily thinkable that, first, more ambitious rules are harder to implement, and second, outvoted states 'sabotage' the project by giving little attention to compliance and implementation. Moreover, a distinction also has to be made with regard to formal rules and rules in practice. What is the relationship between formalities and realities in our cases, then?

Table 6.2   Decision-making rules: the overview picture

	OSCON	PARCON	North Sea Conf.	LRTAP	OZONE
Forma-lities	Unanimity required both for procedural and substantial matters. 'Differen-tiated' deci-sions from 1988 on, opening up opportunities for different policy routes and different timetables for compliance in other parts of the Convention area than the North Sea.	Initially: emphasis on unanimity, but an explicit opening for 3/4 majority decisions 'should unanimity not be attainable' (Art.18); these would be binding only for those states that voted for the measures. As in the case of OSCON: 'differentiated' decisions from 1988 on. No formal changes in the 1992 OSPAR Convention, but further codification of 'differentiation' (Art. 24 on 'regionalization').	No formal rules.	Art.12 in 1979 Convention stated that amendments to the Convention should be adopted by consensus.	Emphasis on consensus, but also elements of majority voting. Vienna Conven-tion: Art. 9: possible qualified (3/4) majority decisions on amendments to the Convention and protocols. In §9(5), a basic right of reservation. Montreal Protocol: on regulated substances, further measures can be adopted by a 2/3 majority of parties present and voting, repre-senting at least 50% of the com-bined consump-tion of the parties. No right of reser-vation. On new substances, same procedures as in the Vienna Con-vention, with rights of reser-vation.
Realities	Emphasis on unanimity. Important effects of 'differen-tiation' with regard to the implemen-tation of NSC measures.	In the 1970s and 1980s, emphasis on consensus (i.e. accepting reservations from 'small' polluters). In the 1990s, increasing use of reservations and a sort of majority voting.	Emphasis on unani-mity.	A flexible consen-sus; e.g. the majority securing a formal acceptance from Convention Parties not willing to join the 1985 Sulphur Protocol. Greater willingness over time to push reluctants harder, but consensus integral within the regime.	Emphasis on con-sensus; no votes taken. Possible 'hidden stick' effects. A certain 'differentiation' effect related to the different targets and time-tables for developing countries.

Regarding OSCON and PARCON, is there a development from practical similarities to both formal and practical differences? Overall, although PARCON did include formal elements of majority voting, this was never meant as a possibility to bind unwilling parties, and had no practical significance in the 1970s and 1980s. Unanimity (with a certain flexibility) ruled the day in both regimes. Also within both regimes, the 1988 introduction of the 'regionalization' principle had decision-making implications, but this had more practical effects within OSCON than PARCON. This indicates that the virtues of differentiation and flexibility in this context is dependent upon issue characteristics and the related constellation of party preferences. In the 1990s, there has been an interesting increased use of reservations and a sort of majority voting within PARCON; clarifying leaders and laggards, but not binding the laggards.

Turning to the two most effective regimes – OSCON and ozone – the natural question becomes: are they characterized by particularly effective decision-making rules? Overall, there are clearly some procedural differences between the regimes, with the ozone regime as the formally most advanced one, introducing elements of majority voting and emphasizing consensus instead of unanimity. Practice has however been quite similar, with a flexible consensus as the main keyword. Hence, although the ozone regime has been hailed by legal experts as a 'great novelty in international environmental law', no votes have ever been taken within the regime, which is probably also related to the lack of a right of reservation with regard to adjustments of the Montreal Protocol.

Has this 'novelty' meant little or nothing in practice, then? Seemingly little, although 'hidden stick' effects of course are possible. Both participants in the regime and the Secretariat emphasize the practical spirit of consensus and willingness to seek pragmatic solutions, not least in the light of the global character of the problem and the need for global participation. Moreover, and not least important, the consent of the developing countries has been achieved by the design of differentiated reduction targets and timetables. Hence, although increased flexibility and differentiation clearly played a role in both cases, and not least OSCON, the prime keys to the success of these two regimes are not found in their complex legal arrangements.

So what about the two less effective regimes, PARCON and LRTAP? Are they less advanced? As a general comment, it is interesting to note that there has been a similar increased willingness to clarify and push laggards harder over time within both regimes, most explicitly within the PARCON regime. This is probably related both to internal factors within the regimes, with a general cooperative trust and foundation well-established, and especially in the case of LRTAP, more external factors like a changed East–West relationship.

Concluding comments: formal differences; practical similarities

Overall, it is interesting to note that although the formal variations are quite marked, practice is very similar. In fact, several of the regimes assessed here contain some clauses opening up opportunities for some sort of majority decisions. However, these clauses have been quite dormant, and consensual decisions have been the order of the day. Hence, taking practice as our key interest, the practical differences between the regimes in this regard seem so marginal that little if any light on the differences in effectiveness between the regimes is provided by this institutional factor.

This does not mean that the case studies do not contain interesting aspects in terms of practical lessons. First and foremost, it should be noted that states have utilized several means to beat 'the least ambitious programme' implications of unanimity. The north-east Atlantic and North Sea regimes have utilized differentiated decisions; the acid rain regime has done something similar in that protocols have been established with the abstention of several parties to the initial Convention; the ozone regime has utilized different reduction targets and timetables for different parties. This slight variety indicates that the particular choice of means to beat the slowest boat rule must be adapted to the problem and political situation at hand.

Generally, the picture above also indicates something about the relationship between law formalities and the practical power realities in an anarchical international society. Consensual decision-making often means slow decision-making, but at least states within the regimes studied here do not seem generally to regard voting down reluctants as a viable long-term option for speeding things up. This should also be a sobering reminder that it is not possible to infer from formal and often 'advanced' rules to actual, 'advanced' practice. However, it is also interesting to note that there has been an increased willingness to clarify and push laggards harder over time within several of the regimes.

6.4.3 The Role of the Secretariats: The Stronger and More Active the Better?

Some have suggested that an effective secretariat is a necessary condition for an effective regime. Along those lines, the analytical point of departure here was that regimes with secretariats which have a financially strong and relatively autonomous and active position tended to be more effective than regimes with less financially strong and active secretariats. A strong financial position (either provided directly by contributions from the parties or provided through a link to a supportive organization like UNEP) and a relatively autonomous position were factors assumed to allow the secretariat to enhance the parties' and regime's capacity to establish and implement agreements. However, the importance of the role of the secretariat was assumed to be dependent upon the administrative capacities of the parties themselves; this is more important in a situation where several or all the cooperative parties have weak domestic administrative capacities; less important when the parties' administrative capacities are quite high.

Table 6.3   The role of the secretariats: the overview picture

	PARCON	OSCON	North Sea Confe-rences	LRTAP	OZONE
Resources (in relation to workload)	First decade one secretary, two deputy secretaries and three clerks. Definitely limited financial resources. Somewhat increasing resources in the last decade (i.e. five executive staff members and six assistants in the 1990s), but work-load also increasing considerably. Responsibility also for North Sea Task Force.	Same as PARCON (shared secretariat)	ad hoc secretarial services, primarily provided by host countries.	Secretariat functions provided by Air Pollution Unit within ECE. Increasing workload and constant manning: five professional staff members. ECE/UN financial problems also mean LRTAP constraints.	Roughly same staff size as OSCON (currently five professionals and eight support staff). The ozone budget (Convention and Protocol) roughly three times bigger than OSCON; but much higher number and heteroge-neous parties. UNEP link must be seen as organizational 'back up' strength.
Practical role	'Moderately passive'; the Conventions mostly about administrative duties; most weight given to adminis-trative issues; some-times a more active, mediating role, with own proposals for solutions. In the 1990s, more active role on reporting and compliance questions.	Same as PARCON		Traditional stage-hand functions; an increasingly complex scientific–political complex to serve.	Initial ideas on 'activist' secretariat rejected; but several text drafting contributions and more active role in reporting and compliance issues over time.

Regarding OSCON and PARCON, have the parties got more than they deserved? Were there changes in the role of the secretariat which may throw some light upon the increasing effectiveness from the late 1980s on?

As a general comment, the OSCON and PARCON secretarial story lends support to the theory that the effectiveness of a regime is not critically dependent on formally huge secretarial resources as long as the parties' own administrative resources are relatively strong. This seems more or less to be the situation in this case: the effectiveness of the two regimes developed and increased over time, with the assistance of an only 'moderately resource-rich' secretariat. The well-functioning secretariat contributed to the gradual establishment of an important platform of knowledge and trust.

Have the two most effective regimes, OSCON and ozone, been served by particularly effective secretariats? Overall, they have at least been served by increasingly effective secretariats. However, none of them can be classified as particularly 'rich' and activist, and for instance the global and increasingly complex ozone regime has been served by roughly the same number of staff as has been the case in the regional and overall 'richer' north-east Atlantic and North Sea context.

Finally, regarding PARCON and LRTAP, are the two less effective regimes served by particularly weak secretariats? Despite certain formal institutional differences, there are several practical similarities. Both secretariats must be characterized as quite weak resource-wise and staff-wise, with the LRTAP regime in the most unfavourable position, given process and administrative development and considering the higher number and more heterogeneous character of the parties involved. However, both secretariats have functioned effectively within these structural constraints, and the functioning of the secretariats cannot be seen as serious impediments in the cooperative and implementation processes.

Concluding comments: more a 'critical minimum' than 'big is beautiful'?

With reference to Sandford's (1994) question whether international environmental treaty secretariats are stage-hands or actors, the regimes studied in this context clearly fit more in the stage-hand than in the actor category. All the secretariats discussed here are in fact staffed by five professionals(!), and are more or less constantly resource-starved, for instance with little money for travel to keep up regular contact with the parties. Formal mandates have been mainly administrative, and although actual 'entrepreneurial' practice seems to have varied a bit, the main picture is a quite low-lying one. Still, it is important to be aware of the fact that secretariat 'activism' may necessarily be quite hidden and discreet, and hard to trace for analysts. Moreover, a trend can be noted in all the cases in the direction of the secretariat taking a more important and active role with regard to reporting and compliance assessment functions.

Hence, although the limited number of cases and marginal differences in the strength and role of secretariats do not allow a very critical scrutiny of the main assumptions formulated, the evidence available does indicate that the conditional elements referring to the administrative strength of the parties themselves should be further refined. The case studies indicate that having a very active and resource-strong secretariat is by no means a necessary condition for reasonably effective cooperation to take place, as long as the secretariat's budgetary and administrative resources are above a certain minimum, and the parties themselves have overall reasonable administrative capacities. This budgetary and administrative minimum is seemingly quite low. For instance, both OSCON and the ozone regime have achieved clear results with modest – but still effective! – secretarial assistance. In the case of OSCON, the parties themselves have overall reasonable administrative capacities. This is less the case within the ozone regime. However, the ozone secretariat has developed an interesting and well-functioning interplay with other regime bodies, something which indicates that the role of secretariats should always be considered in the light of other elements in the administrative setting of regimes.

But even if a large, resource-rich and active secretariat is not a necessary condition for an effective cooperation, the seemingly quite impressive results achieved so far by modest means could mean that modest increases in resources could give disproportionally good results – especially in regimes where present administrative capacity among the parties varies widely. However, given for instance the experience within the ozone regime, where plans for an 'activist', strong secretariat were firmly rejected, the political room in practice for strengthened secretariats is probably limited.

6.4.4 The Structuring of the Agenda: Potentially Important, but Analytically Elusive

On a very general level, it may seem as though an optimal agenda belongs closer to the comprehensive end of the continuum than the narrow end, in order to provide possibilities for flexibly adding and subtracting issues in different phases of the regime's development. Hence, the following main overall assumption was formulated: regimes with comprehensive agendas and the achievement of a flexible adding and subtracting of issues tend to adopt stronger regulations than regimes with narrower agendas and less possibilities for such flexibility. But the practical importance of the structure of the agenda in the broader effectiveness context is clearly more complex. First, utilizing the flexibility advantages requires effective political leadership. Workable package deals must be constructed by skilful entrepreneurs. Second, the links to the decisive national-level policy processes are complex.

Table 6.4   The structuring of the agendas: the overview picture

	OSCON	PARCON	North Sea Conferences	LRTAP	OZONE
Struc-turing of the agenda	The Convention formulated quite generally with regard to dumping issues; a 'black' and 'grey' list gave few structuring signals. Hence, up to the mid-1980s, the agenda was basically only increasing, with no problems getting solved. After breakthrough at the 1987 NSC, gradual follow-up and problem-solving within OSCON.	The Convention contained a 'black' and 'grey' list of land-based substances, which influen-ced the following years' agenda more than within OSCON. In the first decade, focus on a quite small group of substances, including mercury, cadmium, aldrin, dieldrin and endrin. Broader agenda at 1987 NSC a contributing factor to the break-through 50% reduction measures. This Conference also introduced the Best Available Technology (BAT) principle. Increasingly packed agenda over time. The 1992 Conven-tion also includes dumping and radioactive issues.	Combined dumping and land-based issues. The issue of nutrients (phosphorus and nitrogen) came up in connection with the 1984 NSC. The combination of issues potentially important at the 1987 NSC: it has been indicated that the earlier main 'stumbling block' (the UK) would never have agreed to the 50% land-based measures if it had not been given special treatment in connection with the dumping issues.	The Convention can be characte-rized as general and open-ended. Sequential deve-lopment of the LRTAP agenda; with an initial focus on SO_2, turning to the NO_x problem, and then on to the VOC pro-blem, before the Parties returned to SO_2 in 1991. Probably both due to a rational ability to decompose a complex issue and deal with the components gradually as knowledge has improved, and due to some countries consciously avoiding a 'diversion' of regulatory attention. Presently a broader agenda, with negotia-tions on new and combined NO_x and VOC requirements; heavy metals; and persistent organic pollutants (POPs).	Loosely defined agenda in the Vienna Convention, no specific activities or substances men-tioned. However, as there had already been an unsuccess-ful effort in Vienna to establish a CFC protocol, an infor-mal agenda targe-ting these substan-ces and the halons quickly formed. Use of several informal workshops; broke the problems down into smaller components, developed consensus by incremental stages, and established personal relation-ships and mutual confidence. Over time, the agenda has been 'relieved' of scien-tific and technolo-gical complicating issues through establishment of review panels. A flexible agenda has been adopted as a formal principle. Luckily, a gradual adding of new substances and complex issues like the special needs of the developing countries has allo-wed a beneficial institutional adap-tation and assimilation.

Overall, the OSCON and PARCON picture indicates steady growth and occasional flexibility. The issue linkage at the 1987 NSC stands out as the most conspicuous event in this connection. This issue linkage may have contributed to making the turning-point 50% NSC reduction measures and the related vitalization of PARCON possible. The effects of this Conference on OSCON were perhaps even more profound, but this had less to do with the structuring of the agenda itself. In other respects, agenda-related issues do not seem to throw much light on the development of either the OSCON or the PARCON regime.

Regarding OSCON and ozone, are there different problems and no similarities? As will be recalled, the high effectiveness of OSCON does not seem to be particularly related to a very effective way of structuring the agenda. So what about ozone? Overall, the structuring of the agendas is difficult to compare due to marked differences in underlying problem characteristics. Although this issue seems to throw moderate light on the regulations decided upon and degree of effectiveness of these regimes, the ozone negotiators may have utilized available techniques with regard to sequencing and flexibility more consistently than in the dumping case. If this impression is correct, it may be related to a host of other factors, like generally stronger scientific and political leadership in the ozone process.

Finally, are there few similarities between PARCON and LRTAP in terms of agenda approaches and developments? Overall, the approaches chosen with regard to the structuring of the agenda are obviously quite different, which is partly due to the more structural aspects of the problems. Briefly stated, there was no 'focal' relationship between a certain substance and its international effects within the PARCON context, comparable to the relationship between sulphur emissions and acidified lakes within the LRTAP context. The more sequential and focused LRTAP agenda, expressed in the various protocol regulatory processes, was partly a reflection of a somewhat more 'decomposable' problem than the land-based marine pollution problems.

However, the present discussions on a more comprehensive and combined NO_x and VOC Protocol indicate that the basically 'narrow' approach utilized so far has not been totally satisfactory either – although clearly the improvement of knowledge must also be brought into the picture. Overall causal relevance is uncertain; at least there are no indications of significantly less comprehensiveness and flexibility in these cases than in the more effective ones.

Concluding comments: analytically elusive – and seemingly of limited relevance

First of all, these cases show clearly the analytical difficulties involved in efforts to track the importance of conscious efforts to structure the agenda. Quite naturally, different types of problems give different starting points for negotiators' efforts to structure agendas. Some starting points may simply be better suited for sequential and more narrowly focused decision-making than others, while other starting points more naturally point towards broader, comprehensive approaches. In short, the potential entrepreneurial room in this respect may often be severely limited. Overall, there are certain institutional techniques utilized in all of the regimes. The most apparent of these is the establishment of scientific and technical working groups or review panels, which moved a lot of complicated issues out of the main negotiating forums. As discussed in the next section, the organization of these scientific–political complexes varies quite a bit, but the interesting thing in this connection is the common function of 'relieving' the main regime agenda.

Although the 'comprehensiveness' question is also hard to address, as the underlying problems vary so much, it still seems that all these regimes have settled for what must be termed basically a 'narrow' approach, with more or less successful attempts at sequential decision-making. The atmospheric regimes seem to have been the most successful regimes in terms of sequential decision-making. But the latest developments towards, and discussions on, more formally comprehensive approaches both within OSPAR and LRTAP give further support to the thesis that there is no timeless, ideal model in this field; various problems and various phases may require different solutions. Furthermore, it must not be forgotten that the 1987 breakthrough within the PARCON/North Sea context was seemingly strongly related to the temporary issue broadening and linkage possibilities of the North Sea Conferences. Causal relevance is uncertain, but probably limited: it is for instance possible to achieve quite high degrees of effectiveness with quite different approaches with regard to the structuring of the agenda, as indicated by the dumping and ozone experiences. Hence, although the main comprehensiveness and flexibility assumption still makes sense, these cases indicate that it is too general and in need of specification in order to be tested more properly.

6.4.5 The Science–Politics Interface: Organizational 'Buffers' in Order to Combine Scientific Integrity with Political Involvement?

Knowledge production processes related to international environmental regimes may be assumed to be important, given the complex character of environmental problems. However, to what extent and how this importance is dependent on specific forms of organization is more uncertain. A central theme is the need to balance the autonomy and integrity of science on the one hand and involvement and responsiveness to the concerns and needs of decision-makers on the other. Given the fact that important regime decisions and substantial progress can probably be made in the initial regime phase based on quite rough knowledge and imperfect communication, it is reasonable to assume that the balancing and communication challenges identified above become increasingly important

Table 6.5　The organization of the science–politics interface: the overview picture

	OSCON	PARCON
Scientific–political complex	*Technical/scientific body*: 'Standing Advisory Committee for Scientific Advice' (SACSA). Composed of 'technical bureaucrats' from all the countries. From 1993 on: 'Programmes and Measures Committee' (PRAM) *Monitoring*: 'Joint Monitoring Group' (JMG); its work based on national marine monitoring programmes. From 1993 on: Environmental Assessment and Monitoring Committee' (ASMO). ad hoc subsidiary bodies and working groups. *'independent' scientific input*: JMG has received regular inputs from the ICES (International Council for the Exploration of the Sea). Closer integration of ICES from 1993 on.	*Technical/scientific body*: 'Technical Working Group' (TWG). From 1993 on: 'Programmes and Measures Committee' (PRAM). *Monitoring:* same as OSCON ad hoc subsidiary bodies and working groups *'independent' scientific input:* same as OSCON.
Functioning	First decade: the JMG was malfunctioning, and did not play the action-initiating role it was envisaged to do. Moreover, the Oslo and Paris Commissions meetings had limited time to deal with scientific issues. Largely due to the work of the North Sea Task Force, improved functioning in recent decade.	Same as OSCON.
The buffer issue	SACSA, with a combined technical and political mandate, carried out some communicative buffer functions.	TWG, with a combined technical and political mandate, carried out some communicative buffer functions.

North Sea Conferences	LRTAP	OZONE
Ad hoc groups producing 'Quality Status of the North Sea' reports (QSRs) prior to the 1984 and 1987 Conferences Establishment of specific North Sea Task Force (NSTF) at the 1987 Conference, to better coordinate and carry out monitoring, modelling and research activities, and present improved QSR in 1993.	*Technical/scientific bodies*: - 'Working Group on Effects' - 'Working Group on Technology' - EMEP Steering Body. *Under the Working Groups*: 'International Cooperative Programs' and Task Forces. *Monitoring*: EMEP program, with around 100 stations in 33 countries; funding based on a specific 1984 Protocol. *'Independent' scientific input*: work on 'critical loads' has been assisted by the RAINS model developed at IIASA.	Before 1988, the ozone regime had a rather loose scientific–political complex. The scientific process was US-dominated. In addition, the 'Coordinating Committee on the Ozone Layer' (CCOL), established by UNEP in the late 1970s, issuing periodic reports on the risks to the ozone layer. After 1988, and related to the Montreal Protocol, the scientific–political complex became more institutionalized in three main assessment panels: the Scientific Assessment Panel; the Technology and Economics Panel; and the Environmental Effects Panel. Related to the Vienna Convention, there is a Meeting of Ozone Research Managers, convening every three years.
The work of the NSTF has undoubtedly improved and vitalized the scientific–political complex.	The EMEP system has represented a strong scientific foundation and core; a far better functioning and more centrally placed monitoring system than within PARCON. The scientific–political complex has made significant contributions to agenda setting and knowledge improvement within the NO_x, VOC, and most recent sulphur processes.	Differences compared to OSCON: The explicit separation of functions/dimensions in the ozone regime into four panels. The more explicit weight given to the economic issues in the ozone regime. The somewhat ambiguous recruitment policy of the panels. On the one hand, weight on scholarly merits and peer review procedures; on the other hand, emphasis on 'the widest possible geographical balance' in the selection of experts.
The core NSTF functioned as a communicative body, with an explicit national/ administrative dimension.	The Working Group on Strategies can be seen as a mediating buffer – a 'not too formal' meetingplace for scientists and administrators, allowing the building of consensual knowledge on both scientific and political strategic matters.	Before 1988, CCOL can reasonably be seen as a buffer. In 1988, an 'Open-Ended Working Group' and hence an intergovernmental body which reviews and synthesizes knowledge from panels, was established.

over time, when regime regulations need to be revised and finely tuned in relation to environmental and societal conditions in order to remain legitimate and effective. Hence, a main assumption in this connection was formulated as follows: regimes which over time succeed in balancing the need for both independent and usable scientific inputs tend to be more effective than regimes with less success in this regard.

A specific organizational idea in this connection is the establishment of a mediating buffer between scientific processes and policy processes. This idea has two dimensions: on the one hand, 'integration' in order to increase and facilitate communication between scientists and decision-makers; and on the other hand, 'separation' of the scientific and political activities themselves and the avoidance of politicization of regime meetings. Hence, although a precise understanding of the nature of such buffer bodies is lacking, a related, sub-assumption was formulated in the following manner: regimes with a buffer body in the interface between science and politics tend over time to be more effective than regimes with no such buffer body. (See Table 6.5.)

With regard to OSCON and PARCON, are there gradual improvements, but of marginal importance? Overall, the scientific–political complex within these regimes has improved over time, especially related to the work of the North Sea Task Force in the wake of the 1987 North Sea Conference. Hence, the evolving organization has over time given the regimes a well-functioning scientific platform where scientific integrity has been enhanced by greater ICES involvement, and communication and political usability has been enhanced through the more action-oriented NSTF. With regard to the buffer issue, both SACSA, TWG and the core NSTF have functioned as fairly important communicative forums for the science–politics dialogue. However, given the rather uncertain and vague scientific inputs in most of the time periods in question, and the few at best direct distributive policy consequences flowing from the scientific information, the need for such buffers to avoid politicization and contamination of science has been minimal.

Overall, the main causes for changing overall effectiveness must still be sought elsewhere. First, NSTF was a direct outcome of the 1987 North Sea Conference, and possible effects must be sought for in the 1990s, not mid-1980s. Second, it is reasonable to see the rather low scientific–political effectiveness in the first phase of the regimes as a reflection of the generally moderate priority given to North Sea and north-east Atlantic pollution matters by the cooperating states. Hence, it is tempting to see the later scientific vitalization as much more a consequence of the political vitalization taking place than the other way around.

Comparing OSCON and ozone, are there any similarities between the two most effective regimes? The somewhat grey OSCON model was established in the early 1970s, when international environmental regimes and cooperation were really in their infant days. The ozone model was created over a decade later. Do we then have a situation with a more advanced and refined ozone science–politics model? If there are any practical similarities, how can they throw light on the effectiveness scores of the two regimes? As a brief comment, although the OSCON and ozone models are definitely formally quite different, the practical effects of these differences in organization are hard to track down precisely. Both organizational models have (in the case of OSCON, over time) functioned adequately, but seemingly with more important effects for regime development in the ozone case than in the dumping case.

Finally, are there both formal and practical differences between PARCON and LRTAP? The point of departure here is that LRTAP has been hailed as a knowledge-production success. Does this mean, then, that there are both formal and practical contrasts to the PARCON model? Overall, there seem to be both formal and practical/functioning differences between the PARCON and LRTAP scientific–political complexes. An important difference lies in the higher priority given to and better functioning of the LRTAP monitoring system, but there are also several other ways in which the LRTAP complex has made more important contributions to agenda setting and policy making than the PARCON system. Hence, the key to understanding the more moderate effectiveness of the regimes does not lie in the organization of the science–politics interface; especially in the case of LRTAP, quite the contrary.

Concluding comments: the importance of communicative buffers and science with a national flavour

Judging from the cases scrutinized here, scientific knowledge clearly matters for the speed and form of development of international environmental regimes. Especially the acid rain and ozone processes seem to have been very much knowledge-driven all along, and the regimes have played important roles in developing that knowledge. This does not mean that important policy milestones within the regimes, like for instance the 1985 LRTAP 30% Sulphur Protocol, were directly derived from science – far from it (although the 1994 Sulphur Protocol based on 'critical loads' takes an important step in that direction). No, the influence is much more continuous, sublime and diffuse. The scientific–political complexes of these regimes exhibit several structural differences, which are partly derived from the different fundamental characteristics of the environmental problems that motivated the establishment of these regimes. Hence, clear-cut organizational lessons are complicated by the close interplay between policy development and organizational development. For instance, the obvious importance of finding substitute substances within the ozone regime casts light on the establishment of the specific technological panel (and perhaps also the economic panel) within this regime. With regard to the main balancing of the 'integrity' and 'usability' assumption formulated, at least OSCON, PARCON and ozone offer, over time, a certain support for this logic. Improving organizational design has been an element in processes leading to increased effectiveness. But it is interesting to note that the balance within all the regimes studied here has been somewhat tilted towards the 'national control' and 'usability' pole – without creating heated 'politicization' debates. This may have something to do with the generally diffuse relationship between scientific development and policy development within these regimes, with few direct distributional implications. Moreover, it may have something to do with the overall moderate economic implications involved, at least compared to issues like global climate change (see Chapter 7). But it may also mean that the ideal notion of a rough balance between 'integrity' and 'involvement' may simply be unrealistic and not called for at the international level.

Regarding the buffer question, all the regimes analysed here contain some kind of buffer body between scientific activities and decision-making activities, probably most marked in the acid rain regime's Working Group on Strategies. Hence, although there are differences between the regimes, these are not marked enough to throw any light on the differences in regime development and effectiveness. Moreover, with regard to the integration and separation dimensions related to the buffer function, the emphasis in all cases has been on the communicative and integrative function. Hence, the separation function has apparently not been so necessary within these regimes. As indicated above, this may have something to do with basic problem characteristics related to these regimes.

6.4.6 Verification and Compliance Strengthening Mechanisms: Towards Tougher Procedures and Mechanisms?

Two central clusters of questions can be discerned here. The first cluster of questions are related to the issue of reporting and verification, and cover issues related to compliance reporting and the existence of specific bodies to assess and follow up compliance and implementation questions which may spring out of such reports. Without well-functioning reporting systems and implementation bodies, it is a distinct possibility that suspicions of cheating will undermine the stability of regimes over time. Hence, it seemed reasonable to assume that regimes with well-functioning reporting systems and related implementation review bodies tend to be more effective than regimes with lax reporting systems and no specific implementation bodies.

The second cluster of questions are more specifically related to compliance strengthening mechanisms, and highlight the positive incentive and 'carrot' part of the issue. This is of course primarily relevant in international contexts where a significant number of the parties have weak economic and administrative capacities and hence weak abilities to take on and follow up regime requirements. The establishment of a specific fund for the assistance of economically and administratively weaker parties is the most obvious organizational idea. Hence, it was suggested that in international settings with a significant number of economically and administratively weak parties, regimes which succeed in establishing a well-functioning financial mechanism tend to be more effective than regimes which fail in this regard.

First, regarding OSCON and PARCON, can changes in verification and compliance mechanisms throw light over the increase in effectiveness within these regimes? Overall, verification within these regimes has been based on self-reporting. After an initial period of lax procedures and practice, both reporting procedures and practice itself have improved considerably in the 1990s, and the last decade has seen the establishment of a parallel, more policy-oriented North Sea Conference system. However: the 'soft' initial system, with a variable coverage with regard to data, did not cause the slow development of the regimes, and likewise, the recent verification strengthening should be seen more as an interrelated factor than an independent force behind generally increasing effectiveness. (See Table 6.6 for the overview picture.)

Comparing OSCON and ozone, are there particularly effective compliance strengthening mechanisms? There are clearly several procedural and institutional verification and compliance differences between the regimes, with the ozone regime both much more procedurally complex and with a more diverse and complicated practice. However, they still share a basic soft, non-confrontational nature. The ozone regime has so far experienced serious reporting problems, and it is only more recently that the institutional potential inherent in the specific implementation committee and the Fund have contributed to practical improvements. Hence, much like the OSCON case, procedural and practical verification and compliance improvements may have contributed to more recent regime development and effectiveness, but apart from the symbolically and over time also practically important establishment of the Fund within the ozone context, these factors cannot really be regarded as more fundamental causal factors.

Finally, do PARCON and LRTAP exhibit less effective procedures? Overall, there seem to be both similarities and clear differences between the PARCON and LRTAP systems. As a brief comment: if LRTAP has been unique in terms of verification and compliance so far, then this must be related to the EMEP's system capacity for independent verification and not to the compliance procedures – although these have been strengthened relatively recently, with the establishment of a specific implementation committee. But the actual effects of this additional verification capacity on states' reporting practice and confidence-building more generally seem moderate. Hence, despite some differences, the practical functioning of the compliance strengthening

Designing Effective Environmental Regimes

Table 6.6   Verification and compliance mechanisms: the overview picture

	OSCON	PARCON
Formal procedures	Annual reports from the parties on issued dumping permits and approvals.	First decade, annual reports from the parties on type and quantities of emitted substances. Arbitration procedure laid out in Art. 21 in Convention. Recent decade, substantial procedural development and improvement, with a closer relationship between international measures and national reporting.
Functioning	Reporting was steadily improving and functioned well, but largely irrelevant in the initial years due to lack of regime decisions. Increased in relevance when regime decisions started to fall into place.	First decade, quite variable reporting, but unproblematic due to few and loose regime decisions. In line with regulatory development, improved procedures and national practice. The Secretariat in a more active role.
The financial mechanism issue	Not relevant.	Not relevant.

The North Sea Conferences	LRTAP	OZONE
Based on national reports, comprehensive Progress Reports were produced in connection with the 1990 and 1995 Conferences.	Annual reports to the Secretariat on emissions and procedures adopted for the abatement of emissions and the measurement of acid precipitation. In addition to the annual reports, there is a more comprehensive review of national abatement strategies and policies every four years. Implementation Committee established in connection with 1994 Sulphur Protocol.	Annual reports from the parties on production, export and destruction of relevant substances form the basis for annual report produced by the Secretariat for the Meeting of the Parties (Montreal Protocol). Specific Implementation Committee established in 1990. Specific Non-Compliance procedure established in 1992 (Montreal Protocol). Trade sanctions against non-parties (Montreal Protocol). Dispute settlement procedures (Vienna Convention).
Increasingly well-functioning processes, which have contributed to PARCON improvements. In addition, independent progress reports produced by e.g. Greenpeace.	'Reasonable' reporting, but some delayed and also missing data. EMEP monitoring system adds additional verification capacity not much utilized in practice. No critical compliance discussions initially, partly due to East–West considerations. Establishment of Implementation Committee in 1994 may signal a tougher phase.	Less than ideal (but improving!) reporting coverage and quality, but not bad within such a global, heterogeneous context. Self-declared non-compliance in the mid-1990s handled non-confrontationally and successfully, with several regime bodies involved.
Not relevant.	A financial mechanism has been on the agenda for some years, to facilitate burden sharing in connection with the additional abatement costs envisaged for meeting critical loads in different parts of Europe. So far, little progress has been made.	A Multilateral Fund established in 1990; problems with staffing delays and turf battles between involved agencies. Shortfall of voluntary contributions from industrialized countries. Improving situation and performance over time, though.

mechanisms has been quite similar in the two regimes. Procedures and systems have not been weaker than in the other regimes, but not very much stronger either.

Concluding comments: procedural differences; practical similarities; and the crucial interplay between regulatory development and compliance mechanisms

Procedurally, there are both similarities and differences between these regimes. A basic similarity is that the crucial ingredient in all these systems is self-reporting. In other respects, the regimes differ somewhat. For instance, LRTAP has the strongest independent verification element in principle, through its EMEP monitoring system. But PARCON/OSPAR also has a kind of parallel verification system, related to the North Sea Conferences. The ozone regime and LRTAP have implementation committees, with minor procedural differences with regard to composition and so on. And in fact formally, the PARCON regime has the strongest dispute settlement procedures, providing for compulsory third-party settlement.

However, in practice, despite these procedural and institutional differences, the models have functioned in a very similarly soft and non-confrontational way. Slow reporting and missing data have largely been accepted, with only occasionally mild pressure from the secretariats and/or the parties. Implementation committees and dispute settlement procedures have so far had little practical relevance. However, even on this sobering basis, it would be wrong to conclude that the verification and compliance mechanisms reviewed here have not contributed to general confidence-building and the increasing degree of effectiveness witnessed within all these regimes. But given the fundamental functioning similarities, the specific lessons with regard to effective 'verification designs' to be drawn out of these cases need to be formulated carefully.

There are several interesting design observations. One seems to be that the functioning of these mechanisms is closely related to the *functional requirements* of the regimes in different phases. For instance, in the first decade of the PARCON regime, regime regulations were diffuse and provided few precise yardsticks which would need very specific follow-up checking. When regulations got more specific with regard to targets and timetables, reporting procedures and practice improved – related to and strengthening the generally increasing effectiveness, but not initially causing it. Hence, diachronic evidence from the cases gives a certain support to the assumption that regimes with well-functioning reporting systems and related implementation bodies tend to be more effective than regimes with lax reporting systems and no specific implementation bodies. But the evidence clearly suggests that a more precise hypothesis should be refined and reformulated with greater attention to the functional requirements in the various phases of regimes' development and the nature of regulations decided upon. There seems to be an important interplay between regulatory development and the development of verification and compliance mechanisms. This is also related to the more specific *nature* of the regulations typically utilized in the international environmental context so far; for instance with 30% or 50% reductions of a given substance within a specified time frame. As the yearly development of emissions in the period in between has not been specified, the precise reference points for critical compliance discussions along the way have been largely missing – even when regulations generally have become more precise in content and time frame. This has clearly reduced the potential importance of this aspect of environmental regimes, compared for instance to arms control agreements.

With regard to the 'carrot' part of the compliance mechanisms discussion, the limited evidence at hand does not run contrary to the financial mechanism assumption related to the compliance issue. The ozone fund has undoubtedly contributed to the results achieved within the ozone regime, but financial and organizational problems experienced within this regime indicate the inherent problems in all efforts to redress the economic and political imbalances between North and South.

6.5 SUMMING UP: ASSUMPTIONS AND EVIDENCE

Let us go through the summary picture regarding the assumptions and the evidence at hand.

6.5.1 Access and Participation

- *In a short-term perspective, regimes with few and homogeneous participants tend to be more effective than regimes with many and heterogeneous participants. Problem scope shapes more long-term perspectives. Related to this: regional regimes tend to be more effective than global ones.*

These case studies basically support these assumptions, for instance witnessed in the relationship between the wider OSCON/PARCON and the more homogeneous North Sea Conference system. Another highly relevant aspect in this context is the differentiation within the ozone regime between industrialized countries as a more limited 'ozone motor' and the developing countries with a ten-year implementation delay. However, all these regimes have found ways to transcend the requirements for rather broad state participation (be it global or regional) set by problem scopes and long-term legitimacy, by combining broader forums with narrower and more politically effective institutional contexts. This may indicate that *both* the global and regional contexts may be too broad to combine political and problem-solving effectiveness over time; it may be necessary to develop smaller and more homogeneous 'clubs within the clubs'.

- *Regimes with an inclusive decision-making style tend to be more effective than more exclusive regimes.*

Although some diachronic supporting evidence can at first glance be noted, the assumption as formulated is not unambiguously supported by these cases. The main finding is that practical variation in this respect is much less than the first, formal picture would suggest. All regimes over time utilized both inclusive and exclusive approaches. Hence, the case studies point to the need for more nuanced thinking, with differentiated access as the main keyword. A general model suggested is one with open access to plenary meetings and preparatory stages, and more restricted access to meetings on details and fine print, and the final stages of processes.

- *Regimes with regular frequent higher-level political participation in regime activities tend to be more effective than regimes which do not have, or have not such political participation.*

Diachronic evidence is generally supportive. However, the case studies suggest that the positive effects of political participation may be conditional upon bureaucratic groundwork and hence that there is a crucial balance to be found over time. Moreover, political and ministerial inputs may be more important in regimes regulating low visibility activities than regimes regulating more visible and easily politicized activities in themselves.

6.5.2 Decision-Making Procedures

- *The decision-making rules of unanimity and consensus tend to lead to weaker regime decisions and less effective regimes than cases of (qualified) majority voting rules.*

Despite some formal majority voting clauses, the reliance in practice on a basically consensual approach made a strict 'testing' of the assumption less relevant than indicated by the formal picture. Still, the case studies contained interesting examples of flexible application of the consensus procedure: the north-east Atlantic/North Sea regimes utilized differentiated decisions; the acid rain regime did something similar in that protocols were established with the agreed abstention of reluctant parties; the ozone regime utilized different reduction targets and timetables for different parties. Hence, the case studies indicate the need for a more nuanced perception of the limiting effects of the consensus requirement and hence the need not to interpret 'decision-making procedures' too narrowly.

6.5.3 The Role of the Secretariat

- *Overall: regimes with secretariats which have a financially strong and relatively autonomous and active position (up to a certain optimal point) tend to be more effective than regimes with less financially strong and active secretariats; however, the importance of the role of the secretariat may be seen as conditional upon the administrative capacities of the parties themselves.*

Closer scrutiny of the secretariats operating within the case studies showed little practical difference: they clearly fit more in the stage-hand than in the actor category (although 'activism' may necessarily be quite hidden and hard to trace); contain the 'magical' number of five professionals; and are more or less constantly resource-starved. Still, a trend can be noted in all the case studies in the direction of the secretariat taking a more important and active role with regard to reporting and compliance assessment functions. This goes some way to indicate that the effectiveness of regimes is not critically dependent upon the financial strength and political activism of their secretariats, as long as secretariat resources are above a certain minimum. Moreover, the ozone case, in particular, suggests a need to place more emphasis on the interplay with other regime bodies in further studies of the role of the regime secretariats.

6.5.4 The Structure of the Agenda

- *Regimes with comprehensive agendas and flexible adding and subtracting of issues tend to adopt stronger regulations than regimes with narrower agendas and less possibility for such flexibility.*

The ceteris paribus condition is again both critical and complicating. It is very hard to separate the discussion on the structuring of the agenda from basic aspects of the problems being regulated. Even with this caveat, evidence at hand is ambiguous. Some diachronic bits and pieces from the cases, and especially the OSPARCON/NSC context, give a certain support to the logic suggested in the assumption. On the other hand, the overall impression of regime negotiators mainly struggling to narrow down and sequentially focus agendas indicates that the reasoning related to the flexible adding and subtracting of issues may be more theoretically interesting than practically feasible.

6.5.5 The Organization of the Scientific–Political Complex

- *Regimes which succeed in balancing the need for both independent and usable scientific inputs tend to be more effective than regimes with less success in this regard.*

Also in this context, variations between the regimes are heavily dependent upon intellectual problem characteristics, and hence 'pure' differences in approaches are hard to discern. So, in many ways, the fairest conclusion is that the evidence at hand is inconclusive in relation to the formulated assumption. The development of the OSPARCON/NSC case at first glance supports the suggested pattern, but these cases indicate that the organizational development must be seen more as a related and intermediate factor rather than a basic causal factor for the regulative development witnessed. Moreover, it is interesting to note that the overall balance has been tilted towards the usability pole in all the relatively low politicized cases studied in this context. This may indicate that high independence may be most critically important in cases with grave distributional economic issues and/or strongly value-laden issues.

- *Regimes with a buffer body in the interface between science and politics tend to be more effective than regimes with no such buffer body.*

As all the regimes scrutinized contain some form of buffer bodies, the assumption could not be strongly tested. However, it was noted with interest that increasing attention has been given to the communication dimension of the science–politics issue, reflected among other things in the mandates and functioning of the Working Group on Strategies within the acid rain context, the North Sea Task Force within the marine pollution context, and the Open-Ended Working Group related to the panel reports within the ozone regime.

6.5.6 Verification and Compliance

- *Regimes with well-functioning reporting systems and related implementation review bodies tend to be more effective than regimes with lax reporting systems and no specific implementation bodies.*

At first glance, there is diachronic supporting evidence found in all the case studies, as verification and compliance mechanisms have improved in functioning over time and the degree of effectiveness has increased. Procedural development was marked within OSCON and PARCON in the 1990s; a specific non-compliance procedure and an implementation committee were established within the ozone regime in the beginning of the 1990s; and LRTAP saw the establishment of an implementation committee in 1994. But a closer scrutiny of these cases indicates that the organizational development again must be seen more as a related and intermediate factor than a basic causal factor for changes and variances in effectiveness. Why? An important factor is the nature of the regulations decided upon within these regimes so far: relatively general, and with yearly emissions reduction requirements not specified. Hence, these cases support thinking within this field which gives close attention to the interplay between regulative developments and requirements and the design of verification and compliance mechanisms. Also in this matter, there may be no simple timeless model to be found, making sense across all issue-areas and in all phases.

6.5.7 'Institutional Density'

- *Regimes which contain many meeting-points for different types of actors tend to be more effective than regimes which contain relatively few meeting-points.*

The ideas and assumption related to 'institutional density' were less elaborated than the other institutional issues and assumptions. Hence, only some very general observations from the case studies can be noted. Within the ozone case, the varied and 'dense' participation at a number of meetings and conferences within and outside the regime in the important first five years of the regime's functioning contributed to increasing concern and learning among the parties. In the LRTAP regime, the steady development of a 'dense' scientific–political complex created a well-functioning backdrop for gradual learning and confidence-building. In general, the 'density' dimension needs to be elaborated further, both analytically and empirically.

Let us then move on and see how these findings and lessons may shed light on the development of the global climate change regime, before we wind up this book with some general methodological reflections and suggestions for the effective design of international environmental regimes in Chapter 8.

NOTES

1. This is earlier considered and discussed in Wettestad and Andresen (1991) and Andresen and Wettestad (1995). However, as indicated in Chapter 1, tentative results from Miles et al. (1999) indicate that bringing in a broader range of regimes weakens this correlation; malign problems are in fact sometimes solved effectively.
2. As noted in Chapter 2, all the assumptions are formulated under the condition of 'all other things being equal'.

7.   Designing an Effective Climate Change Regime: A Task 'Too Hot to Handle'?[1]

7.1 INTRODUCTION

As indicated in the introduction, the analytical and comparative exercise performed in the previous chapters should ideally also have some practical relevance for negotiators in other environmental regimes, especially regimes in their early stages, when institutional structures are less fixed and there are several possible routes ahead. One of the most interesting – though also challenging – international environmental issues is the problem of global climate change and the related regime established in 1992. Before winding up this book with some final conclusions and reflections, let us discuss how and to what extent institutional insights and lessons from the other regimes analysed in this book can throw light on institutional choices made so far, and future challenges in the climate context.[2]

Section 7.2 will present a brief description of the climate issue and an account of the negotiations, to indicate the degree of malignancy of the issue and hence the rough degree of similarity with the other regimes analysed in this book. Without such a rough comparative basis and context, there is a clear risk of misinterpreting preceding developments and prescribing institutional 'cures' not adapted to the types of problems experienced by the regime 'patient' in question. Then, in section 7.3, the six focused institutional issues will be discussed within the climate context, using the general case lessons as points of departure. Section 7.4 will sum up and present some concluding reflections.

7.2 THE GLOBAL CLIMATE CHANGE ISSUE: MAIN CHARACTERISTICS AND A BRIEF REVIEW OF THE INTERNATIONAL POLITICAL PROCESS SO FAR[3]

7.2.1 The Global Climate Change Problem: A Malign Point of Departure

When the negotiators of the Intergovernmental Negotiating Committee (INC) for a Framework Convention on Climate Change convened for the first time in February 1991, various types of scientific groundwork had made it clear that they were about to deal with a potentially very malign problem both in an intellectual and political sense.[4] Intellectually, given that the natural greenhouse effect is in fact essential for life on Earth, the principal challenge was to isolate the potentially disturbing long-term effects of human activity from a picture dominated by naturally occurring atmospheric conditions and changes. Hence, the level of complexity was (and is) very high, and uncertainty was (and still is) considerable. It was clear that a number of gases were involved, with much initial focus on carbon dioxide (CO_2), but also with attention given to gases like methane (CH_4) and nitrous oxide (N_2O). Given the functioning of ecosystems, not only emissions were significant, but also the role of large carbon 'sinks' like the ocean and the forests. Moreover, the central role of CO_2 and methane automatically implied that important sources of the problem were related to energy production and consumption, transportation and agriculture – and hence went to the heart of both traditional and modern societies. Furthermore, both the origins and characteristics of the problem appeared to be truly global. Somewhat like the issue of ozone layer depletion, this problem had mainly been created by the industrialized countries, although the future role of developing countries was crucial. In addition, there were no cheap or easy technological 'fixes' to the problem. As opposed to the marine pollution and acid rain contexts, installing clean-up devices could not do the job; and in contrast to the ozone depletion case, substituting a group of substances could definitely not do the job! More fundamental changes were probably required in vital national activities such as transportation and the production and consumption of energy.

7.2.2 The Regime Creation Phase, Culminating in the 1992 Framework Convention

What was it, then, that triggered the establishment of the Intergovernmental Negotiating Committee (INC) in 1990? With the more long-standing scientific attention given to the issue, a combination of a general rise in interest in environmental issues and specific 'events' like the 1988 US heatwave and drought surely played a role. The general upsurge in interest in environmental issues was reflected for instance in international events like the 1987 World Commission on Environment and Development (WCED) report, and important agenda-setting meetings like the Toronto Conference on the Changing Atmosphere (June 1988), the Ottawa International Meeting of Legal and Policy Experts on the Protection of the Atmosphere (June 1989), the Hague Ministerial Conference on Atmospheric Pollution and Climate Change (March 1989), and the Nordwijk Ministerial Conference on Atmospheric Pollution and Climate Change (November 1989).[5] Moreover, the up-coming United Nations Conference on Environment and Development (UNCED) became a natural focal point for such a global issue.[6] The link to the UNCED process made it natural for the work of the INC to be placed under the auspices of the UN General Assembly, as urged by the developing countries. During the five rounds of INC negotiations leading up to the 1992 UNCED Summit, some main trends can be identified. First, despite clear US scientific leadership on this issue, it quickly became clear that the sobering policy line signalled by the Americans at previous international meetings was kept up in the formal negotiating forum. Second, the European Community, fronted by its very outspoken Environmental Commissioner Ripa di Meana, exercised strong rhetorical leadership; and the Community had in 1990 committed itself to CO_2 stabilization by the year 2000. Third, except for Japan and Russia, the tentative positions of most other developed countries were closer to the EC than the US, generally supporting a call for the adoption of specific reduction targets and related timetables. Fourth, in a process so far highly dominated by the actors above, the developing countries increased their involvement in the process, stressing the responsibility of the developed countries for creating the problems. In other respects, the interests of these countries varied widely, with the small, low-lying island states on the 'progressive' side – organized in the Alliance of Small Island States (AOSIS) – and the Organization of Petroleum-Exporting Countries (OPEC) countries on the other, 'reluctant' side.

When the UNCED in Rio de Janeiro drew closer, the EC failed to establish the crucial carbon tax which was supposed to bolster its negotiating position in Rio; the pivotal, reluctant US stance stood firm in spite of massive attacks; and many developed countries were probably at heart uncomfortable with the sheer complexity of climate politics. With this background, the outcome in Rio offered few surprises. Similar to other international environmental contexts, a Framework Convention on Climate Change was adopted,[7] with the most specific commitments being related to the reporting of greenhouse gas inventories and national plans to address climate change. The Convention contained a loose call for a return to the 1990 level of greenhouse gas emissions by the end of the decade, 'either individually or jointly' by the developed country parties (the Annex 1 parties). Furthermore, emphasis was placed on 'new and additional' resource transfers to the developing countries in order, first, to meet their reporting requirements, and later to assist in their implementation efforts. A Conference of the Parties (CoP) was established as the main decision-making forum, and two main subsidiary bodies were appointed: the Subsidiary Body for Scientific and Technological Advice (SBSTA) and the Subsidiary Body for Implementation (SBI) (see Figure 7.1). In addition, an interim Secretariat was established in Geneva. The 1992 Convention was signed in Rio by 153 countries.

Figure 7.1   The climate regime: organizational setup

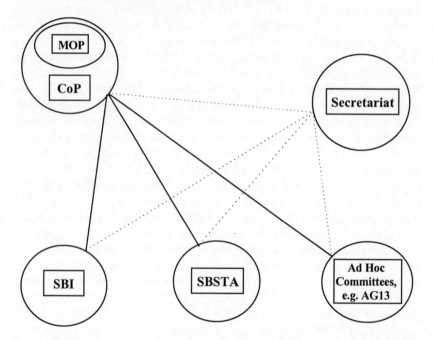

Notes: After the Kyoto Protocol enters into force, its main decision-making body wil be The Conference of the Parties serving as the Meeting of the Parties (or CoP/MOP). Ad hoc committees, which may be established by the CoP (or the CoP/MOP, once the Protocol enters into force), are generally of limited duration.

7.2.3 From Rio to Berlin: 1992–95

In anticipation of the national ratification processes and entry into force of the Convention, it was decided to continue with the INC meetings after 1992. These six meetings largely focused on procedural and methodological development related to the national communications and subsidiary bodies.

However, at the closing of the final session, substantial procedural disagreement remained regarding so-called 'Joint Implementation' (JI) projects[8] and various rules of procedure. In 1994, with the fiftieth ratification, the Convention entered into force, setting the stage for the first CoP (to be held within one year after entry into force). Two rough protocol drafts were launched, one by AOSIS calling for a 20% reduction of CO_2 emissions by 2005, and one 'elements paper' by Germany. The first CoP (CoP One) was then held in Berlin from 28 March to 7 April 1995 as the second climate regime milestone. The main outcome of the Conference was the adoption of the so-called Berlin Mandate. Here, a process was explicitly set in motion to negotiate by 1997 a protocol or other legally binding instrument to set targets and timetables for the reduction of greenhouse gas emissions in the post-2000 period (such as 2005, 2010 and 2020) by the developed countries. In this connection, a specific Ad-Hoc Group on the Berlin Mandate (AGBM) was instituted. Moreover, with regard to the sensitive issues of international implementation and assistance, a compromise was adopted concerning a four-year pilot phase of 'Activities Implemented Jointly' (AIJ) with no formal emission credits given. In addition, some further work was announced on the issue of technology transfer. With regard to the institutional and procedural issues, it was decided to place the permanent Secretariat in Bonn, but some procedural deadlock remained regarding membership of the CoP's Bureau and decision-making procedures (further elaborated in section 7.3.2).

What, then, were the main forces shaping this outcome? The overall mood was one of general sobriety. For instance, the EC held a less ambitious rhetorical profile than in the heated pre-Rio days. The emerging so-called JUSCANZ coalition of other developed countries – including countries like Japan, the US, Canada, Australia, New Zealand, and Norway – emphasized first and foremost flexibility in the international process due to the special circumstances in these countries. The developing countries generally opposed flexibility in terms of JI projects, and the OPEC countries and others were generally no less reluctant than before. The basic message of the Intergovernmental Panel on Climatic Change (IPCC) had not changed since Rio. So how did the Mandate come about at all? First, a more flexible and balanced US position clearly played a role. Moreover, a positive dynamic between an expanding 'Green Group' of developing countries with India in a key position and the more 'low-key progressive' EC must be mentioned. This dynamic reduced developing country reluctance through the mentioned compromise on a pilot phase for 'Activities Implemented Jointly' and put pressure on other actors like the JUSCANZ group. In addition, entrepreneurial efforts from the Conference and future Secretariat host country Germany, as well as effective procedural leadership by the Conference President and the INC Chair, have been emphasized.[9]

7.2.4 From Berlin to Kyoto: 1995–97

Minimal further progress was made before CoP Two, held in Geneva in July 1996. Prior to the Conference, the second IPCC assessment report was presented, explicitly stating for the first time that human interference with the climate was already discernible. The US endorsed the main message of the IPCC report at CoP Two, and explicitly supported the adoption of binding commitments at CoP Three – acts very important both symbolically and politically – though it still included a call for commitments from both developed and developing countries. Still, together with, among other things, a more 'activist' stance by the UK, this contributed to an atmosphere where a specific Berlin Mandate was adopted as the Geneva Declaration. The Declaration endorsed the IPCC report and called unequivocally for a legally binding instrument to be adopted in Kyoto at CoP Three. However, 16 countries did not endorse the Declaration, among them Australia, New Zealand, Saudi Arabia, Russia, and Venezuela.[10]

Progress soon slowed down within the following AGBM meetings. Just to indicate some of the complexity with regard to issues and positions: the US emphasized maximum policy flexibility, both in terms of geographical space (that is, the implementation context) and timing of measures. They also stressed the inclusion of all known greenhouse gases, enthusiastically backed by countries like Japan and Norway on both accounts, but were sceptical about the call for differentiated targets by Norway and other countries and increasingly emphasized the need for commitments also from developing countries. The EC was critical of measures like emission trading and the general idea of differentiated targets for different (groups of) countries, and was also sceptical about including the full range of greenhouse gases, but emphasized internal differentiation within the EC as a crucial element of the negotiations. When the EC launched the specifics of its approach in March 1997, with differentiated reduction ambitions among the EC countries adding up to an overall 15% reduction by 2010 of a 'basket' of greenhouse gases with 1990 as baseline year, the process picked up some speed. However, other specific proposals like the Japanese (overall 5% reductions during the years 2008–12) and the American (emissions stabilization during the same period) were not launched until late autumn, and negotiators and observers travelled to Kyoto and CoP Three with a strong feeling of uncertainty.

The outcome in Kyoto was more ambitious than many had expected. The overall ambition is to reduce developed countries' greenhouse gas emissions by at least 5% by the period 2008–12, compared to 1990 levels.[11] Moreover, a surprising degree of differentiation between the more specific commitments of countries was achieved, with Iceland (+10%), Australia (+8%), and Norway (+1%) as the only countries actually allowed to increase their emissions, and important actors like the US and the EC having to reduce their emissions 7 and 8% respectively, which in the case of the US was more than expected. Other important elements in the Kyoto outcome were a last minute agreement in principle concerning the establishment of an emission permit trading system, the opening up of opportunities for Joint Implementation between developed countries, and the establishment of a 'Clean Development Mechanism' allowing developed countries to pay for emission reductions in developing countries and partly to use such reductions in the achievement of their own commitments.

So how did it come about? Given the pivotal role of the US, the more flexible American attitude announced by Vice President Al Gore during his brief visit to Kyoto definitely played an important role. However, according to participants in the process, central American positions did not in fact change very much along the way. The flexibility was primarily reflected in a more silent, exhausted resignation to pressure from developing countries and the Chairman during the very last minutes of the Conference.[12] Hence, in narrow bargaining terms and as regards the major actors, the US probably gave or 'lost' most compared to its original position, although the picture is somewhat complicated by the inclusion of six gases.[13] The role of the EC was somewhat ambiguous, although it was more positive than negative in terms of effect on the progress of the discussions. On the one hand, based largely on its rather ambitious 15% emission reduction target and internal differentiation scheme, it played a more offensive role than at CoP One, especially with regard to numbers and targets, and scored high points with environmentalists. On the other hand, criticism for lacking negotiation flexibility was voiced by non-EC countries in Kyoto, and such criticism has also been voiced by actors within the EC in the aftermath of the Conference.[14] This is primarily related to the EC emphasis on a lengthy list of policies and measures designed to reduce emissions, to be made binding on Annex 1 countries.[15] In terms of actor interests, the overall compromise has been aptly described by Andresen (1998:32): 'The EU got their numbers, the US got their institutions, Japan maybe got some prestige, the developing countries avoided their commitments, and there were even some prospects of progress on the North/South dimension through the Clean Development Mechanism'. However, in forging this compromise, the role of the Chairman, Raul Estrada-Oyuela from Argentina, was very important, not least in managing to get a deal accepted during the final hours. This important role was rooted in several factors.[16] First, the high complexity and related 'veil of uncertainty' of the negotiations gave additional power to the few (systemic) actors who both had formal integrative and oversight functions and managed to fulfil these functions in practice. Second, and related to the practice part already mentioned, Estrada-Oyuela was personally up to the formidable task. Third, the stakes were high in terms of coming up with an agreement, and the role of the Chairman only increased as time passed on and total failure became an increasingly probable outcome.

Concluding this background section, then: in five and a half years, the regulatory strength of the climate change regime has increased substantially – from a loose and common stabilization target in the 1992 Convention to differentiated commitments in the 1997 Kyoto Protocol, adding up to an overall 5% reduction target. Given the malign character of the issue, this is no small achievement – although probably grossly inadequate in terms of coping with the looming threat of global climate change. The Kyoto Protocol's ultimate success is of course dependent on the tricky task of implementation and behavioural change. If we then, reluctantly, call the climate regime a political success so far, it becomes interesting to examine whether this political success also means that the evolving institutional design has been successful so far. Furthermore, what are the main institutional challenges ahead? This indicates that it is time to zoom in on a more detailed institutional discussion, primarily focused on the most recent, dynamic regime functioning phase, from the first formal Conference of the Parties in 1995 on. Main findings and lessons from the other regimes discussed in this book will form important analytical points of departure.

7.3 CLIMATE INSTITUTIONAL POSSIBILITIES AND FALLACIES IN THE LIGHT OF LESSONS FROM OTHER REGIMES[17]

7.3.1 Access and Participation: An Inclusive and 'Dense' Process, but are All Flexibility Options Utilized?

Regarding the scope of state participation, the case evidence suggested the strength of more limited, homogeneous approaches compared to wider approaches with more heterogeneous participation. For instance, the experiences of the more homogenous North Sea Conference system as a motor for the wider OSCON and PARCON regimes indicate the potential value of identifying similar, more limited 'climate process motors'. Also highly relevant in this context was the differentiation within the ozone regime between industrialized countries as a more limited vanguarding group, primarily responsible for the initial problem, and the developing countries with a ten-year implementation delay. However, all these regimes have found ways to transcend the requirements for rather broad state participation (global or regional) determined by problem scope and long-term legitimacy, by combining broader forums with more narrow and politically effective institutional contexts. This may indicate that *both* the global and the regional contexts are too broad to combine political and problem-solving effectiveness in the course of time; it may be necessary to develop smaller, more homogeneous 'clubs within the clubs'.

Turning to the more specific climate context, an inclusive, global approach has so far been dominant with regard to state participation. For instance, some 150 states took part in the INC meetings leading up to the 1992 Convention; 170 delegations participated in the Berlin CoP One; and 161 nations took part in CoP Three in Kyoto. This broad participation is clearly related to central problem characteristics. First, both emission sources and climate effects are global, although on both accounts with regional variations. Moreover, and quite similar to the ozone regime, the growing, and in the future crucial, greenhouse gas emissions of the developing countries, as well as the need for global legitimacy for the adopted regulations, have pointed towards including these countries in the negotiations from the very beginning. Hence, the climate change issue was from the start placed in a broader environment and development context. In addition, the evolving ideas on potentially global policy measures like joint implementation and international trading of emission quotas have become further elements suggesting a global participatory context. However, the overall global approach has not prevented a flexible utilization of different participatory contexts at regime meetings: the all-inclusive plenary meetings; meetings of several Open-Ended Working Groups like the Ad Hoc Group on Article 13; private meetings of the various negotiation coalitions; and contact groups of key representatives of each of these groups.[18] Tellingly, the final phase of CoP One has been described thus: 'After negotiations during the meeting's ministerial segment developed into discussion among 24, and then 15 parties ("Friends of the President"), agreement on a mandate was reached in the early hours of the final day'.[19] The same dynamic was witnessed in Kyoto. During the final, rather exclusive negotiating rounds, the stage was dominated by the major actors and the smaller actors were put on the sidelines.

Moreover, as an additional element 'softening up' the global context, a gradual regionalization of commitments has been developed, reminiscent of the development within the ozone regime. The 1995 Berlin Mandate explicitly recognized the prime responsibility of the *developed* countries – in this context also termed the Annex 1 countries – to agree upon new policies and measures within specified time-frames by 1997. Although disputed to the last minute, the Kyoto commitments only contain reduction targets for the developed countries. On the one hand, in the light of the ozone experiences, this can be seen as a necessary balancing of effectiveness and legitimacy or equity. As further discussed in connection with the ozone regime, such a differentiation downplays more short-term problem-solving effectiveness in return for increased short-term regime legitimacy and hopefully increased long-term problem-solving effectiveness. On the other hand, it can be argued that the increased regionalization of commitments has led to a certain mismatch between the inclusive participatory approach and the more limited group of countries willing to take on binding commitments at this stage. This has been reflected in the fact that a large majority of states present in the negotiations do not participate in the active meaning of the word. Hence, in principle, one possible solution to this mismatch could be a temporarily increased further formal regionalization within the regime. Moreover, within such a scenario, the most obvious, specific and well-established organizational potential sub-context would be the Organization for Economic Cooperation and Development (OECD).[20] This particular organizational context has not been given much attention so far, however. Why is this? The first obvious point is that the OECD has come to include at least three major groups in the negotiations: the EC; JUSCANZ; and several of the Countries with Economies in Transition (CEIT) – with very varying interests and positions in the negotiations. Moreover, the EC has been making progress in its internal burden-sharing game. One of the critical questions is what the EC may gain by entering into more formalized arrangements with the other OECD sub-groups. If such mutual gains are hard to envisage, then interestingly, more general discussions of potential OECD burden-sharing arrangements are of little practical relevance.[21] Be this as it may, given the global nature of the problem, the OECD option cannot avoid complicated questions of legitimacy, burden-sharing and joint implementation far beyond the OECD context. Hence, although it generally makes sense to be aware of the possibilities for more regional 'vanguarding' efforts, a key role for the global, comprehensive context as an important forum for securing global legitimacy and hence strengthen longer term problem-solving seems absolutely crucial.

Shifting the focus, then, from governments and regime parties to the access and participation of various 'outsider' non-governmental actors, one of the key lessons in this connection from the regimes analysed in previous chapters was the importance of striking an optimal balance between inclusive phases and forums and more exclusive phases and forums, in order to utilize fully the different strengths of both approaches. In terms of stages and development over time, the importance of inclusive and open initial phases was suggested. Overall, the increasing emphasis given in particular to the value of open access suggests that the balance should be tilted as far as possible towards the inclusive pole. This point seems to have been well taken within the climate context. Similar to the ozone regime, the climate negotiators have opted for an overall inclusive model. With regard to the Conference of the Parties (CoP), any body or agency, whether international or national, 'which is qualified in matters covered by the Convention', and which has informed the Secretariat of its wish to participate at the CoP as observer, may do so unless one third of the parties object. In practice, this meant for instance in connection with the important first

CoP in Berlin in 1995 (which established the Berlin Mandate), that almost 200 observer organizations participated – UN specialized agencies, inter-governmental organizations, and non-governmental organizations. Moreover, more than 2000 journalists were registered, and it has been maintained that a total of around 4000 participants followed the Conference proceedings.[22] The picture at CoP Three in Kyoto was quite similar.

In addition to the CoPs, NGOs have also participated as observers in Working Groups, for instance in the AGBM, and in the Ad Hoc Group on Article 13 (AG 13). Moreover, a few states included NGO representatives in their delegations. The NGO participation has been highly diverse, with a rough distinction to be made between the environmental organizations (like Greenpeace) and the business organizations. Within the latter category, a new distinction can be made between the 'grey' or 'black' organizations (like the Global Climate Coalition representing the fossil fuel industry), and the 'greener' organizations representing renewable energy industries (like the Business Council for a Sustainable Energy Future) and the insurance industries. It has been maintained that the participation of the latter, the 'green' business organizations, has increased over time.[23] However, as noted earlier, it may generally be assumed that the business organizations have favourable access to decision-makers via several channels and have less need for, and interest in, utilizing the international meetings for lobbying purposes. Not surprisingly, Heads of Delegations meetings and similar forums have had an exclusive character. Moreover, as the pre-Kyoto process went into its final stages, inclusiveness was reduced. For instance, at the seventh AGBM meeting in August 1997, interest groups were barred from all sessions. The Chairman of the AGBM process, Mr Estrada-Oyuela, tellingly stated that this was due to the fact that 'we are now in the process of negotiations that requires a more private atmosphere'.[24] Still, the overall balance has been somewhat tilted in favour of inclusiveness, and this balance seems to have functioned well.

Turning finally, then, to the issue of ministerial participation and the degree of 'political energy' infused into the process, case evidence definitely indicated the positive effects of regular and frequent higher-level political participation in regime activities. However, the case studies also suggested that the positive effects of political participation were conditional upon bureaucratic ground-work and hence that there was a crucial balance to be found over time. In the climate case, an important lesson so far seems to be that the vitalizing effects so easily related to high-profile political participation do not require the actual presence of ministers. Although ministerial participation has so far been substantial, with all three CoPs winding up with crucial concluding ministerial segments,[25] even meetings without a single minister have attracted considerable media attention. Hence, these experiences support the assumption that the need for high-level political participation is partly dependent on issue-area characteristics. In this case especially, the potential regulatory costs involved are apparently enough to keep the political momentum up, at least so far. So, if a balance point and an 'optimal' level of politicization is to be found, the pertinent question is rather whether the necessary bureaucratic footwork has been, and will be given, adequate room in relation to the political and symbolic processes. The Kyoto meeting is obviously important as a regime milestone and symbolic event, but an important challenge is no doubt to come up with *implementable* decisions and adequate national follow-up capacity.[26] The international regime part of this challenge brings up questions like Secretariat capacity and the functioning and adequacy of the climate organizational machinery so far. Hence, one of the first post-Kyoto tasks should be to examine critically the organizational setup and process development so far, and the requirements related to the present and probable future design of commitments and protocols. Given that the political and attention-raising part of this issue seems well taken care of, at least for the time being, such an organizational review and streamlining process could secure the smooth functioning of the bureaucratic part of the overall balance with regard to processes. In this connection, the complaints being voiced about real progress only being accomplished during the final rounds of the main negotiation phases should clearly be noted. Process streamlining could well mean overall fewer meetings, with the actual frequency being made dependent on the existence and presentation of substantial new proposals and ideas to be discussed. Still, one should keep in mind that the progress of negotiations is very much a matter of bargaining tactics, in which institutional effects and matters may only be the tip of the iceberg.

Concluding this section, the organizational access and participation dilemmas and balancing acts suggested by experiences from other environmental regimes seem to have been well handled within the climate regime so far. With regard to the scope of state participation, the inclusive, global approach utilized is closely related to central problem characteristics. Both emission sources and climate effects are global, although with regional variations. Similar to the ozone regime, the increasing, and in future crucial, greenhouse gas emissions of the developing countries, as well as the need for global legitimacy for the adopted regulations, have pointed to including these countries in the negotiations from the very start. Moreover, a basic North–South regionalization of commitments has balanced the somewhat conflicting requirements for effective and legitimate processes. However, there have been costs in the form of a certain mismatch between the global scope of the forum and the exclusive Northern scope of the first phase commitments, and especially within the US, criticism has been raised regarding this approach. With regard to outsiders' access, much like the ozone process, an overall inclusive and open approach has been chosen, although with increasing use of closed sessions during the concluding phases of negotiation rounds. Regarding ministerial and high-level political input into processes, a fruitful interplay between political and bureaucratic processes and meetings has been established. As the political, 'vitalizing' part seems well taken care of, the main challenge ahead may be more in the field of bureaucratic and international streamlining of organizations. Overall, it should be noted that this first phase of the climate regime has been characterized by a high, perhaps unprecedented, institutional 'density'.[27] Hence, at least in this respect, the malign, complicated character of the issue has been institutionally counterbalanced.

7.3.2 Conflict over Decision-Making Rules: A 'Fig Leaf' for Underlying Tensions?

In terms of decision-making rules, lessons from other cases suggested the importance of distinguishing between procedural formalities and political realities with regard to the issue of decision-making rules. Despite several formal majority voting clauses, there was a general reliance in practice on a basically consensual approach. However, several interesting elements were noted which made the consensual approach more flexible, like geographically differentiated decisions in terms of application and stringency, and the agreed abstention of reluctant parties. Let us first, then, briefly describe the climate formalities. The 1992 Climate Convention laid down a basically consensual approach. It stated that the parties should make every effort to reach agreement on any proposed amendment or annex to the Convention by consensus. If all efforts at consensus were exhausted, the amendment should as a last resort be adopted by a three-quarters majority vote. However, according to Articles 7.2(k) and 7.3 in the Convention, the first CoP session had to decide by consensus on the Rules of Procedure for itself and subsidiary bodies. At the following INC meetings, this issue turned out to be controversial. For instance, at the final INC session in February 1995, a diverse group of countries including Australia, Brazil, the Czech Republic, Japan and the EC countries, backed the option indicated in the Convention, but with an emphasis on the three-fourths majority option. Opposing this position and emphasizing a consensual approach was a group of mainly G-77 countries including China, Colombia, Nigeria, Kuwait and Saudi Arabia.[28] At the first CoP in 1995, several sub-issues within this context were increasingly uncovered. For example, important OECD actors like the EC and the US insisted that voting on financial matters should require unanimity, fearing the possibility of losing financial control. Moreover, sustaining the basic position launched by Kuwait and Saudi Arabia in the INC sessions, the OPEC states insisted that unanimity should apply with regard to the adoption of protocols and other substantive decisions related to the development of the Convention.[29] Hence, the issue was deferred to the second CoP. Formally, the second CoP did not make much progress on this issue. Still, the adoption of the Geneva Ministerial Declaration against a number of dissenting voices[30] can be interpreted as a small victory for parties not supporting a 'total unanimity' position.[31] No progress was made on this issue at CoP Three in Kyoto. Hence, the formal situation is still basically unresolved and open with regard to the issue of decision-making rules.

Before we discuss the practical effects of this situation and some implications for the process ahead, let us first briefly suggest some important background factors shaping this development. Given the consensual and prudent experiences from other regimes, are there specific, potential climate regime circumstances that can shed light on the fairly heated discussions on these matters? In general, the potentially grave economic and competitive consequences for almost all actors involved, not least for the oil-exporting countries, can be noted. It can be argued that 'strong' international climate commitments challenge national economies in a hitherto unprecedented manner. It seems likely that, in particular, major oil producers like Kuwait and Saudi Arabia have regarded a procedure emphasizing unanimity as a potential instrument to block the adoption of 'strong' new commitments.[32] The reluctance of industrialized countries concerning 'strong' rules on financial matters is clearly a reflection of an underlying complex North–South tug-of-war over economic and political power. From an outside perspective, one may of course wonder if the heated discussions are really worth it. Lessons from other regimes clearly suggest a basically cautious and restrained approach with regard to the use of formal voting possibilities. Given the high economic stakes involved in the climate context, there is no reason to expect a different overall approach in this context. Hence, clearly there are also more specific, tactical institutional linkage dimensions to this issue. At CoP One, several oil-producing developing countries, and especially Saudi Arabia and Kuwait, demanded a permanent seat on the Bureau of the Conference, partly on the grounds that such a seat had been granted to the Alliance of Small Island States (AOSIS).[33] The other parties were, and have remained, less enthusiastic about this demand, as the combination of a seat for OPEC in the Bureau and unanimity procedures would give these countries a strong vetoing position within the regime.[34] Hence, lacking progress on the composition of the Bureau issue has 'spilled over' to the issue of decision-making rules.

Has this conflict really mattered much in practice? Apparently very little. Several types of decisions have been made in the absence of an agreement on formal rules. For instance, at CoP One, the seating of the Secretariat was decided by a vote. Moreover, at CoP Three, various aspects of the Kyoto Protocol were adopted by some sort of 'consensus', greatly aided by an active Chairman cleverly adapting the consensus requirement in relation to the various decision challenges at hand. These skills were described by observers of the process in the following telling manner: 'Several times objectors were left open mouthed as Mr Estrada-Oyuela brought down the gavel to declare a paragraph adopted by consensus when they had hardly finished their opposition ... What saved his approach from being draconian was his unflagging good humour and strictly unpartisan approach.'[35] Finally, looking ahead, assuming that the formalities will fall into place in the near future, it makes sense to devote some attention to a systematic exploration of the potential for employing the many flexibility options available within a consensual framework in order to secure strong as well as legitimate international decisions – a combination which is practically a prerequisite for achieving both political and problem-solving effectiveness. We are then back to the discussion of the possibilities of formalized, regional options. Moreover, given the multitude of flexibility options available, it also makes sense to find ways to utilize as many as possible without drowning in a much too complex totality. This theme will be further explored in section 7.3.4 below on the structuring of the agenda.

7.3.3 The Role and Resources of the Secretariat: Clearly Above the Critical Minimum, but Below the Optimal Level?[36]

General logic and evidence from the other case studies suggest that, in order to perform the necessary back-up functions, regime secretariats must have a critical minimum level in terms of financial and human resources. When there are many parties, and the vast majority of the parties have moderate administrative capacity, this critical minimum level will tend to be higher. However, in none of the cases studied in this context was there a need for a large bureaucracy. Moreover, the ozone case in particular suggests the importance of assessing the role of the secretariat in the light of the total organization of regime bodies, with obvious potential for synergy effects. Turning then to the climate context, a Secretariat supporting the INC process was established in Geneva in 1990/91, based on personnel who had been working for UNCTAD, UNEP, and WMO. In connection with the adoption of the 1992 Climate Convention, this became the interim climate Secretariat in Geneva, with six professionals and seven support staff. Organizationally, it was under the UN General Assembly. The costs of the interim Secretariat were covered by the UN regular budget under the then Department for Policy Co-ordination and Sustainable Development, with additional contributions from UNEP, WMO, and bilateral donors. In addition, there were particular financial resources to support participation in the process, and also supplementary activities by the Secretariat.[37] With regard to the mandate of the Secretariat, it was formulated in Article 8 of the Convention in a rather standard way for international environmental politics: to support sessions of the CoP and subsidiary bodies by compiling and issuing reports on various types of national follow-ups; to 'facilitate assistance to the Parties, especially developing country Parties, on request, in the compilation and communication of (required) information' (2c); and to ensure the necessary coordination with the secretariats of other relevant international bodies. Regarding these tasks, the explicit mention of reporting assistance to parties, and especially developing countries, should be noted. However, at least in the initial phase of the regime, this had few practical effects; specific assistance to developing countries was mainly financed by 'extra-budgetary funds'.

In connection with the entry into force of the Convention, the issue of finding a permanent home for the Secretariat became more important. This was discussed at the first CoP in Berlin in 1995, where four main alternatives were proposed: Toronto, Montevideo, Geneva, and Bonn. Important decision-making criteria included convenient access for delegations to the Secretariat and regime meetings, and possible budgetary savings by having the Secretariat located near other UN bodies, as well as contributions offered by the potential host government.[38] Although Geneva was the favourite, when the issue was finally settled through a vote, Bonn somewhat surprisingly was the winner.[39] By March 1998, staffing had increased to 35 professionals and 17 support staff, augmented by short-term support staff and consultants as needed.[40] The approved 1998 core budget is US$9 727 100. Moreover, with regard to the internal organization of the Secretariat, five main sections have been established. In addition to a directing 'Executive Direction and Management Section', there are sections for 'Communication Assessment Review' (CAR); 'Financial and Technical Cooperation' (FTC); 'Implementation and Planning'; and 'Inter-governmental and Information Support' (IIS).[41] This new organization corresponds roughly to the overall organization of the regime bodies.

How, then, can we assess this Secretariat development? Are the current administrative and financial resources adequate in relation to the various tasks involved? And what about the post-Kyoto perspectives? Although direct comparisons are always tricky, compared to the resources of the ozone Secretariat (currently five professionals; eight support staff; and a total budget for the Convention and Montreal Protocol of a little under 5 million US dollars), the climate Secretariat situation does not look that bad – given that the number and type of parties are quite similar in the two contexts, and that there are similarities also with regard to subsidiary bodies. The climate resources at least seem to be clearly above the critical minimum. Moreover, the location in Germany has been hailed as a strength. As maintained by Jäger and O'Riordan (1996:26): 'The patronage of a key, and committed, big emitter, with considerable resources of cash and other support for the Secretariat, should not be underestimated'. However, both the complexity of the climate issue, the high ambitions of the parties, and the large – and probably unprecedented – interest in the negotiation rounds from a multitude of state and non-state actors, the media, researchers, and the public at large, represent formidable information and servicing challenges for the Secretariat. The various subsidiary bodies under the Convention have a dual character in this connection: they both require Secretariat attention and work, and carry out supporting administrative work.

Looking ahead, there are good reasons for careful consideration of the adequacy of administrative capacity. With the move of the Secretariat from Geneva to Bonn, and the limited time so far for administrative consolidation, training and fine tuning, it is only natural that it will still take some time to find the optimal organization of regime back-up functions. In terms of more specific functions to watch, as indicated by Victor and Salt (1995), building a well-functioning reporting system is a task where the Secretariat has an important role to play. Given the ambitious approach chosen, with national reports supplemented by country visits and in-depth reviews, this has till now meant a heavy workload for the Secretariat, and this workload will only increase with the increasingly global reporting and review process. Moreover, and not least important, the progress towards a more structured and formal system for various types of international implementation efforts – most notably joint implementation and trading of international emission permits (see section 7.3.6) – may require substantial Secretariat support and supervision efforts, depending, however, on the ultimate design.

In summary: climate Secretariat capacity seems clearly above a 'critical minimum' requirement. Whether the resource situation is 'optimal' is a very difficult question to answer, however. This depends, among other things, on what the parties would like the Secretariat to do and at what speed. It is generally clear that the tasks are formidable, given the global context, the many issue dimensions, and the considerable interest in the negotiations.

7.3.4 The Structuring of the Agenda: Many Comprehensiveness Dimensions and Virtues, but will the Totality be Destructive?

Experiences from other regimes support the general idea of the virtue of a sequential and incremental development of regime regulatory agendas, related to the gradual development of scientific and technological knowledge. The practical feasibility of a flexible adding and subtracting of issues can be questioned, though, on the basis of the cases previously analysed in this book. Moreover, the obvious close relationship between the structuring of the agenda and central problem characteristics must be emphasized.

Therefore, turning to the climate context, the complex and comprehensive causes of the climate change problem indicate a certain fundamental and structural 'drive' towards comprehensiveness.[42] This has been reflected in negotiations with many sub-issues and sub-dimensions, where calls for flexibility and comprehensiveness have gained increasing support, as states have gradually realized the complexity of the climate policy challenges. Perhaps the most obvious example concerns the issue of greenhouse gas comprehensiveness. In the early days of the regime, much focus was understandably directed at the issue of CO_2 emissions, as these emissions had the best knowledge base and CO_2 is in many contexts the most important greenhouse gas. In the course of time, based especially on the work carried out by the Intergovernmental Panel on Climatic Change (IPCC), knowledge on the range of relevant gases has increased considerably, and the issue of sinks has also made progress.[43] Among the most relevant gases, in addition to CO_2, are methane (CH_4); nitrous oxide (N_2O); hydrofluorocarbons (HFCs); perfluorocarbons (PFCs); and sulphur hexafluoride (SF_6). As noted in section 7.2.4, the Kyoto Protocol includes all these six gases. In addition, both the issues related to target differentiation and the implementation context deserve a brief mention in this context.[44] Target differentiation refers to the fundamental choice between 'flat rate' international commitments (as in the 1985 Sulphur Protocol, calling for a common 30% cut of emissions) and differing international commitments (as in the 1994 Sulphur Protocol, with differing reduction requirements for different states). In this context it should be noted that differentiation was in fact explicitly called for in the Berlin Mandate.[45] However, the basis for such differentiation is of course a long and complicated discussion in itself.[46] In the implementation context, this refers to the issue of whether emission reductions must be achieved unilaterally or within a multilateral context through joint implementation projects and arrangements for the trading of emission permits. Although perfectly understandable and reasonable in the light of the complex and inevitably global scope of climate change policies, such an international context raises a number of tricky institutional questions, related to the establishment and effective operation of such systems.[47]

How can we assess this development? On the one hand, the drive towards comprehensiveness has functioned positively. For instance, the increasingly constructive and 'progressive' role of key actors like the US seems highly dependent on a negotiating agenda in which flexibility and comprehensiveness are central concepts. This has also been reflected in many conditional statements of positions, where a possible support for more ambitious targets and timetables has been made dependent on aspects like a broad basket of greenhouse gases, the inclusion of both sources and sinks of greenhouse gases, and a flexible and international implementation perspective. Hence, loose, informal package deals have already played a role within the regime. For instance in Kyoto at CoP Three, it seems very likely that the US accepted a tougher overall reduction target than initially proposed 'in return for' a basic acceptance within the regime of the design of a more flexible approach, especially related to a system of emission permit trading. On the other hand, developing inter-issue connections and more or less explicit package deals implies a distinct risk of deadlock, and of situations where lacking progress on one issue leads to deadlock in the whole process. The increasing complexity and interconnectedness may of course be tactically exploited and CoP Three offered several examples. Nevertheless, given the essentially positive aspects of comprehensiveness, the alternative to a complex game with risks of tactical exploitation could easily be a game without the attendance of central actors. In other words, central problem characteristics have seriously limited the practical scope for setting up a more 'narrow', less complicated negotiation game. Still, post-Kyoto progress may partly be dependent on the ability of negotiators to once again temporarily limit the scope of the agenda and deal with issues in a prioritized, sequential manner. This may be easier in a situation where the Kyoto Protocol for now has settled a lot of specific issues of principle. An obvious candidate for focused attention is the building of institutional capacity for the effective operation and supervision of a system for the international implementation of commitments.

7.3.5 The Science–Politics Interface: Both Well-Functioning Application of Lessons and Institutional Innovation?

In other international environmental arenas, there has been increased focus on the communication factor of the science–politics issue, reflected in the establishment of 'buffer' bodies as meeting places for scientists and policy-makers. Moreover, and interestingly, an essentially 'national' and governmental flavour to the composition of bodies has not created significant problems, at least not within moderately politicized contexts like transboundary air pollution and land-based marine pollution. In addition, a close relationship between organization and specific issue characteristics was noted also in this connection. Turning then to the climate change context, 'scientific organization' preceded 'political organization', in a somewhat similar way as it did in the ozone depletion context. In 1979, the First World Climate Conference was held in Geneva, and the World Climate Program was launched. The next important milestone was the 1985 Villach climate conference under the auspices of WMO, UNEP and ICSU (International Council of Scientific Unions), marked by the broad participation of scientists from different climate research communities representing 29 countries. The establishment in 1987 of the Advisory Group on Greenhouse Gases under the auspices of WMO and UNEP was followed by the founding in 1988 of the Intergovernmental Panel on Climatic Change (IPCC) under the auspices of the same two organizations. In the period up to the first CoP in 1995 in Berlin, two main phases can be discerned in the organization and functioning of the IPCC.[48]

From 1988 to 1992, the function of the IPCC was to coordinate and initiate climate research in order to fulfil three tasks: (1) to assess available scientific information on climate change (Working Group I); (2) to assess the environmental and socio-economic impacts of climate change (Working Group II); and (3) to formulate response strategies (Working Group III). In addition to the Working Groups (WGs), some task forces, and the WGs' plenaries, there was an IPCC Plenary, a Bureau, and a Special Committee for Developing Countries. In 1990 the first IPCC Assessment Report was presented to the Second World Climate Conference. Despite complaints about lacking communication between the WGs, this design was quite successful. On the one hand, a certain separation of science and politics was achieved first by the distinction between the 'scientific' WGs and task forces and the more politically geared plenary forums responsible for formulating summaries for policy makers; second, by having WG I as a strong natural scientific core and by having 'softer', more value-laden and political issues discussed in WG II and especially WG III. On the other hand, communication and the linking of science and politics was achieved first by the very establishment of the IPCC as an intergovernmental body; second, the governmental nomination of participants; third, an explicit clause calling for 'balanced geographic representation';[49] fourth, the explicit unifying and advisory role of the plenary bodies; and fifth, the very openness of the process, with the active encouragement of participation from environmentalists and industry experts.[50]

In 1992, the IPCC was reorganized. WGs II and III were merged into a new WG II, and a new WG III was set up to deal with socio-economic and other cross-cutting issues related to climate change.[51] This reorganization did not, however, change the basic functioning of the scientific–political complex. Moreover, the 1992 Climate Convention also marked the formal establishment of a Subsidiary Body for Scientific and Technological Advice (SBSTA), open to government representatives from all parties.[52] However, it was not until 1995 that the SBSTA started to function in practice. At the first CoP, the role of the SBSTA was further developed, and it was described as 'the link between the scientific, technical and technological assessments and the information provided by competent international bodies, and the policy-oriented needs of the Conference of the Parties'.[53] Hence, important tasks of the SBSTA should include a summary of scientific findings by the IPCC and other competent bodies; a consideration of scientific, technical and socio-economic aspects of the in-depth review of national communications; a consideration of methodological issues in the preparation and aggregation of national greenhouse inventories; issues related to technology transfer; and also the general adequacy of Convention progress in terms of 'environmental requirements' as indicated more or less clearly by scientists. At its first meeting in August 1995, the dilemma of fundamental scientific integrity versus national control cropped up in debates on the composition of subsidiary Technical Advisory Panels (TAPs), both with regard to the degree of national control and the geographical balance of representation. Due to differences in political culture and the fact that a majority of experts come from developed countries, these countries prefer a more independent expert-dominated model, while developing countries prefer a model giving more weight to political and national criteria for participation.[54] This conflict has not been resolved at subsequent meetings.

Why, then, would there be a need for the SBSTA, when the IPCC was already there and had an explicit and well-functioning advisory role? One probable explanatory factor was that the parties regarded the IPCC as too detached and independent, feeling the need for a body that was more formally and practically incorporated in the regime. The outcome is that the climate regime has an extraordinarily well-developed scientific–political complex, with several organizational entities and bodies fulfilling advisory and communicatory functions. Hence, it is probably symptomatic of this 'institutional density' that the former IPCC Chairman Bert Bolin in August 1997 downplayed the IPCC's advisory role.[55] However, like several other organizational issues within the regime, developing an optimal interaction and division of labour between the various regime bodies takes time. This seems to have been the case with regard to the relationship between the more established, scientifically pure IPCC and the more, by nature, politically geared and staffed 'newcomer' SBSTA. For instance, according to Lanchbery (1997:167), 'long sessions of the SBSTA have been devoted to some Parties refighting battles concerning science that they had previously lost in meetings of the IPCC'. However, the relationship between the two bodies and the functioning of the SBSTA have improved in the course of time.[56]

In conclusion, the institutional design of the scientific–political complex can be interpreted as a successful application of the main lessons from other regimes concerning the creation of institutional prospects for positive communication between scientists and policy-makers, and a more issue-specific fine tuning of an extremely complex intellectual issue. The fact that accusations of politicization of science and complicated discussions concerning national control have been more striking within the climate context than other contexts is probably more a reflection of the higher stakes within the climate 'game' than a sign of serious organizational defects. Thus, it follows that the formidable gap so far between the scientific call for an immediate 60% reduction in greenhouse gas emissions to stabilize atmospheric conditions, and the most recent 5% cut decided upon in Kyoto, has not been caused by organizational defects of the regime; on the contrary, results might in fact have been worse with a less trustworthy and consensual scientific input. The 1992

Convention may not have been ratified,[57] and the 1995 adoption of the Berlin Mandate and ensuing process leading up to the Kyoto Protocol can also be regarded as proof that most countries take the scientific message seriously. However, the climate context is uniquely complex in an international comparative perspective, and the organizational handling of the science–politics interface is neither finished nor 'perfect'. Hence, refining the organization of the science–politics relationship may have significant positive effects on the process in a longer term perspective. Among the important challenges are, first, the further development of broad-based participation in the scientific work, not least with regard to participation from developing countries. Moreover, the further clarification and fruitful division of labour between the IPCC and the SBSTA must be kept up. In potential situations of more temporary sharp upsurges or declines in the general public's interest and attention, it may be crucial to have well-functioning, legitimate forums to keep political responses as rational and effective as possible.

7.3.6 Verification and Compliance: Institutionally Advanced, though Still Quite 'Soft'

The verification and compliance discussion includes many dimensions – from the design of reporting systems, through procedures for dispute settlement, to the design of financial mechanisms for bolstering compliance. Although other regimes discussed in this book functioned initially and for a long time in a soft, non-confrontational way, they have in the course of time developed sharper 'teeth', with better reporting procedures, separate implementation review bodies, and generally more critical discussions. This may suggest that developing more 'intrusive' procedures requires an initial period of general confidence-building among the parties. Moreover, although this development in some cases was also related to a generally more trusting atmosphere between East and West, a second main lesson implies that there is a certain relationship between regulatory design and the verification and compliance instruments required. In the early phases of the regimes studied, regulations were in several respects diffuse, and the checking of progress did not require advanced procedures. When regulations became more precise and complex, the interest in improved verification procedures increased considerably. Thirdly, in the global ozone context with a marked North–South dimension, the establishment of a Multilateral Fund was important. In a design perspective, such financial mechanisms bring up more general dilemmas related to the balancing of effectiveness and legitimacy. When donors feel that effectiveness is not given enough priority, they definitely have their ways of showing discontent by delaying or halting their contributions.

Turning then to the climate context, with the economic and political costs involved in climate gas reductions being potentially higher than in other environmental regimes so far, it is likely that the climate discussion must search for lessons outside the environmental realm and also be innovative. Discussions and practice so far support such a thesis. At least three main related dimensions can be discerned: the design of reporting procedures and potential problems; the organizational handling of implementation and non-compliance issues; and the role of a financial mechanism in this connection. Turning first to the question of the design of the reporting system, the 1992 Convention established that all parties were obliged to submit 'national communications' providing information on their national greenhouse gas inventories, emissions projections, and the policies and measures they were taking to limit future emissions. Annex 1 developed country parties were obliged to provide particularly detailed information on a regular basis. It was generally stated that these communications were to be internationally reviewed. At the first CoP, it was decided that the Annex 1 reports, focusing on ten main issues, should be subject to in-depth reviews carried out by expert review teams within one year of being received by the Secretariat. Review teams would consist of experts nominated by the parties and from international organizations, selected under the guidance of the Chairs of the SBSTA and the Subsidiary Body for Implementation (SBI). Balance in expertise and origin should be sought.[58] Team reports should be written in 'non-confrontational language', and submitted to the SBI and SBSTA for consideration. In the first round of communications and reviews up to the beginning of 1997, synthesis reports were prepared for the first CoP (based on the 15 first communications) and the second CoP (based on 34 communications). By the end of 1996, 31 country visits and reviews had been carried out. By spring 1997, Annex 1 countries had completed their second round of communications, and developing countries started on their first round of communications.[59]

In terms of practical experience, both parties and observers assess progress so far in overall positive terms.[60] Although there have been some delayed reports both within the group of Annex 1 countries and not least with regard to developing countries, this process has functioned quite well. One may perhaps say surprisingly well, compared with other environmental regimes, and taking into consideration the complexity of many of the reporting issues and the still early phase of the process. The country visits and in-depth reviews must also be characterized as an institutionally advanced dimension, compared to most other environmental regimes. In composing the review teams, there seems to have been a successful balance between commonly witnessed concerns for national control and the need for teams to have a certain independent 'bite'. With regard to background factors for the results achieved so far, first, reporting was emphasized in the 1992 Convention and emerged as a sort of substitute for more specific action in the follow-up work. Second, an important actor like the US has given high priority to the reporting issues. However, some reporting problems have been noted, for instance in terms of lacking data and varying base years,[61] and experiences not least from the ozone regime indicate that several types of problem are likely to arise and should be anticipated. In general, good reporting is dependent on Secretariat capacity to produce clear procedures and in turn handle the incoming data – and reporting states' willingness and capacity to report. As noted earlier, Secretariat capacity seems good, but also clearly not unlimited, and a point to watch for Parties seeking optimal follow-up of international decisions. If we regard willingness to report as a factor that is scarcely manipulated, then the chief remaining critical point is state capacity. As the 'old' OECD countries overall have adequate capacity, this question concerns primarily the developing countries and the CEIT group, linked to the financial mechanism. A couple of discussion points may be noted here. First, as several of these countries have increasingly run into reporting trouble within the ozone regime, comprehensive solutions involving at least these two regimes could be envisioned. Second, so far, the technological and financial mechanism within the regime has focused on the developing countries, which is reasonable in a long-term perspective. However, to the extent that reporting capacities in the CEIT countries are inadequate, a gradual temporary redirection of attention may be required.

Regarding the organizational handling of the implementation and non-compliance issues, first, the Subsidiary Body on Implementation (SBI) clearly has a role to play. The main function of the SBI was to assist the CoP in the assessment and review of the effective implementation of the Convention, including advice on the development of the financial mechanism and technology transfer. In practice so far, the main contribution of the SBI has been in the preparation of synthesis reports of the national communications. A more critical review function resembling the Implementation Committee within the ozone regime has not yet been developed, which is only natural given the lack of precise regime regulatory benchmarks prior to the Kyoto Protocol. Moreover, a second main element in the compliance context is the so-called Article 13 process. The first CoP established an Ad Hoc Group on Article 13 in the 1992 Convention,[62] based on the idea that it would be useful to have a forum where concerns about failing to implement, and implementation problems, could be discussed in a non-confrontational way; obviously inspired by the non-compliance procedures developed in the ozone regime context.[63] The process has been inclusive, with substantial inputs from both states and NGOs. In general, discussions so far have rather stressed methods of positively enhancing implementation than methods of highlighting non-compliance.[64] A third, additional element in the compliance context is the formal dispute resolution procedures laid out in Article 14 in the Convention; in a fairly standard way, one might say. Given previous regime experiences and the general interest in developing non-confrontational and positive implementation mechanisms within the regime, these procedures are likely to be of little practical interest.

Some concluding notes, then, on the financial mechanism. Article 4.3 in the 1992 Convention called for the developed country parties to provide new and additional financial resources to assist reporting in developing countries.[65] Moreover, financial resources, 'including the transfer of technology' should be provided to meet the full incremental costs related to the implementation of future commitments. In addition, Article 11 called for 'a mechanism for the provision of financial resources on a grant or concessional basis, including ... the transfer of technology', with its operation entrusted 'to one or more existing international entities'. In this context, Article 21 established an interim arrangement, with the Global Environment Facility (GEF) as the entity entrusted with the interim operation of the financial mechanism – despite developing countries' more general discontent with representation on the GEF. The restructuring of GEF in 1994 reduced developing countries' discontent, but not entirely.[66] At the first CoP, it was decided to continue the interim solution for four more years. So far, GEF's main role has been in the field of reporting assistance. According to official sources, 'in total US\$53 million has been provided by GEF to support 75 countries in preparing ... their first national communications'.[67] Problems have been noted with regard to reports on action taken to provide financial and technical assistance to developing countries, especially with regard to the novel and climate-specific nature of the contributions.[68] As mentioned, the Kyoto Protocol establishes a new 'Clean Development Mechanism' (CDM). According to Article 12.2 in the Protocol, the purpose of the CDM is both to assist non-Annex 1 parties 'in achieving sustainable development and in contributing to the ultimate objective of the Convention', and to assist Annex 1 parties in achieving compliance with their commitments. Moreover, and not least important, Annex 1 parties 'may use the certified emissions reductions accruing from such project activities to contribute to compliance'. Who, then, will gain most from the CDM? It has been argued that, among other things, this depends on its final location and whether the GEF or the World Bank will control the new mechanism.[69] Others have emphasized the need to avoid getting bogged down in such issues, and to focus on more general institutional clarification related to the certification, verification and approval of emissions reductions and the role and functions of the executive board.[70]

In conclusion, the institutional development within the climate regime related to verification and compliance can be interpreted in several ways. The *combination* of 'soft' elements, reflected for instance in the non-confrontational emphasis of the Article 13 process and reporting support for developing countries, and the somewhat 'harder' elements, reflected for instance in the country reviews, can be interpreted as signs of learning; especially from the development of the ozone process and procedures, but also from review procedures within organizations like IMF and GATT. However, much of it can also be interpreted as developing more independent responses to a singularly complex global problem, which requires specially adapted and to some extent innovative institutional responses. Considerable progress has been made, but the system is not completed, both with regard to the separate parts and not least the division of labour and the interplay between the various bodies. Moreover, finding the optimal balance between 'soft' and 'hard' elements will remain a critical challenge in the years ahead. Luckily, critical tests are still some years away.

7.4 CONCLUDING INSTITUTIONAL COMMENTS: MORE 'ISSUE-SPECIFIC INCREMENTALISM' THAN 'LESSONS LEARNT FROM OTHER REGIMES'?

Important institutional dimensions of the climate regime have evolved in accordance with the main lessons from other regimes. Obvious examples are the organization of the science–politics interface, with a quite successful combination of the often conflicting concerns of integrity and involvement achieved, and the weight given to developing procedures and mechanisms for enhancing confidence-building, reporting and implementation capacity in developing countries. However, there are clear limits to the usefulness of a 'lessons learnt' approach in terms of understanding institutional development so far. Much of the institutional development can best be understood as responses to the specific characteristics of the climate change issue – what perhaps may be termed 'issue-specific incrementalism'. For instance, the overall inclusiveness and broad scope of participation emanated naturally from central problem characteristics, like global emission sources and climate effects; the future crucial greenhouse gas emissions of the developing countries and the need for global legitimacy for the regulations adopted; and the developing ideas on potentially global policy measures like joint implementation and international trading of emission permits. Moreover, the broad agenda, with a number of issues and sub-issues, reflects a very complex issue. Much of the same 'response to complexity' goes for the unusually well-developed scientific–political complex, with the IPCC, SBSTA, and several other bodies. With regard to verification procedures, the unique (within the environmental realm) design of an approach including in-depth review teams and week-long country visits may also be interpreted as an 'extraordinary response to an extraordinary and complex problem'. Given the potentially serious economic implications of international regulations, reliable progress data may become crucially important to uphold regime legitimacy and stability over time. To some extent, the institutional issues have been 'hot to handle', especially as issues like the design of decision-making procedures have been used by parties for other, tactical political purposes. However, given the complexity of the issue, rather remarkable institutional progress has overall been achieved in a limited time span.

Has this 'remarkable' institutional development influenced outcomes so far? As in the cases analysed in earlier chapters, institutional influence is to some extent quite subtle; it is related to the arena function of the regime, and less related to the specific design features developed so far. Sticking my neck out, I would still in particular point to institutional 'density', with many meeting points and substantial high level political involvement within a limited time span; the broad agenda, clearly paving the way for the important compromise of the Kyoto Protocol; and the somewhat controversial regionalization of commitments (that is, giving developing countries a grace period). However, as a possible weak point, it has been suggested that if this regionalization had been carried out more forcefully and an approach only including the Annex 1 countries had been chosen as the main negotiation forum, more progress could have been made earlier.[71] This is possible, but in a more long-term perspective, the inclusive approach chosen makes very much sense.

NOTES

1. I owe inspiration for this title to Skjærseth (1993).
2. For other contributions that touch upon institutional matters within the climate regime context, see for instance Sebenius (1993); Victor and Salt (1994); Jäger and O'Riordan (1996); Greene and Lanchbery (1996); Børsting and Fermann (1997); Mitchell (1997); Andresen (1998).
3. See for instance Børsting and Fermann (1997) and Andresen (1998) for a more comprehensive review of the process.
4. The scientific story goes back to the work of the Swedish scientist Arrhenius more than a century ago, through measurements of atmospheric carbon dioxide initiated in the International Geophysical Year in 1957, via US dominated science in the 1970s and 1980s, up to the creation and performance of the Intergovernmental Panel on Climatic Change (IPCC). For a more comprehensive review, see for instance Lunde (1991).
5. See for instance Børsting and Fermann (1997) for further information on these meetings.
6. The UN link dated back to the 1987 WCED report and its call for a climate treaty, and the 1988 UN General Assembly Resolution urging the world to treat climate change as a priority issue. See Børsting and Fermann (1997:62).
7. The United Nations Framework Convention on Climate Change (FCCC).
8. Joint Implementation (JI) can be described as a system by which countries with high greenhouse gas emissions abatement costs finance and are given credit for abatement or other climate measures related to sources or sinks in countries with lower abatement costs. See for instance Loske and Oberthur (1994).
9. See for instance Oberthur and Ott (1995); Greene and Lanchbery (1996:6).
10. For a summary of CoP Two, see for instance Oberthur (1996).

11. The regulatory basket includes six gases: carbon dioxide (CO_2), methane (NH_4), nitrous oxide (N_2O), hydrofluorocarbons (HFCs), perfluorocarbons (PFCs), and sulphur hexafluoride (SF_6).
12. Norwegian interviews, February 1998.
13. See Andresen (1998:30).
14. This is primarily based on unpublished proceedings from the EU Climate Leadership Project Meeting on lessons from Kyoto, 5 March 1998. See Schjølset (1998) for a Norwegian perspective.
15. See for instance *ENDS Report* (1997:17).
16. Norwegian interviews, February 1998.
17. This section has benefited from interviews with and comments from several ·Norwegian participants in the processes: H. Dovland, Ministry of Environment (October 1996); G. Børsting, Ministry of Environment (May 1997; February 1998; May 1998), G. Sjøberg, Ministry of Foreign Affairs (September 1997); P. Stiansen, formerly with the Convention Secretariat and now Ministry of Environment (October 1997; February 1998). For an early discussion of many of the same institutional issues within the climate context, see Andresen and Wettestad (1992).
18. This is further described in Greene and Lanchbery (1996).
19. Dunn (1995:440).
20. Such a 'small-scale agreement', encompassing the OECD or Economic Commission for Europe, is for instance suggested by Sebenius (1993; particularly pp.212–214).
21. See for example Rowlands (1996).
22. Oberthur and Ott (1995).
23. Newell and Paterson (1996:731).
24. *International Environment Reporter*, 20 August 1997, pp.781–782.
25. For instance in connection with CoP One, Greene and Lanchbery (1996:328) state: 'by the time the government Ministers arrived in the middle of the second week, little had been achieved. Then the negotiations began to proceed rapidly'.
26. This is emphasized for instance in Victor and Salt (1994).
27. As commented by Andresen (1998:35-36): 'over the last seven years, thousands of climate negotiators and lobbyists have spent well over half a year together discussing these issues'.
28. *International Environment Reporter* (1995A:136).
29. See for instance *ENDS Report* (1995B:44); and Oberthur and Ott (1995).
30. Notably Australia, and Saudi Arabia on behalf of a group of oil-exporting countries and Russia. See Oberthur (1996:200).
31. Oberthur (ibid.).
32. Oberthur and Ott (1995:148–149).
33. Ibid.
34. See Børsting and Fermann (1997:76-77).
35. *The Financial Times* (12 December 1997).
36. This section has benefited greatly from Norwegian interviews in 1997 and 1998, and from inputs and comments by Øystein B. Thommesen, FNI.
37. *Green Globe Yearbook* (1997:90).
38. Børsting and Fermann (1997:77).
39. See for instance Oberthur and Ott (1995:150).
40. Based on information provided to the *Yearbook of International Co-operation on Environment and Development* 1998/99.
41. FCCC Website information.
42. The virtues and hazards of comprehensiveness both generally and in the more specific climate context are further discussed in the chapter by Sebenius in Sjøstedt (ed. 1993).
43. The IPCC has identified more than 25 climate gases, including 15 hydrofluorocarbon gases (HFCs) alone, for which Global Warming Potentials (GWPs) have been calculated. See Fuglestvedt and Skodvin (1996).
44. For a more systematic discussion of key climate policy dimensions, see Ringius and Wettestad (1997).

45. According to Article 4.2 in the Berlin Mandate, when OECD countries develop climate policy targets and strengthen their commitments, they should do this by 'taking into account the differences in these Parties' starting points and approaches, economic structures and resource bases, the need to maintain strong and sustainable economic growth, available technologies and other individual circumstances'.
46. For an analysis of the issue of differentiation and the FCCC and the Berlin Mandate, see for instance Ringius and Torvanger (1997).
47. See for instance Loske and Oberthur (1994) and Greene and Lanchbery (1996).
48. See for instance Lunde (1991) and Skodvin (1994; forthcoming 1998) for more extensive assessments.
49. Hence, developing country participation in the work of the IPCC increased from ten in early 1989 to 40 by August 1990. See Skodvin (forthcoming 1999B).
50. See Shackley (1997).
51. The IPCC provided interim reports in 1992 and 1994 and a full-fledged Second IPCC Assessment Report in December 1995.
52. For the complete mandate, see Article 9 in the 1992 Convention.
53. Report of the Conference of the Parties on its first session, p. 21.
54. See for instance Greene and Lanchbery (1996:332–333) and Andresen (1998:54).
55. Skodvin (forthcoming 1999B), referring to an interview with Bolin in the Norwegian newspaper Arbeiderbladet, 18 August 1997.
56. See for instance Andresen (1998:53).
57. As pointed out by Skodvin (forthcoming 1999B).
58. It has informally been agreed that, wherever possible, there should be at least three representatives of the parties within each team, including one from a developing country, and nominees from parties should constitute a majority of the team. See Greene and Lanchbery (1996:10).
59. *Green Globe Yearbook* (1997:91).
60. This is based on a series of Norwegian interviews during 1997. With regard to 'observers', see for instance Greene and Lanchbery (1996); Andresen (1998) and Morlot (1998).
61. See Morlot (ibid.).
62. Article 13, 'Resolution of questions regarding implementation' states: 'The Conference of the Parties shall, at its first session, consider the establishment of a multilateral consultative process, available to Parties on their request, for the resolution of questions regarding the implementation of the Convention'.
63. However, as pointed out by Bodansky (1997:13), in contrast to the Montreal Protocol, no such procedure is mandated, and the more sensitive wording of 'non compliance' is not utilized.
64. See for instance Lanchbery (1997:166).
65. For a general discussion of this provision, see for instance Jordan and Werksman (1996).
66. GEF was made functionally autonomous from the World Bank and a 32-member Council was created, with equal representation between developing and developed countries. For discussions on the role of GEF, see for instance Sjøberg (1996), Fairman (1996), Bodansky (1997) and Botnen (1997).
67. UNFCC/CP/1996/8. Decisons to Promote the Effective Implementation of the Convention. Financial Mechanism. Report of the Global Environmental Facility to the Conference of the Parties.
68. Mitchell (1997:5).
69. See *Earth Negotiations Bulletin* (1997).
70. See Lunde (1998).
71. See Andresen (1998).

8. Designing Effective Environmental Regimes: Launching the Three Conditional Ps (Problems, Phases, and Processes)

8.1 SUMMING UP THE KEYS TO THE INSTITUTIONAL DILEMMAS: THE THREE CONDITIONAL Ps[1]

What then are the main substantive and methodological conclusions arising from the work on this book? Starting with the more substantive institutional findings and reflections, let us first address the question to what extent regimes matter in relation to more fundamental problem characteristics. The main answer here is simply that 'regimes clearly matter'. Within all of the regimes, there is a strong feeling that we would not have been where we are today both in terms of issue-specific policies and environmental development without the regime, so the notion of a 'sterile' debate about 'whether regimes matter or not' is supported.[2] However, moving very much further in terms of a more precise measurement is definitely risky on the basis of the data I have had access to. True, there are probably differences and nuances with regard to institutional impact between the regimes, as reflected in a somewhat differing effectiveness score. But as differences of issue malignness also co-vary with the differing effectiveness scores, that is, that more malign issues correlate with more moderate degrees of effectiveness and vice versa, the 'true' institutional impact is still elusive. Moreover, the degree of interplay between regime development and changes in problem characteristics is strong, not least in terms of knowledge development increasingly being organized within the regimes. This has contributed significantly to making problems intellectually less complicated to deal with in the subsequent rounds of regime development. Hence, this is a relevant and interesting finding, but serves in this context also to increase the difficulty in disentangling the respective influence of regimes and institutions in relation to problems.

This is of course a quite sobering backdrop for the more specific discussion on *how* institutional factors have mattered. But sobering does not mean irrelevant, especially if one also takes into consideration the 'windows of opportunity' perspective on institutional design. In other words, when temporary political 'windows of opportunity' open, the existence of effectively designed institutions may be crucially important in order to transform a more benign interest constellation rapidly into strengthened international commitments. Hopefully a little encouraged, let us then go through the main findings in relation to the institutional dilemmas introduced in Section I of this book. First, access procedures and participation issues were one of the more important institutional issues.

- **Should Access be Inclusive or Exclusive?**

Both, depending on problem characteristics, timing, and type of process. With regard to the scope of state participation, all the regimes had found ways to transcend the requirements for rather broad state participation (be it global or regional) set by problem scopes and long-term legitimacy. They combined broader forums with narrower and politically effective institutional contexts. This may indicate that *both* the global and regional contexts may be too broad to combine political and problem-solving effectiveness over time; it is necessary to develop smaller and more homogeneous 'clubs'. Also in terms of 'outsiders' access', all the regimes found ways to combine the wide spectrum of inputs and political energy related to the open model with the intimacy and oversight more easily achieved in more secluded forums. Hence, differentiated access has also been the keyword here, with open access to plenary meetings and preparatory stages, and more restricted access to meetings on details and fine print, and final stages.

- **Should National Participants be Bureaucrats or Ministers?**

Both, but sequentially, and with the role of the latter also dependent upon problem characteristics. In the case studies, high-level and ministerial inputs to processes were clearly important, as for instance witnessed in the marine pollution context. But there was also an important interplay between solid administrative groundwork and spectacular ministerial gatherings, and an important balance to be struck. A general rule of thumb may be that regimes regulating low visibility activities need more high profile and regular political input than regimes regulating more visible and specific activities more suited for general political attention and public campaigns.

- **Should Decision-Making be Consensual or Rely on Majority Voting?**

The room for the latter seems limited, but increasing over time. Although there were some formal variations, and several of the regimes opened up opportunities for some sort of majority decisions, consensual decisions were the general order of the day. As increasing decision-making capacity by the use of majority voting was generally and initially not seen as a viable option, the parties within the different regimes instead developed a sort of differentiation between the parties in order to beat 'the least ambitious programme' implications of consensus. The north-east Atlantic/North Sea regimes developed differentiated decisions between the states bordering the North Sea and the rest; the acid rain regime established protocols with the agreed abstention of reluctant convention parties; the ozone regime utilized different reduction targets and timetables for developed and developing countries. The particular choice of approach to beat the slowest boat rule was adapted to the problem and political situation at hand. However, over time, moves towards tougher decision-making practices were noticed within several of the regimes.

- **Should the Secretariat be a Low-Lying Stage-Hand for the Parties or a Driving Entrepreneurial Actor?**

High hopes for the latter should be tempered, but the balance is among other things dependent upon problem characteristics and the cooperative phase. Although the role of international secretariats is by nature low-key and easy to underestimate, the regimes studied here did not bolster notions of the effectiveness of such secretariats being some sort of necessary condition for overall regime effectiveness, at least in cases where the parties themselves have overall reasonable administrative capacities. In general, the secretariats functioned efficiently in relation to quite limited financial and administrative resources. Although they fit more into the stage-hand category than into the actor category, a trend could be noted in the direction of the secretariats taking a more important and active role with regard to reporting and compliance assessment functions over time. Moreover, the secretariats developed over time an interesting and well-functioning interplay with other regime bodies, indicating that the role of such secretariats should always be considered in the light of other elements in the administrative setting of regimes.

- **Should the Agenda be Comprehensive or Narrow?**

Possibilities for the latter are heavily conditioned by problem characteristics, but the strengths of both options should in principle be sequentially utilized. In general, the structuring of the agenda was the institutional issue which was most difficult to handle empirically, and hence also in terms of possible impact on processes. This is much related to the close relationship between this issue and basic issue characteristics. Issues starting out with a natural concern about one or a small group of substances and related environmental problems (like sulphur dioxide and acid rain) were simply better suited for sequential and more narrowly focused decision-making than other issue areas with a more diffuse picture (like land-based marine pollution). Nevertheless, it still seems that all these regimes have settled for what must be termed basically a narrow approach, with more or less successful attempts at sequential decision-making. The atmospheric regimes seem to have been the most successful regimes in terms of sequential decision-making. But for instance in the case of LRTAP, where single pollutant processes and protocols have been replaced by more multi-pollutant approaches, this is closely related to the development of knowledge on the various types of interplay between pollutants.

- **Should the Scientific–Political Complex Emphasize Scientific Integrity or Political Involvement?**

Although a combination is in principle optimal, the importance of the former dimension increases when issues and regime development imply high regulatory costs. Generally, it was clear that scientific knowledge mattered for the development of these regimes, and the acid rain and ozone processes especially were very much knowledge-driven all along. Moreover, over time, the regimes played important roles in developing that knowledge. However, more specific institutional lessons must definitely take issue-specific characteristics into consideration. For instance, the obvious importance of finding substitute substances within the ozone regime shed light on the establishment of the specific technological panel within this regime. Moreover, with regard to the generally difficult institutional balancing of scientific integrity versus national control and involvement in political processes, apart from the somewhat special case of the climate regime, the balance within the other regimes was tilted towards the latter pole without giving rise to much conflict and complaints about 'politicization' of science. This may have something to do with the generally diffuse relationship between scientific development and policy development within these regimes, with few direct distributional implications and moderate economic implications. In these regimes, the buffer bodies between science and politics have been used for purposes of communication and integration, not for separation. The general logic here is supported by the climate regime experiences. The graver regulatory and economic implications within this regime have led to a more heated debate about the functioning of the scientific–political complex than within the other regimes, and it makes sense to see the IPCC's Working Group III also as a separating buffer between science and politics.

- **Should Verification Procedures be 'Intrusive' or 'Non-Intrusive'?**

The need for and possibilities of 'intrusiveness' increase over time. Although there were certain procedural variations, with for instance the ozone regime and LRTAP having specific implementation committees, a basic similarity was the central place of systems of self-reporting. Moreover, in practice, despite certain procedural and institutional differences, the models have initially functioned in a very similarly soft and non-confrontational way. Slow reporting and missing data have largely been accepted, with only occasionally mild pressure from the secretariats and/or the parties. Implementation committees and dispute settlement procedures have so far had little practical relevance. However, even on this sobering basis, it would be wrong to conclude that the verification and compliance mechanisms reviewed here have not contributed to general confidence-building and an increasing degree of effectiveness witnessed within all these regimes. An interesting observation seems to be that the functioning of these mechanisms is closely related to the *functional requirements* of the regimes in different phases. When regulations got more specified with regard to targets and timetables, the parties sharpened and improved reporting procedures and practice.

- **Should Compliance Mechanisms Rely on 'Sticks' or 'Carrots'?**

In the environmental arena, 'sticks' seem mainly theoretically interesting, while the need for 'carrots' depends on problem characteristics. Generally, 'sticks' were only formal paper tigers within the regimes. This may have something to do with the generally diffuse character of international environmental politics, with lots of scientific and technological complexity, moderate economic regulatory implications, and, at least in the early phases, quite vague and general regulatory yardsticks. However, the debate within the at least more economically 'threatening' climate context does not so far point towards a more significant role for sanctions and 'sticks' in general. With regard to the financial 'carrot' part of the compliance mechanisms discussion, the evidence at hand was limited to the ozone Multilateral Fund. The need for and establishment of this Fund was clearly related to global and heterogeneous ozone problem characteristics and actors. The Fund undoubtedly contributed to the results achieved within the ozone regime, but financial and organizational problems experienced within this regime are clearly related to far more general conflicts in terms of redressing economic and political power imbalances between the North and the South.

Hence, in summary, *designing effective regimes is primarily a matter of optimal and flexible combinations of all these institutional possibilities.* The case evidence has indicated at least three main conditional keys to locating the more specific institutional optimum balancing point in specific cases: Problem characteristics; Phases; and Process types – **the Three Ps**. First, *there is a close interplay between problem characteristics and the optimum institutional design.* For instance: low visibility problems require more continuous high-level, attention-raising institutional input than more high visibility problems. Value-laden conflicts and problems are more in need of voting mechanisms to cut through decision deadlocks than less value-laden problems more amenable to compromise and the development of consensus. Comprehensive, often global, problems with many and heterogeneous parties require a strong secretariat, capable of providing various forms of process assistance. Complex problems require more elaborated scientific–political complexes. Issues starting out with a natural concern about one or a small group of substances and related environmental problems are better suited for sequential and more narrowly focused decision-making than issue areas with a more diffuse picture. Second, *certain institutional options go more naturally together with certain phases in the development.* Take for instance what may be termed the early, institutional 'warm-up' phase after the initial convention has been established. This phase generally calls for inclusive access, bureaucratic footwork, the building of consensual decision-making, and 'non-intrusive' confidence-building verification and compliance mechanisms. Over time, when knowledge increases and the parties' ambitions also increase, there is a greater need for higher decision-making and aggregation capacity, perhaps enhanced by the temporary and vitalizing participation of ministers and politicians in the process. When regulations become more ambitious and specific, the need for sharper verification and compliance instruments also increases. Hopefully, the previous 'softer' phase has provided the general foundation of mutual trust which allows such a move towards tougher institutions. Third, irrespective of the phase dimension, *there are certain processes which go better together with certain institutional options.* This is clearly skating on thinner ice than in the cases of the two previous Ps. The prime example here is probably that more 'exploratory' processes point towards inclusive, open access and participation, while more concluding, decision-shaping processes are generally enhanced by more exclusive access and 'closed' processes.

Although designing effective environmental regimes should not be seen as a 'mission impossible', it is most likely a *mission delicate*. Intellectual exercises related to 'optimum' institutional designs as indicated above will often and easily run hard aground in the real world political games. Take for instance the initial idea for a strong and activist secretariat in the ozone context, sensible for instance in the light of the many and heterogeneous potential parties to the regime. This idea was quickly shot down by, at the time, more reluctant actors. The aborted efforts to involve NGOs in the work of the ozone Implementation Committee also spring to mind. A recent example of the challenges one is easily faced with is the discussion on the possible establishment of a permit trading system within the climate regime. There is little experience to draw on from other regimes; it makes a lot of sense in overall effectiveness terms, given the specific climate problem structure; and several actors are sceptical because they apparently see increased flexibility as a 'fig leaf' for the promotion of particular actors' political interests.

8.2 IF I COULD START ALL OVER AGAIN: A METHODOLOGICAL BLUES

Moving on then to some final more methodological reflections, an interesting point of departure is the question 'how would I have gone about it if I could start writing the book from scratch again?' At least two main dimensions would have been given more emphasis, related to context and case selection. Let us go through these blues lessons in turn. With regard to the need for more contextual analysis, let me first briefly explain why the 'institutional cut-up' approach utilized in this book was chosen. This was very much related to my initial ambition to utilize systematic and specified comparative analyses as an important method in making a contribution to knowledge development in this field. In order to compare, there was a need for a specification and isolation of a limited group of institutional factors. As my understanding of the true tallness of the analytical order has improved (not least due to the work of several colleagues at the Fridtjof Nansen Institute), as further elaborated below, I have become increasingly aware of the limits of, and challenges involved in, applying the comparative method in this field. However, given the comparative ambition, the 'cut-up' approach initially made very much sense. With the benefit of hindsight, it is easy to see that this approach tends to complicate a more contextual and evolutionary understanding of the regime processes, where institutional arrangements have developed in relation to a complex web of issue-specific changes. Still, the 'cut-up' approach definitely also has its merits, especially in terms of accessibility and oversight. Hence, an institutionally focused, but more evolutionary approach is probably more optimal.

Turning then to the issue of case selection, the first sub-issue here is related to the number of cases studied. As indicated above, the need for detailed tracing of institutional 'paths' of influence makes cross-regime comparisons very time- and resource-demanding. Hence, a natural solution would be either to concentrate on one or two regimes or to put together larger teams of people with responsibility for one or two regimes each. Fewer case studies would generally of course allow more in-depth studies, for instance in terms of conducting more in-depth and institutionally focused interviews in all the major countries involved in the chosen regime(s). Moreover, such more in-depth studies could also allow the exploration of tricky but interesting issues like differential institutional impact; in other words, the way and the extent to which institutional mechanisms like the ozone trade sanctions influenced some parties, but not others. Putting together larger teams of people is of course an attractive and often utilized option, but is not without its flaws in relation to the comparative, synthesizing challenge which clearly exists in this field. We all know that analysts interpret concepts and empirical data differently, so there is after all a room for synthesizing solo ventures like the one carried out in this book. But please be aware that it does take time and tends to give you a considerable headache at times.

Finally, a few words about the need for a more conscious choice of cases. As indicated in the introduction, and further elaborated in the theoretical and methodological chapter, an important reason for choosing the four main regimes initially discussed in this book was simply data availability and my own previous research experience. At least with regard to the interest of myself and others at the Fridtjof Nansen Institute in the OSCON/PARCON and LRTAP regimes, this is partly related to the importance for Norway of effective international solutions to the problems addressed by these regimes. Luckily, the regimes and problems addressed in this book also contained some important differences and similarities which enhanced the general relevance of the main findings. On the other hand, it is certainly true that a more conscious choice of cases could have enhanced the value of the conclusions and findings further. For instance, by holding central key control characteristics more constant, for example, by only looking at regimes regulating the same basic types of activities, or being at precisely the same stage in their development, the challenge of control could have been handled better. Another approach would have been only to have chosen regimes which had some very specific characteristics in terms of issues or institutional characteristics. This could have increased variation in the focused institutional variables, and/or special issues or institutions could have functioned as 'critical' cases.

Enough said. Much could have been done differently. Hopefully, this concluding section has provided some clues on how to develop this important, but challenging, field of study further. Good blues basically says that 'yes, I've made mistakes, but I'm not giving up'. This is also a fitting note on which to end this book.

NOTES

1. Loosely echoing the three Cs launched in Haas, Keohane and Levy (1993): increase Concern, enhance Capacity-Building, and strengthen the Contractual Environment.
2. Compare endnote 11 in Chapter 1 and the reference to Young's (1998) contribution.

References

Abrahamsen, G. (1988). Science, politics and environmental issues, Keynote paper presented at the Conference on Air Pollution in Europe, September, Stockholm.

Andresen, S. (1993). The effectiveness of the International Whaling Commission, *Arctic*, vol. 46, no. 4; pp. 108–116.

Andresen, S. (1996). Effectiveness and implementation within the 'North Sea/North East Atlantic Cooperation': development, status and future perspectives, in *The Effectiveness of Multilateral Environmental Agreements,* Workshop Proceedings and Study Reports, Nord 1996:18, Nordic Council of Ministers, Copenhagen, pp. 60–83.

Andresen, S. (1998). Evaluating the climate regime: achievements, positions, and lessons, SAMRAM Working Paper, April, The Fridtjof Nansen Institute.

Andresen, S. (forthcoming 1999). The effectiveness of the international convention for the regulation of whaling, in Miles, E. et al. *Explaining Regime Effectiveness: Confronting Theory with Evidence*, Cambridge, MA, MIT Press.

Andresen, S. and Wettestad, J. (1992). International resource cooperation and the greenhouse problem, *Global Environmental Change,* vol. 2, no. 4, December, pp. 277–291.

Andresen, S. and Wettestad, J. (1993). The effectiveness of international resource cooperation: some preliminary notes on institutional design, *International Challenges*, vol. 13, no. 2, pp. 61–75.

Andresen, S. and Wettestad, J. (1995). International problem-solving effectiveness: the Oslo Project story so far, *International Environmental Affairs*, vol. 7, no. 2, Spring, pp. 127–150.

Andresen, S.; Skjærseth, J.B. and Wettestad, J. (1995). Regime, the state and society: analyzing the implementation of international environmental commitments, Laxenburg, IIASA Working Paper WP–95–43, June.

Andresen, S.; Skodvin, T.; Underdal, A. and Wettestad, J. (1994). 'Scientific' management of the environment? science, politics and institutional design, R:006–1994, The Fridtjof Nansen Institute.

Annual Reports on the Activities of the Paris Commission 1978–93, The Oslo and Paris Commissions, London.

Axelrod, R. and Keohane, R. (1985). Achieving cooperation under anarchy: strategies and institutions, in Oye, K. (ed.), *Cooperation under Anarchy*, Princeton, Princeton University Press, pp.226-254.

Bakken, P. (1989). Science and politics in the protection of the ozone layer, in Andresen, S. and Østreng, W. (eds), *International Resource Management*, London, Belhaven Press, pp. 198–205.

Barrat-Brown, E.P. (1991). Building a monitoring and compliance regime under the Montreal Protocol, *Yale Journal of International Law*, vol. 16, pp. 519–70.

Benedick, R.E. (1991). *Ozone Diplomacy*, Cambridge, MA, Harvard University Press.

Bernauer, T. (1995). The effect of international environmental institutions: how we might learn more, *International Organization*, vol. 49, no. 2, Spring, pp. 251–277.

Bernauer, T. and Mitchell, R. (1997). Empirical research on international environmental policy – designing qualitative case studies, paper prepared for the annual Meeting of the International Studies Association (ISA), Toronto, 18–22 March.

Biermann, F. (1997). Financing environmental policies in the South – experiences from the Multilateral Ozone Fund, *International Environmental Affairs*, vol. 9, no. 3, Summer, pp. 179–219.

Biersteker, T.J. (1993). Constructing historical counterfactuals to assess the consequences of international regimes, in Rittberger, V. (ed.), *Regime Theory and International Relations*, Oxford, Clarendon Press, pp. 315–338.

Blix, H. and Emerson, J.H. (1973). *The Treaty Maker's Handbook*, Stockholm, Almquist & Wiksell.

Bodansky, D. (1997). The history and legal structure of the global climate change regime, in Sprintz, D. and Luterbacher, U. (eds), *International Relations and Global Climate Change*, Potsdam, Potsdam Institute for Climate Impact Research.

Boehmer-Christiansen, S. (1990). Environmental quality objectives versus uniform emission standards, Special North Sea Issue of *International Journal of Coastal and Estuarine Law*, pp. 139–50.

Boehmer-Christiansen, S. and Skea, J. (1987). The development of the acid rain issue in West Germany and the UK, paper presented at ENER meeting, Brussels, June.

Boehmer-Christiansen, S. and Skea, J. (1991). *Acid Politics: Environmental and Energy Policies in Britain and Germany*, London, Belhaven Press.

Botnen, T.K. (1997). Funding for the global environment – determined by national or common objectives?, Development and Multilateral Institutions Programme Report 2/1997, The Fridtjof Nansen Institute.

Brack, D. (1996). *International Trade and the Montreal Protocol*, London, The Royal Institute of International Affairs.

Brackley, P. (1987). *Acid Deposition and Vehicle Emissions: European Environmental Pressures on Britain*, Hampshire, Gower.

Breitmeier, H. et al. (1996). The international regimes database as a tool for the study of international cooperation, Laxenburg, IIASA Working Paper WP–96–160.

Broadus, J. et al. (1993). Comparative assessment of regional international programs to control landbased marine pollution: The Baltic, North Sea and Mediterranean, Marine Policy Center, Woods Hole.

Brown, L. et al. (1997). *Vital Signs*, Worldwatch Institute, New York and London.

Brown-Weiss, E. and Jacobson, H. (1994). Strengthening compliance with international environmental accords: some preliminary observations from a collaborative project, paper presented at the 35th Convention of the International Studies Association, Washington, DC, 31 March.

Brown-Weiss, E. and Jacobson, H. (eds) (1998). *Engaging Countries: Strengthening Compliance with International Accords*, Cambridge, MA, MIT Press.

Børsting, G. and Fermann, G. (1997). Climate change turning political: conference-diplomacy and institution-building to Rio and beyond, in Fermann, G. (ed.), *International Politics of Climate Change – Key Issues and Critical Actors*, Oslo, Scandinavian University Press, pp. 53–82.

Cameron, J.; Werksman, J. and Roderick, P. (1996). *Improving Compliance with International Environmental Law*, London, Earthscan.

Chayes, A. and Chayes, A. (1991). Compliance without enforcement: state behavior under regulatory treaties, *Negotiation Journal*, July, pp. 311–330.

Chayes, A. and Chayes, A. (1993). On compliance, *International Organization*, vol. 47, no. 2, Spring, pp. 175–205.

Chayes, A. and Chayes, A. (1995). *The New Sovereignty: Compliance with International Regulatory Agreements*, Cambridge, MA, Harvard University Press.

Chossudovsky, E. (1989). *East–West Diplomacy for Environment in the United Nations*, New York, UNITAR.

Churchill, R,: Kutting, G. and Warren, L.M. (1995). The 1994 UN ECE Sulphur Protocol, *Journal of Environmental Law*, vol. 7, no. 2, pp. 169–197.

Clark, W. et al. (forthcoming). *Learning to Manage Global Environmental Risks*.

DeSombre, E. and Kaufman, J. (1996), The Montreal Protocol Multilateral Fund: partial success, in Keohane, R. and Levy, M. (eds), *Institutions for Environmental Aid: Pitfalls and Promise*, Cambridge MA, MIT Press, pp. 89–126.

di Primio, J.C. (1996). Monitoring and verification in the european air pollution regime, Laxenburg, IIASA Working Paper WP–96–47.

Dovland, H. (1987). Monitoring European air pollution, *Environment*, vol. 29, December, pp. 10–15.

Ducrotoy, J. (1997). Scientific management in Europe: the case of the North Sea, in Brooks, L.A. and VanDeveer, S.D. (eds), *Saving the Seas – Values, Scientists, and International Governance*, Maryland Sea Grant College, pp. 175–193.

Dunn, S. (1995). The Berlin climate change Summit: implications for international environmental law, *International Environment Reporter*, 31 May, pp. 439–444.

Earth Negotiations Bulletin (1997). Report of the Third Conference of the Parties to the United Nations Framework Convention on Climate Change, 1–11 December 1997, vol. 12, no. 76, pp. 1–32.

ECE/LRTAP (1995). *Strategies and Policies for Air Pollution Abatement – 1994 Major Review*, Geneva.

Elster, J. (1989). *Nuts and Bolts for the Social Sciences*, Cambridge, Cambridge University Press.

ENDS Report (1986). Opening skirmishes on the health of the North Sea, no. 141, October, pp. 4–6.

ENDS Report (1987A). Public opinion on the environment: a warning to government, no. 146, March, pp. 16–17.

ENDS Report (1987B). UK policy shifts on dumping, discharges pave way for successful North Sea meeting, no. 154, November, pp. 3–4.

ENDS Report (1995A). Ozone layer left at risk at risk as talks stumble on funding, no. 251, December, pp. 35–37.

ENDS Report (1995B). First climate conference agrees further talks on emission cuts, no. 243, April, pp. 43–44.

ENDS Report (1995C). Ministers agree new curbs on ozone depleters, no. 272, September, pp. 44–45.

ENDS Report (1997). The unfinished climate business after Kyoto, no. 275, December, pp. 16–20.

Environmental Policy and Law (1989). Non-compliance with ozone agreement, vol. 19, no. 5, pp. 147–148.

Environmental Policy and Law (1993). The Copenhagen Meeting, vol. 23, no. 1, pp. 6–12.

Environmental Policy and Law (1996). The Vienna Meeting, vol. 26, nos. 2–3, pp. 66–71.

Fairman, D. (1996). The global environment facility: haunted by the shadow of the future, in Keohane, R. and Levy, M. (eds), *Institutions for Environmental Aid – Pitfalls and Promise*, Cambridge, MA, MIT Press, pp. 55–87.

Fearon, J.D. (1991). Counterfactuals and hypothesis testing in political science, *World Politics*, vol. 43, January, pp. 169–95.

The Financial Times (12 December 1997).

French, H. (1994). Making environmental treaties work, *Scientific American*, December 1994, pp. 62–65.

Fuglestvedt, J. and Skodvin, T. (1996). *A Comprehensive Approach to Climate Change: Options and Obstacles*, CICERO Report 1996:4.

Gehring, T. (1994). *Dynamic International Regimes: Institutions for International Environmental Governance*, Berlin, Peter Lang Verlag.

George, A.L. (1979). Case studies and theory development: the method of structured, focused comparison, in Lauren, P.G. (ed.), *Diplomacy: New Approaches in History, Theory and Policy*, New York, Free Press, pp. 43–69.

Global Environmental Change Report (1996). Funding and MDIs addressed at ozone summit, 13 December.

Green Globe Yearbook (1992–1998), Oxford, The Fridtjof Nansen Institute/Oxford University Press/Earthscan (from 1998 on, *The Yearbook of International Co-operation on Environment and Development*).

Greene, O. (1994). On verifiability, and how it could matter for international environmental agreement, IIASA Working Paper WP–94–116.

Greene, O. (1996). The Montreal Protocol: implementation and development in 1995, in Poole, J. and Guthrie, R. (eds), *Verification 1996: Arms Control, Environment and Peacekeeping*, Westview Press, pp. 407–426.

Greene, O. and Lanchbery, J. (1996). Developing the climate change regime: the process in 1995, in Poole, J. and Guthrie, R. (eds), *Verification 96: Arms Control, Environment and Peacekeeping,* Westview Press, pp. 321–338.

Haas, E. (1980). Why collaborate? Issue-linkage and international regimes, *World Politics*, vol. 32, no. 3, pp. 357–405.

Haas, P. (1990A). Obtaining international environmental protection through epistemic communities, *Millennium*, vol. 19, no. 3, pp. 347–363.

Haas, P. (1990B). *Saving the Mediterranean: The Politics of International Environmental Cooperation*, New York, Columbia University Press.

Haas, P.; Keohane, R. and Levy, M. (eds) (1993). *Institutions for the Earth – Sources of Effective International Environmental Protection*, Cambridge MA, MIT Press.

The Hague Declaration on the Environment, The Hague, 11 March 1989. See *Environmental Policy and Law* (1989), vol. 19, no. 2, p. 78.

Hagerhall, B. (1993). The evolving role of NGOs, in Hagerhall, B. (ed.), *International Environmental Negotiations – Process, Issues and Contexts*, The Swedish Institute of International Affairs.

Haggard, S. and Simmons, B.A. (1987). Theories of international regimes, *International Organization*, vol. 41, no. 3, Summer, pp. 491–517.

Haigh, N. (1987). *EEC Environmental Policy and Britain*, Essex, Longman.

Haigh, N. (1989). New tools for European air pollution control, *International Environmental Affairs*, vol. 1, Winter, pp. 26–38.

Hajer, M.A. (1995). *The Politics of Environmental Discourse: Ecological Modernization and the Policy Process*, New York, Oxford University Press.

Hasenclever, A.; Meyer, P. and Rittberger, V. (1996). *Theories of International Regimes*, Cambridge, Cambridge University Press.

Hayward, P. (1990). The Oslo and Paris Commissions, special North Sea issue of *International Journal of Coastal and Estuarine Law*, pp. 91–101.

Hey, E.; Ijlstra, T. and Nollkaemper, A. (1993). The 1992 Paris Convention for the protection of the marine environment of the North–East Atlantic: a critical analysis, *International Journal of Marine and Coastal Law*, vol. 8, no. 1, pp. 1–76.

International Environment Reporter (1993). UK urges postponement of directive on waste water treatment because of cost, 1 December, p. 890.

International Environment Reporter (1995A). INC-11 concludes with little of substance to send to first meeting of treaty parties, 22 February, pp. 135–136.

International Environment Reporter (1995B). Montreal Protocol working group puts off new proposals until November, 17 May, pp. 361–362.

International Environment Reporter (1995C). Montreal Protocol successful in reducing methyl chloroform levels, scientists say, 26 July, pp. 566–567.

International Environment Reporter (1995D). Bjerregaard urges global phaseout of methyl bromide, faster phaseout of HCFCs, 20 September, pp. 711–712.

International Environment Reporter (1996). Effectiveness of Montreal Protocol in stemming ozone loss hailed by scientists, 2 October, pp. 867–868.

International Environment Reporter (1997A). Top climate change official says negotiators should be concerned at talks sluggish pace, 20 August, pp. 781–782.

International Environment Reporter (1997B). Methyl Bromide among issues unresolved as Montreal Protocol meeting nears end, 17 September, pp. 861–862.

International Environment Reporter (1997C). Methyl Bromide phaseout plans, CFC licensing system only gains in Montreal, 1 October, pp. 903–904.

Jachtenfuchs, M. (1990). The European Community and the protection of the ozone layer, *Journal of Common Market Studies*, vol. 28, no. 3, pp. 261–277.

Jackson, C.I. (1990). A tenth anniversary review of the ECE Convention on Long-Range Transboundary Air Pollution, *International Environmental Affairs*, vol. 2, no. 3, Summer, pp. 217–226.

Jäger J. and O'Riordan, T. (1996). The history of climate change science and politics, in O'Riordan, T. and Jäger, J. (eds), *Politics of Climate Change – a European Perspective*, London, Routledge, pp. 1–31.

Jordan, A. and Werksman, J. (1996). Financing global environmental protection, in Cameron, J.; Werksman, J. and Roderick, P. (eds), *Improving Compliance with International Environmental Law*, London, Earthscan Publications Limited, pp. 247–256.

Kay, D. and Jacobson, H.K. (1983). *Environmental Protection: The International Dimension*, New Jersey, Allanheld, Osman.

Keohane, R. (1985). *After Hegemony: Cooperation and Discord in the World Political Economy*, Princeton, Princeton University Press.

Keohane, R. (ed.) (1986). *Neorealism and its Critics*, New York, Columbia University Press.

Keohane, R. (1990). Multilateralism: an agenda for research, *International Journal*, vol. xi, no. V, autumn 1990, pp. 731–795.

Keohane, R. (1993). The analysis of international regimes: towards a European-American research programme, in Rittberger, V. (ed.), *Regime Theory and International Relations*, Oxford, Clarendon Press, pp. 23–49.

Keohane, R. and Levy, M. (eds) (1996). *Institutions for Environmental Aid: Pitfalls and Promise*, Cambridge MA, MIT Press.

King, G.; Keohane, R. and Verba, S. (1994). *Designing Social Inquiry: Scientific Inference in Qualitative Research*, Princeton NJ, Princeton University Press.

Kingdon, J.W. (1984). *Agendas, Alternatives, and Policy Alternatives*, Boston, Little and Brown.

Koskenniemi, M. (1992). Breach of treaty or non-compliance? Reflections on the enforcement of the Montreal Protocol, in Handl, G. (ed.), *Yearbook of International Environmental Law*, vol. 3, Graham and Trotman, pp. 123–162.

Krasner, S. (ed.) (1983). *International Regimes*, Ithaca, Cornell University Press.

Lanchbery, J. (1997). Whither the Climate Convention? in Guthrie, R. (ed.), *Verification 1997 – The Vertic Yearbook*, Oxford, Westview Press, pp. 159–170.

Laugen, T. (1995). Compliance with international environmental agreements – Norway and the Acid Rain Convention, R:003–1995, The Fridtjof Nansen Institute.

Levy, M. (1993). European Acid Rain: The Power of Toteboard Diplomacy, in Haas, P.; Keohane, R. and Levy, M. (eds), *Institutions for the Earth*, Cambridge MA, MIT Press, pp. 75–133.

Levy, M. (1995). International co-operation to combat acid rain, *Green Globe Yearbook*, the Fridtjof Nansen Institute/Oxford University Press, pp. 59–69.

Levy, M. and Young, O.R. (1993). The effectiveness of international regimes, draft.

Levy, M; Young, O.R. and Zürn, M. (1994). The study of international regimes, Laxenburg, IIASA Working Paper WP–94–113.

Liberatore, A. (1993). The European Community's Acid Rain Policy, draft for the project on 'Social Learning in the Management of Global Environmental Risks'.

Lijphart, A. (1971). Comparative politics and the comparative method, *American Political Science Review*, vol. 65, September, pp. 682–693.

Litfin, K. (1994). *Ozone Discourses: Science and Politics in Global Environmental Cooperation*, New York, Columbia University Press.

Loske, R. and Oberthur, S. (1994). Joint implementation under the Climate Change Convention, *International Environmental Affairs,* vol. 6, pp. 45–58.

Lunde, L. (1991). *Science and Politics in the Global Greenhouse: A Study of the Development towards Scientific Consensus on Climate Change*, EED Report 8, The Fridtjof Nansen Institute.

Lunde, L. (1998). The Kyoto Protocol: flexibility mechanisms after Kyoto, keynote address to the Conference 'Climate after Kyoto – Implications for Energy', The Royal Institute for Environmental Affairs, London, 5–6 February, 1998.

McCormick, J. (1989). *Acid Earth*, London, Earthscan.

Malnes, R. (1992). 'Leader' and 'entrepreneur' in international negotiations: a conceptual analysis, EED Report 1992/9, The Fridtjof Nansen Institute.

March, J.G. and Olsen, J.P. (1989). *Rediscovering Institutions: The Organizational Basis of Politics*, New York, The Free Press.

Mearsheimer, J. (1995). The false promise of international institutions, *International Security*, vol. 19, no. 3, Winter 1994/95, pp. 5–50.

Mensbrugghe, Y. (1990). Legal status of international North Sea Declarations, Special North Sea Issue of *International Journal of Coastal and Estuarine Law,* pp. 15–23.

Miles, E.L. (1987). Science, politics, and international ocean management: the uses of scientific knowledge in international negotiations, *Policy Papers in International Affairs*, no. 33, Institute of International Studies, University of California, Berkeley.

Miles, E.L. (1989). Scientific and technological knowledge and international cooperation in resource management, in Andresen, S. and Østreng, W. (eds), *International Resource Management: The Role of Science and Politics*, London, Belhaven Press, pp. 46–88.

Miles, E.L. et al. (forthcoming 1999). *Explaining Regime Effectiveness: Confronting Theory with Evidence*, Cambridge MA, MIT Press.

Milne, R. (1987). Pollution and politics in the North Sea, *New Scientist*, 19 November 1987.

Miller, K. (1989). The greenhouse effect: potential for effective regional response, thesis, Seattle, Institute for Marine Studies.

Mitchell, R.B. (1994A). *International Oil Pollution at Sea – Environmental Policy and Treaty Compliance*, Cambridge MA, MIT Press.

Mitchell, R.B. (1994B). Regime design matters: intentional oil pollution and treaty compliance, *International Organization*, vol. 48, no. 3, Summer, pp. 425–458.

Mitchell, R.B. (1997). Implementation of the IPCC – compliance, effectiveness and institutional design, in Sprinz, D. and Luterbacher, U. (eds), *International Relations and Global Climate Change*, Potsdam, Potsdam Institute for Climate Change.

Morisette, P. (1989). The evolution of policy responses to stratospheric ozone depletion, *Natural Resources Journal*, vol. 29, pp. 793–820.

Morisette, P. et al. (1990). *Lessons from other International Agreements for a Global CO$_2$ Accord*, paper, Washington, Resources for the Future.

Morlot, J.F. (1998). Ensuring compliance with a global climate agreement, OECD Information Paper, Draft 21 January 1998.

Newell, P. and Paterson, M. (1996). From Geneva to Kyoto: The Second Conference of the Parties to the UN Framework Convention on Climate Change, *Environmental Politics*, vol. 5, no. 4, Winter, pp. 729–735.

Nollkaemper, A. (1993). *The Legal Regime for Transboundary Water Pollution: Between Discretion and Constraint*, Dordrecht, Martinus Nijhoff/ Graham & Trotman.

NOOA, NASA, UNEP and WMO (1994). Scientific Assessment of Ozone Depletion: 1994. Executive Summary, World Meteorological Organization Global Ozone Research and Monitoring Project – Report No. 37, Geneva.

Nordberg, L. (1993). *Combating Air Pollution*, LRTAP 'non-paper', March.

North Sea Conference Progress Report (1995). Report produced to the Fourth International Conference on the Protection of the North Sea, Esbjerg, Denmark, 5–9 June 1995.

Oberthur, S. (1996). The Second Conference of the Parties, *Environmental Policy and Law*, vol. 26, no. 5, pp. 195–201.

Oberthur, S. (1997A). *Production and Consumption of Ozone-Depleting Substances 1986–1995*, Berlin, GTZ, Deutsche Gesellschaft für Technische Zusammenarbeit.

Oberthur, S. (1997B). The role of Europe in the international co-operation for the protection of the stratospheric ozone layer, draft for the 'Strategies for European Leadership of International Climate and Sustainability Regimes', 14 October 1997.

Oberthur, S. and Ott, H. (1995). The First Conference of the Parties, *Environmental Policy and Law*, vol. 24, nos. 4–5, pp. 144–156.

Oden, S. (1968). The acidification of air and precipitation and its consequences in the natural environment, *Ecology Committee Bulletin* no. 1, Swedish National Research Council, Stockholm.

Olson, M. (1965). *The Logic of Collective Action*, Cambridge MA, Harvard University Press.

The Oslo and Paris Commissions (1984). *The Oslo and Paris Commissions: The First Decade*, London.

Oye, K. (1986). Explaining cooperation under anarchy: hypotheses and strategies, in Oye, K. (ed.), *Cooperation under Anarchy*, Princeton, Princeton University Press, pp. 1–24.

Pallemaerts, M. (1992). The North Sea ministerial declarations from Bremen to the Hague: does the process generate any substance?, *International Journal of Estuarine and Coastal Law*, vol. 7, no. 1, pp. 1–26.

Parson, E.A. (1993). Protecting the ozone layer, in Haas, P; Keohane, R. and Levy, M. (eds), *Institutions for the Earth*, Cambridge MA, MIT Press, pp. 27–75.

Parson, E.A. (1996). International protection of the ozone layer, *Green Globe Yearbook*, the Fridtjof Nansen Institute/Oxford University Press, pp. 19–28.

Parson, E.A. (1997). International environmental negotiations: the current state of empirical and analytical study, *International Negotiation*, vol. 13, no. 2, pp. 161–185.

Parson, E.A. and Greene, O. (1995). The complex chemistry of the international ozone agreements, *Environment*, vol. 37, no. 2, pp. 16–20; 35–43.

Princen, T. and Finger, M. (eds) (1994). *Environmental NGOs in World Politics – Linking the Local and Global*, London, Routledge Press.

Quality Status of the North Sea reports (1984; 1987; 1993).

Raustiala, K. (1997). States, NGOs and international environmental institutions, *International Studies Quarterly*, vol. 41, no. 4, December, pp. 719–741.

Reid, P. (1990). The work of the North Sea Task Force, Special North Sea Issue of *International Journal of Coastal and Estuarine Law*, pp. 80–89.

Ringius, L. (1997). Environmental NGOs and regime change: the case of ocean dumping of radioactive waste, *European Journal of International Relations*, vol. 4, no. 1, March, pp. 61–104.

Ringius, L. and Torvanger, A. (1997). Sharing the costs equitably. Manuscript, CICERO, Oslo, March.

Ringius, L. and Wettestad, J. (1997). 'Friedheim in the greenhouse': tracing key positions of key actors on key climate issues, FNI Note N:002–1997, The Fridtjof Nansen Institute.

Rittberger, V. (ed.) (1990). *International Regimes in East–West Politics*, London and New York, Pinter Publishers.

Rittberger, V. (1993). *Regime Theory and International Relations*, Oxford, Clarendon Press.

Rowlands, I.H. (1995). *The Politics of Global Atmospheric Change*, Manchester, Manchester University Press.

Rowlands, I.H. (1996). *International Justice and Global Climate Change*, draft.

Ruggie, John G. (1975). International responses to technology: concepts and trends, *International Organization*, vol. 29, Summer, pp. 557–583.

Sadowski, S. (1996). The Oslo and Paris Commissions: their work, the 1997 Ministerial Meeting, and the role of NGOs, *North Sea Monitor*, December, pp. 14–16.

Sand, P. (1990A). *Lessons Learned in Global Environmental Governance* Washington, World Resources Institute.

Sand, P. (1990B). Regional approaches to transboundary air pollution, in Helm, J. (ed.), *Energy: Production, Consumption and Consequences*, Washington, National Academy Press, pp. 246–263.

Sandford, R. (1992). Secretariats and international environmental negotiations: two new models, in Susskind, L.; Dolin, E.J. and Breslin, W. (eds), *International Environmental Treaty Making*, Cambridge MA, Harvard Program on Negotiation.

Sandford, R. (1994). International environmental treaty secretariats: stage-hands or actors?, *Green Globe Yearbook*, the Fridtjof Nansen Institute/Oxford University Press, pp. 17–31.

Schjølset, S. (1998). EU's role in negotiating the Kyoto Protocol – a Norwegian perspective, unpublished note, March, The Fridtjof Nansen Institute.

Sebenius, J.K. (1990). Negotiating a regime to control global warming, report, Harvard University.

Sebenius, J.K. (1993). The law of the sea conference: lessons for negotiations to control global warming, in Sjøstedt, G. (ed.), *International Environmental Negotiation*, Laxenburg, IIASA, pp. 189–217.

Shackley, S. (1997). The intergovernmental panel on climate change: consensual knowledge and global politics, *Global Environmental Change*, vol. 7, no. 1, pp. 77–79.

Sjøberg, H. (1996). The Global Environment Facility, in Werksman, J. (ed.), *Greening International Institutions*, London, Earthscan Publications Limited, pp. 148–163.

Skjærseth, J.B. (1991). Effektivitet, problem-typer og løsningskapasitet: en studie av Oslo-samarbeidets takling av dumping i Nordsjøen og Nordøstatlanteren, R:009–1991, The Fridtjof Nansen Institute.

Skjærseth, J.B. (1992A). *From Regime Formation to Regime Functioning 'Effectiveness' – Coping with the Problem of Ozone Depletion*, The Fridtjof Nansen Institute, R:007–1992.

Skjærseth, J.B. (1992B). *The Mediterranean Action Plan – More Political Rhetoric than Effective Problem-Solving?*, R:006–1992, The Fridtjof Nansen Institute.

Skjærseth, J.B. (1992C). Towards the end of dumping in the North Sea: an example of effective problem solving?, *Marine Policy*, vol. 16, no. 2, pp. 130–141.

Skjærseth, J.B. (1993). *The Climate Policy of the EC – Too Hot to Handle? A Study of Interests and Preferences versus EC Problem-Solving Capacity*, EED Report 1993/2, The Fridtjof Nansen Institute.

Skjærseth, J.B. (1996). The impact of environmental institutions: implementing North Sea pollution control, paper prepared for the 37th Annual Convention of the International Studies Association, April, San Diego, CA.

Skjærseth, J.B. (forthcoming 1998). The making and implementation of north sea pollution commitments: institutions, rationality and norms, doctoral dissertation, Oslo, The Fridtjof Nansen Institute.

Skodvin, T. (1992). 'Structure' and 'agent' in institutional bargaining: institutional design and political leadership in the United Nations Conference on the Law of the Sea, *Cooperation and Conflict*, vol. 27, no. 2, pp. 163–191.

Skodvin, T. (1994). The ozone regime, in Andresen, S. et al., *'Scientific' Management of the Environment? Science, Politics and Institutional Design*, The Fridtjof Nansen Institute, R:006–1994, ch. 6.

Skodvin, T. (forthcoming 1999A). The ozone regime, in Underdal et al., *Science and International Environmental Regimes: Combining Integrity with Involvement*, Manchester, Manchester University Press.

Skodvin, T. (forthcoming 1999B). The Intergovernmental Panel on Climate Change, in Underdal et al., *Science and International Environmental Regimes: Combining Integrity with Involvement*, Manchester, Manchester University Press.

Snidal, D. (1995). The politics of scope: endogenous actors, heterogeneity and institutions, in Keohane, R. and Ostrom, E. (eds), *Local Commons and Global Interdependence – Heterogeneity and Cooperation in Two Domains*, London, Sage Publications, pp. 47–70.

Sprinz, D. And Vaahtoranta, T. (1994). The interest-based explanation of international environmental policy, *International Organization*, vol. 48, no. 1, Winter, pp. 77–105.

Stairs, K. and Taylor, P. (1992). Non-governmental organizations and the legal protection of the oceans: a case study, in Hurrell, A. and Kingsbury, B. (eds), *The International Politics of the Environment*, Oxford, Clarendon Press, pp. 110–142.

Stenstadvold, M. (1991). The evolution of cooperation: a case study of the NO$_x$ protocol (in Norwegian), unpublished thesis, University of Oslo.

Stokke, O.S. (1992). Environmental performance review: concept and design, in Lykke, E. (ed.), *Achieving Environmental Goals – The Concept and Practice of Environmental Performance Review*, London, Belhaven Press, pp. 3–25.

Strange, S. (1983). Cave! Hic dragones: a critique of regime analysis, in S. Krasner (ed.), *International Regimes*, Ithaca, Cornell University Press, pp. 337–354.

Susskind, Lawrence E. (1994). *Environmental Diplomacy – Negotiating More Effective Global Agreements*, Oxford, Oxford University Press.

Szell, P. (1993). Negotiations on the ozone layer, in Sjøstedt, G. (ed.), *International Environmental Negotiation*, Laxenburg, IIASA, pp. 31–48.

Szell, P. (1995). The Development of Multilateral Mechanisms for Monitoring Compliance, in Lang, W. (ed.), *Sustainable Development and International Law*, London, Graham and Trotman, pp. 97–109.

Szell, P. (1996). Decision making under multilateral environmental agreements, *Environmental Policy and Law*, vol. 26, no. 5, pp. 210–214.

Sætevik, S. (1988). *Environmental Cooperation Between the North Sea States*, London, Belhaven Press.

Ulfstein, G. (1996). The Vienna Convention for the Protection of the Ozone Layer and the Montreal Protocol, in 'The effectiveness of the multilateral environmental agreements', Nordic Council of Ministers Report 1996:18, pp. 105–117.

Underdal, A. (1980). *The Politics of International Fisheries Management: The Case of the Northeast Atlantic*, Oslo, Universitetsforlaget.

Underdal, A. (1989). The politics of science in international resource management: a summary, in Andresen, S. and Østreng, W. (eds), *International Resource Management: The Role of Science and Politics*, London, Belhaven Press, pp. 253–269.

Underdal, A. (1990). Negotiating effective solutions: the art and science of political engineering, unpublished paper, the University of Oslo.

Underdal, A. (1991). Solving collective problems: notes on three modes of leadership, in *Challenges of a Changing World – Festschrift to Willy Østreng*, The Fridtjof Nansen Institute, pp. 139–155.

Underdal, A. (1992). The concept of regime 'effectiveness', *Cooperation and Conflict*, vol. 27, no. 3, pp. 227–240.

Underdal, A. (1995). The study of international regimes, *Journal of Peace Research*, vol. 32, no. 1, pp. 113–119.

Underdal, A. (1997). Draft theory chapter for the Miles et. al. project book (forthcoming 1999).

Underdal, A. et al. (forthcoming 1999). *Science and International Environmental Regimes: Combining Integrity with Involvement*, Manchester, Manchester University Press.

UNFCCC (1996). UNFCCC/CP/1996/8, Decisions to promote the effective implementation of the convention. Financial mechanism. Report of the Global Environment Facility to the Conference of the Parties.

Victor, D.G. (1995). The Montreal Protocol's non-compliance procedure: lessons for making other international regimes more effective, draft presented at the workshop 'The Ozone Treaties and Their Influence on the Building of Environmental Regimes', Vienna, Austria, December.

Victor, D.G. and Ausubel, J. (1992). Verification of international environmental agreements, *Annual Review of Energy and Environment*, vol. 17, pp. 1–43.

Victor, D.G. et al. (1994). Review mechanisms in the effective implementation of international environmental agreements, Laxenburg, IIASA Working Paper WP–94–114.

Victor, D.G. and Salt, J. (1994). From Rio to Berlin: managing climate change, *Environment*, vol. 36, no.10, pp. 6–15 and 25–32.

Victor, D.G.; Raustiala, K. and Skolnikoff, E.B. (eds), *The Implementation and Effectiveness of International Environmental Commitments*, Cambridge MA, MIT Press.

Von Moltke, K. and Young, O.R. (1995). International Secretariats, background paper for the workshop at the Rockefeller Brothers Conference Center, Pocantico, NY, June 15–18.

Waterton, C. (1993). The UK case study for acidification and transboundary air pollution – a preliminary survey, contribution to the 'Social Learning in the Management of Global Environmental Risks' project.

Wetstone, G. (1987). A history of the acid rain issue, in Brooks, H. and Cooper, C.L., *Science for Public Policy*, Oxford, Pergamon Press, pp. 163–195.

Wetstone, G. and Rosencrantz, A. (1983). *Acid Rain in Europe and North America*, Washington DC, Environmental Law Institute.

Wettestad, J. (1988). The outcome of the 1987 North Sea Conference: science counts, but politics decides?, *International Challenges*, no. 2, pp. 31–36.

Wettestad, J. (1989). *Uncertain Science and Matching Policies: Science, Politics and the Organization of North Sea Cooperation*, R:003–1989, The Fridtjof Nansen Institute.

Wettestad, J. (1991A). The Paris Convention for the prevention of marine pollution from landbased sources, in Wettestad, J. and Andresen, S., *The*

Effectiveness of International Resource Cooperation: Some Preliminary Findings, R:007–1991, The Fridtjof Nansen Institute, pp. 57–74.

Wettestad, J. (1991B). The effectiveness of LRTAP, in Wettestad, J. and Andresen, S. (1991), *The Effectiveness of International Resource Cooperation: Some Preliminary Findings*, R:007–1991, The Fridtjof Nansen Institute, pp. 74–94.

Wettestad, J. (1992). The 'effectiveness' of the Paris Convention on marine pollution from landbased sources, *International Environmental Affairs*, vol. 12, no. 4, pp. 101–121.

Wettestad, J. (1994). Science, politics and institutional design: the case of the North–East Atlantic landbased marine pollution regime, *Marine Policy*, vol. 18, no. 3, May, pp. 219–33.

Wettestad, J. (1995A). LRTAP: the jewel in the crown for 'discursive diplomacy'?, in 'Implementing Environmental Conventions', Papers from the Second High-Level Nordic Policy Seminar Copenhagen 27–28 1994, Scandinavian Seminar College, pp. 68–77.

Wettestad, J. (1995B). *Nuts and Bolts for Environmental Negotiators? Institutional Design and the Effectiveness of International Environmental Regimes*, FNI Note N:001–1995, The Fridtjof Nansen Institute.

Wettestad, J. (1995 C). Science, politics and institutional design: some initial notes on the long-range transboundary air pollution regime, *Journal of Environment and Development*, vol. 4, no. 2, Summer 1995, pp. 165–185.

Wettestad, J. (1996). Acid lessons? assessing and explaining LRTAP implementation and effectiveness, Laxenburg IIASA Working Paper WP–96–18. A revised version was published in *Global Environmental Change*, vol. 7, no. 3, 1997, pp. 235–249.

Wettestad, J. (1998), Participation in NO_x policy-making and implementation in the Netherlands, UK and Norway: different approaches, but similar results? In Victor, D.G.; Raustiala, K. and Skolnikoff, E.B. (eds), *The Implementation and Effectiveness of International Environmental Commitments*, Cambridge MA, MIT Press, pp. 381–431.

Wettestad, J. (forthcoming 1999A). Dealing with landbased marine pollution in the North–East Atlantic: The Paris Convention (PARCON) and the North Sea Conferences, in Underdal, A. et al., *Science and International Environmental Regimes: Combining Integrity with Involvement*, Manchester, Manchester University Press.

Wettestad, J. (forthcoming 1999B). From common cuts to critical loads: The ECE Convention on Long-Range Transboundary Air Pollution (LRTAP), in Underdal et al. , *Science and International Environmental Regimes: Combining Integrity with Involvement*, Manchester, Manchester University Press.

Wettestad, J. and Andresen, S. (1991). *The Effectiveness of International Resource Cooperation: Some Preliminary Findings*, R:007–1991, The Fridtjof Nansen Institute.

Young, O.R. (1979). *Compliance and Public Authority: A Theory with International Applications*, Baltimore, Johns Hopkins University Press.

Young, O.R. (1986). International regimes: toward a new theory of institutions, *World Politics*, vol. 39, October, pp. 104–122.

Young, O.R. (1989). *International Cooperation: Building Regimes for Natural Resources and the Environment*, Ithaca, Cornell University Press.

Young, O.R. (1991). Political leadership and regime formation: on the development of institutions in international society, *International Organization*, vol. 45, Summer, pp. 281–308.

Young, O.R. (1992). The effectiveness of international institutions: hard cases and critical variables, in Rosenau, J.N. and Czempiel, E., *Governance without Government: Order and Change in World Politics*, Cambridge MA, Cambridge University Press, pp. 160–195.

Young, O.R. (1994). *International Governance – Protecting the Environment in a Stateless Society*, Ithaca, Cornell University Press.

Young, O.R. (1998). The effectiveness of international environmental regimes. what we know and what we need to know, paper produced for the annual meeting of the American Association for the Advancement of Science, Philadelphia, 12–17 February.

Young, O.R. and Osherenko, G. (eds) (1993). *Polar Politics: Creating International Environmental Regimes*, New York, Cornell University Press.

Young, O.R. and Underdal, A. (1998). Institutional dimensions of global change, scoping report for the International Human Dimensions Programme on Global Environmental Change (IHDP).

Young, O.R. et al. (forthcoming 1999). *The Effectiveness of International Environmental Regimes*.

Yin, R.K. (1989). *Case Study Research: Design and Methods*, London, Sage.

Zürn, M. (1995). The rise of international environmental politics: a review of current research, draft.

Index